THE CAMBRIDGE
COMPANION TO
HENRY JAMES

The Cambridge Companion to Henry James is intended to provide a critical
introduction to James's work. Throughout the major critical shifts of the last
fifty years – and despite suspicions of the traditional high literary culture that
was James's milieu – as a writer he has retained a powerful hold on readers
and critics alike. All essays are newly commissioned for this volume, written
at a level free from technical jargon, and designed to promote accessibility
to the study of James and his work.

Cambridge Companions to Literature

(*Continued on page following the index*)

THE CAMBRIDGE COMPANION TO
HENRY JAMES

EDITED BY
JONATHAN FREEDMAN

The University of Michigan, Ann Arbor

CAMBRIDGE
UNIVERSITY PRESS

PUBLISHED BY THE PRESS SYNDICATE OF THE UNIVERSITY OF CAMBRIDGE
The Pitt Building, Trumpington Street, Cambridge CB2 1RP, United Kingdom

CAMBRIDGE UNIVERSITY PRESS
The Edinburgh Building, Cambridge CB2 2RU, UK   http: //www.cup.cam.ac.uk
40 West 20th Street, New York, NY 10011-4211, USA   http: //www.cup.org
10 Stamford Road, Oakleigh, Melbourne 3166, Australia

First published 1998
Reprinted 1998

Printed in the United States of America

Typeset in Sabon

A catalogue record for this book is available from the British Library

Library of Congress Cataloguing-in-Publication Data is available

ISBN 0-521-49584-9 hardback
ISBN 0-521-49924-0 paperback

CONTENTS

CONTENTS

CONTRIBUTORS

MARTHA BANTA is Professor of English at the University of California, Los Angeles. Her publications include *Henry James and the Occult, Failure and Success in America, Imaging American Women,* and *Taylored Lives,* as well as many articles and contributions to essay collections in which Henry James makes his presence known.

MILLICENT BELL is Professor Emerita at Boston University. She has written extensively on nineteenth- and twentieth-century American literature. Most recently, she has published *Meaning in Henry James* (Harvard University Press, 1991) and is the editor of *The Cambridge Companion to Edith Wharton.*

SARA BLAIR is an Associate Professor at the University of Virginia. She is the author of *Henry James and the Writing of Race and Nation* (Cambridge University Press, 1995) and is working on *The Place of the Literary,* a book about the construction of literary value in sites of urban modernity.

JONATHAN FREEDMAN is an Associate Professor at the University of Michigan. He is the author of *Professions of Taste: Henry James, Commodity Culture, and British Aestheticism,* editor of *Oscar Wilde: New Century Views,* and co-editor of *Hitchcock's America.* He is currently working on *The Temple of Culture,* a book about the relation between Jewish intellectuals and the construction of high culture.

DOROTHY J. HALE is an Associate Professor at the University of California, Berkeley. She is the author of *Social Formalism: The Novel in Theory from Henry James to the Present* (Stanford University Press, 1997) and a number of articles in such journals as *Novel* and *ELH.*

ERIC HARALSON is an Assistant Professor at the State University of New York, Stony Brook. Having received his Ph.D. from Columbia University, he is currently working on a book on James and fin-de-siècle masculinity.

PHILLIP HORNE is Reader in English Literature at University College, London. He is the author of *Henry James and Revision: The New York Edi-*

tion (Oxford University Press, 1990), and has edited Henry James's *A London Life & The Reverberator* for Oxford and *The Tragic Muse* for Penguin. He is presently completing a new selection of James's letters for Penguin.

ROSS POSNOCK is the Highland Professor of English at the University of Washington. He is the author of *Henry James and the Problem of Robert Browning* and *The Trial of Curiosity: Henry James, William James, and the Challenge of Modernity.* He is currently working on a book on African-American intellectuals and the pragmatist tradition.

MARGERY SABIN is Lorraine Chiu Wang Professor of English at Wellesley College. She is the author of *English Romanticism and the French Tradition* and *The Dialect of the Tribe: Speech and Community in Modern Fiction.* Her recent essays and reviews about colonial and postcolonial narrative and about the identity of literary study have appeared in such journals as *Raritan Quarterly, Essays in Criticism, Victorian Studies,* and *College English.*

HUGH STEVENS teaches at the University of York. Author of a number of articles on James, he received his Ph.D. from Trinity Hall, Cambridge, and is currently working on a book on Henry James and queer performativity.

WILLIAM STOWE is a Professor of English at Wesleyan University. He is the author of *Balzac, James and the Realistic Novel* (1983) and *Going Abroad: European Travel in Nineteenth-Century American Culture* (1994), both published by Princeton University Press.

ROBERT WEISBUCH is a Professor of English at the University of Michigan, and has served as chair of the English Department and Dean of the Graduate School. He is the author of *Emily Dickinson's Poetry* (1975) and *Atlantic Double Cross: American Literature and British Influence in the Age of Emerson* (1983).

FRANCES WILSON studied at the Universities of Oxford, Southampton, and Sussex. She is currently teaching at the University of Reading. Her Ph.D. thesis was on Henry James and Freud; she is currently editing a collection of the myths of Byron.

PREFACE

Henry James (1843–1916) is generally acknowledged to be one of America's greatest novelists and critics, although he spent most of his career in England. He is the author of some of the best-known fictions of the later nineteenth and early twentieth century – novels like *Portrait of a Lady* (1881), stories like "Daisy Miller" (1876), tales like *The Turn of the Screw* (1898). His criticism, moreover, offers one of the most definitive accounts of what James called "the art of fiction" – all the more impressive because at the time he wrote, prose fiction was accorded a secondary place in literary judgment, well behind lyric and epic in critical esteem. And in his travel memoir, *The American Scene*, James gave a uniquely perceptive account of America at the turn of the century, forcefully registering the remarkable changes then underway in the racial, economic, and political terrain of his native land.

James is also, however, the author of some of the most mind-bogglingly obscure prose of his, or any, period. Although some of his works make easy claims on reader's sensibilities – as I write, *Portrait of a Lady* is being prepared for Hollywood production – others set out quite consciously to challenge or even to offend them. James spent much of his life lamenting the results, and hoping that he would find readers able to appreciate his efforts. Although the mass audiences of his own time might have disappointed him, critics soon fulfilled his aspirations. Beginning in the 1920s, with a boost from Ezra Pound and T. S. Eliot; accelerating in the 1940s, with a major push from F. O. Matthiessen; gathering further force in the 1950s and 1960s, with the work of a number of so-called "New Critics" (close formalist readers of literary texts), James got installed at the very center of the canon of literary value and esteem. Even as the premises of much of this criticism were thoroughly called into question by critics of the next generations, James remained crucial; some of the most important revisionary works of post-New Critical theorists and critics – those of Shoshona Felman, Leo Bersani, and Caroline Porter, to name three very different ones – were accomplished through re-readings of James.

This volume seeks to measure both James's multiple achievements and his role in critical practice. It can hardly be inclusive of either – there are no essays on James's brilliant autobiographies, for example; and some critical positions are less well-represented than others. Nevertheless, the reader will find virtually all of James's major fictions discussed here, and from virtually every angle current in the last fifty years. Each of the contributors to the volume has been asked to survey a crucial aspect of James, whether a thematic issue, a critical conundrum, or a knotty text, in such a way as both to clarify James's procedures and vividly to put on display her or his own critical sensibility. In an introductory essay, for example, I attempt to account for James's unique contemporaneity – for the fact that, even as a new generation of readers and critics works to question the value or even the possibility of high literary culture itself, the work of that seemingly mandarin aesthete Henry James remains central to their endeavor. Martha Banta situates James in a different cultural politics, those of masculinity in his own era – and, by extension, our own. In *The Golden Bowl* and *The American Scene*, Banta shows, James articulated a rich and powerful critical response to the boisterous masculinity represented by his contemporary, Teddy Roosevelt, and to its role in constructing a uniquely American style of manliness. Frances Wilson places James in the context of his remarkable family, tracing the network of interconnections between the novelist and his philosopher brother and with his less public, but equally brilliant, sister Alice. Wilson shows how the three acted out common obsessions, inherited from their mystical millionaire of a father but taken well beyond his scope, with bodies, performance, utility, and waste.

Philip Horne turns our attention to the questions raised for the student by the multiple texts that exist for James's major works. Perhaps no writer since Shakespeare poses such knotty textual problems: James's habits of publication and revision present the reader with multiple options for experiencing virtually every one of his major fictions. Horne traces some of the conundrums that this proliferation creates for the unwary reader; showing, finally, how they throw into sharp relief such vexing questions as the nature of author and text themselves. Dorothy Hale continues this focus on the legacy of James's authorial practices by focusing on James's theory of the novel. As one of the first and certainly one of the most influential theorists of this perpetually re-invented form, James created an idiom for thinking about the ethical as well as the formal consequences of the fiction-making act. Hale shows how even successors who sought to distance themselves from James's example end up endorsing the Jamesian ethic even as they critique the Jamesian method.

The book then turns to essays that focus more specifically on individual works. Robert Weisbuch shows how powerfully engaged are some of James's most enduring fictions, like *Portrait*, *Daisy Miller*, and *Turn of the Screw*, in delineating a response to Emerson's blitheness in the face of evil. James does so, paradoxically but powerfully, by turning to the epic tradition (especially Milton) to help develop a vocabulary for thinking about the problem even – or especially – in a modern, secular world. Hugh Stevens places James in the context of current writing about "queer" or transgressive identity, suggesting through a reading of James's tale *In the Cage* how rich James's sense of queer transgressivity proves to be, and how fully it can supplement the more reductive side of current critical accounts. Millicent Bell gives a reading to James's tale "The Pupil" that similarly focuses on transgression; but here the subject of shame turns out to be the vulgarity of money, the appalling insistence of the pecuniary, the full shamefulness of which in genteel culture turns out to be central to the meaning of James's tale.

The volume concludes with essays centering on – but extending their concerns well beyond – five of James's most famous and challenging works. Sara Blair shows how James's "realist" novel, *The Bostonians*, crucially grapples not only with questions of gender and national identity in a post–Civil War environment, but with the very possibilities of culture itself. The novel, Blair shows, interrogates the powers of culture at the moment of realism by comparing and contrasting various scenes of culture-making, ranging from reading groups and salons to Lyceums and public lectures to its own fictive endeavor. As such, Blair concludes, James's work points not only backwards – toward the cultural formations of elite Boston – but forward, to those to be organized alongside, rather than in opposition to, the logic of a booming mass culture. Eric Haralson turns to a novel of James's so-called Major Phase (the phrase is Matthiessens's), showing how *The Ambassadors* challenges not only fin-de-siècle notions of masculinity, but the nineteenth and twentieth century's very insistence on the power of sexuality itself. William Stowe places another "Major Phase" novel, *The Wings of the Dove,* in the multiple contexts of gender, sexuality, economy, and the culture of professionalism, suggesting that the great achievement of James's novel is not only to enter into dialogue with each of these, but also to transcend them. Marjorie Sabin centers on questions of empire, particularly at the moment of imperial decline, that moment when the British empire felt itself facing decay in the face of their upstart American cousins. Sabin reads James's text *The Golden Bowl* against Conrad's famous record of the hollowing out of the colonizer in the face of the colonized, *Heart of Darkness;* James's heroine, Maggie Verver, represents a new version of the Conradian virtuous liar, one who gains a new but highly equivocal power by her mastery of an idiom of deceit. This power, Sabin shows, at once attracts and repels James as a model for not only the civilizing process as experienced in a newly decrepit Europe, but in a booming America. And it is with that issue that Ross Posnock concludes the volume. Posnock shows along with Freedman, Banta, Blair, and Stevens – alongside, in some sense, virtually every contributor to the volume – how James not only anatomizes the critical terrain of his own moment, but anticipates the possibilities and problems of a dawning modernity. Boldly comparing James and his African-American contemporary W. E. B. Du Bois, Posnock argues that the racial politics of Jamesian fiction, generally taken to be reactionary at best, actually anticipate a pragmatist pluralism that flourished among African-American writers like Ralph Ellison as well as critics of our own era who are attempting, in Posnock's view, to think beyond race to a cultural politics of hybridity.

Readers will find here, then, many Henry Jameses: Henry James the shrewd anatomist of metaphysical evil, of mass culture at the moment of realism, of novel theory, of economic necessity, of queer identity, of racial mixing, of Rooseveltian masculinity, of female power and imperial destiny – and this is just to name a few. And they will find examples of just about every critical method and possibility of our own moment. It is my hope – and the hope of my fellow authors – that the volume will help them gain better traction on both: will help them to a better knowledge not merely of James and his own era but of the rich and multifarious critical practices and cultural possibilities of our own. For the reader of this volume will discover what its authors have learned, too: that whatever issue one finds oneself confronting, it remains as impossible now as it has been for the past century to do so without coming to terms with Henry James.

One of James's most oft-quoted comments is a sentence from the *Preface* to the New York Edition of *Roderick Hudson:* "Really . . . relations stop nowhere, and the exquisite problem of the artist is eternally, but to draw, by a geometry of his own, the circle within which they *appear* to do so." The same "exquisite problem" faces the editor facing the daunting prospect of acknowledging all the relations, contributions, and suggestions that have gone into the making of a volume. I need to thank Eric Sundquist, for proposing me as editor; an anonymous reader for the proposal, who made a number of very insightful suggestions; Martha Banta, who in addition to contributing a marvelous piece with promptness and ease gave some particularly sage counsel at a crucial moment; T. Susan Chang and Anne Sanow, for shepherding it through its many incarnations; and Katharita Lamoza, copy-editor *extraordinaire* and, finally, of course, the authors of the pieces that follow, who cheerfully wrote and even more cheerfully revised. I also need to thank a number of friends – Liz Barnes, Alison Booth, Monica Feinberg Cohen, Adrienne Donald, Christopher Flint, Daniel Hack, June Howard, John Kucich, Anita Norich, David Scobey, E. Blake Vermeule are just a few of them – for aid and comfort over the time I've spent working on the volume. And everything here is for Sara.

Errata

Chap. 6
P. 128, line 12: should continue "The telegraphist feels deeply implicated in these events."
P. 128, indent: should begin with " She felt . . . as if she might soon be pounced upon. . . ."

Chap. 7
P. 140, line 1: should read " . . . he has difficulty in asking about it; . . . "
P. 140, line 14: "Suede" should read "Suède."
P. 143, line 2: quotation should begin with "Today, after a considerable interval," and run to the end of the paragraph.
P. 144, line 31: "first" should read "fast."
P. 145, line 31: insert "expect to" after "to."
P. 146, line 7: "Zenobie" should read "Zénobie."
P. 147, line 37: "joining" should read "joint."
P. 148, line 7: "connection" should read "connexion."
P. 148, line 9: insert "a" after "benefit of."
P. 148, line 10: "sees" should read "saw."
P. 148, line 11: quotation should close following "it."
P. 150, line 5: "Volume II" should read "Volume XI."

Chap. 9
P. 170, line 32: "amorous arousal" should read "amorously aroused."
P. 171, line 12: "is" should read "it."
P. 173, line 33: insert comma after "soul."
P. 178, line 27: "(s)exploits" should read "exploits."
P. 181, line 7: "term" should read "terms."
P. 183, line 20: "of" should read "or."
P. 185, note 26: should end with "self-preservation."

A HENRY JAMES CHRONOLOGY

1843   Henry James born on April 15 near Washington Square in New York City. His father – Henry James Senior – takes his family (including Henry's older brother William) to England and Europe, where Henry Senior suffers a nervous breakdown, one of the many "vastations" (in his phrase) to affect his family.

1845   The family returns to America, shuttling between Albany and New York City. Garth Wilkinson James born.

1846   Robertson James born.

1848   Alice James born.

1855–60   The family returns to Europe, where Henry Senior seeks a more supple education for the children. A succession of tutors is hired; the children then attend a series of schools. The peripatetic Jameses return to America, this time to live in Newport, Rhode Island; then they go back to Europe, this time to live in Geneva.

1862   The family returns to Newport, where two particularly crucial events occur. First, James becomes acquainted with his orphaned cousin Minnie Temple, generally taken to be the original of Isabel Archer in *Portrait of a Lady*. Second, he suffers a back injury in a stable fire; this "obscure hurt" (as Henry, obscurely, called it) keeps him from serving in the Civil War, unlike his two younger brothers.

1863   After a brief stint at Harvard Law School, Henry devotes himself to writing. His first story is published anonymously the next year.

1865   Henry's first signed tale, "The Story of a Year," is published in the *Atlantic Monthly*. James begins to publish reviews, art criticism, and travel essays in journals like *The Nation* and *The Atlantic*.

1869   While James tours Europe – meeting painters like Dante Rossetti and William Morris, and intellectuals like George Eliot,

Charles Darwin, and Leslie Stephen – Minnie dies of tuberculosis.

1870   *Watch and Ward* is serialized by *The Atlantic.*

1872–75 While shuttling back and forth between Europe and the United States, James writes *Roderick Hudson* (published in 1875). Moves permanently to Europe.

1875   James in Paris, where he befriends Turgenev and hobnobs with Flaubert, Zola, and Maupassant.

1877   *The American* published. After visiting Italy, James moves to England.

1878   *Daisy Miller* published – and becomes an international sensation. This is the year, too, of *The Europeans* and "An International Episode."

1879   *Confidence* and *Hawthorne* published.

1880–81 James is based in London, but spends some months in Italy. Publishes *Washington Square* and *Portrait of a Lady,* which gain him a reputation as the pre-eminent American novelist of his time.

1882   Returns to America for visits punctuated by tragedy: mother and father die, as does brother Wilky (in 1883). Following his final return to England after this series of deaths, James settles into a life of writing, visits to country houses, and dining out – one marked by prodigious literary output for the next two decades.

1884   "The Art of Fiction."

1886   *The Bostonians* and *The Princess Casamassima* published, initiating a period in which James experiments with naturalism. Although public response to this work is respectful, a tone of disappointment creeps into reviews.

1888   *The Reverberator, The Aspern Papers.*

1890   *The Tragic Muse* published to decidedly mixed reviews.

1891   James decides to write for the theater, adapting *The American* for the stage with some success. He also begins a decade-long period of writing many short stories and longer tales.

1892   Alice James dies, after a year-long bout with breast cancer.

1893   *The Real Thing and Other Tales.*

1895   *Guy Domville* opens at the St. James's Theater in London; James takes a bow, and is booed off the stage by this audience. Humiliated (and galled by the success of Oscar Wilde's *Im-*

portance of Being Earnest, which followed it at the same theater), James abandons his new career as playwright. Publishes Terminations, containing many of the fables of the artist's life, which he continues to write during the next few years. James returns to fiction-writing, vowing to bring the lessons of the drama with him.

1896	The Spoils of Poynton; Embarrassments (containing "The Figure in the Carpet" and "The Next Time").
1897	What Maisie Knew. James hires a stenographer and begins to dictate his work, correcting typewritten transcriptions by hand. This is the method he is to employ for the rest of his life.
1898	The Turn of the Screw.
1899	The Awkward Age.
1901	The Sacred Fount published; writes The Ambassadors – published two years later. The novels of the next three years are generally thought of as James's greatest achievement: in F. O. Matthiessen's term, "the Major Phase."
1902	The Wings of the Dove.
1904	The Golden Bowl.
1905	Returns to America, touring the Northeast and the South, and then makes lecture tour to the West by Pullman car.
1907	The American Scene – James's reflections on his native land after more than a generation's absence. Revises many of his novels and tales for publication in the New York Edition, writes eighteen prefaces for the edition, published between 1907–1910.
1908	Italian Hours.
1910	James suffers a nervous breakdown. William comes to England to comfort Henry, then returns to America and dies. Robertson James also dies this year.
1913	A Small Boy and Others.
1914	Notes of a Son and Brother.
1915	Becomes a British citizen. Involves himself in war relief.
1916	After a brief illness, dies on February 28.

JONATHAN FREEDMAN

Introduction: The Moment of Henry James

Why, after a hundred years, Henry James? At a critical moment so leery of traditional notions of literary and cultural value, so impatient with gestures of authorial self-aggrandizement, so suspicious of the prerogatives of class privilege, few writers would seem *less* likely to survive than one thoroughly embedded in the highest of high literary culture, driven by desire for canonical status, fascinated by the intensities of the drawing room and the mores of the country house. And few bodies of work would seem less likely to thrive in our MTV-mediated age of instantaneous apprehension. The thickness, the opacity, the ambiguous range of reference of Jamesian prose demand attention, focus, and, that rarest of contemporary commodities, *time*.

Yet persist he has: indeed, his work has managed to attract devoted readers and inspiring commentaries across and through the major critical shifts of the last fifty years. Each successive wave of theoretical and critical practice – New Criticism, deconstruction, feminism, marxism, New Historicism – staked their claims and exemplified their style of interpretation by offering powerful re-readings of James. And as critical insistences of our own decade have shifted to emphases on postcoloniality, critical race studies, the study of sexual dissidence, James has retained a powerful hold on readers and critics alike. He has done so, moreover, not as a "case," an object of critical scrutiny (if not condescension), he does so as a vital participant in these arenas. Indeed, if there is one surprise that the contributors to this volume (and its editor) persistently note, it is that this snobbish, if not mandarin, aesthete should have responded so intently to the seismic shifts of his own era, a time of enormous transformations in the domains of race, political economy, gender. In so doing, these critics further note with some astonishment, he seems to have registered rumblings we thought all our own.

The essays that follow have much to say about James's relation to these matters, and more to boot. In this essay, I focus on three particular aspects of his work that touch with special power on the concerns of our own moment: the sometimes overlapping, indeed often mutually constitutive, arenas of family, nation, and the literary. My point in doing so is to suggest that in these in particular, as in his work as a whole, James is a uniquely double figure, one richly situated in the cultural possibilities of his own moment but able to rework them in ways that seem profoundly prescient. My aim here, then, is partially to "place" James in the circumstances of his time, partially to suggest some of his saliences to our own. But my major goal is to reinvite the reader to this most difficult and most rewarding of novelists. Many years of teaching James to both undergraduates and graduate students – not to mention the responses of dubious colleagues – reminds me of just how many obstacles James poses to contemporary readers. I hope this volume can help those readers recognize not only how astute but also how persistently challenging James can be – and that one of the things he challenges most fully is the complacency about our historical uniqueness that we bring to reading James.

JAMES AND FAMILY

"We were inhabitants of a distinct country," wrote Henry James's brother, the pragmatist philosopher William, "the country of James." Perhaps no greater uniqueness was possessed by Henry than the rich and idiosyncratic family into which he was born and in which he alternately chafed and thrived. And it was as much this family experience, I want to suggest, as his own affectional sensibilities that made James such a shrewd observer of the crosscurrents of intimacy, the work of relation. For Henry James was from the first pitched outside the newly dominant middle-class institution of the "family" – a position that allowed him to cast a skeptical eye on its effects in all the terrains it touched, both public and private.

To understand the full oddity of James's upbringing, we might want to look briefly at one of the most influential descriptions of nineteenth-century American family life, that offered in Mary Ryan's 1981 *Cradle of the Middle Class*. Through a richly sedimented account of upstate New York's Oneida County, Ryan shows how the institution of the middle-class family grew out of the traditional, patriarchal family grounded in the rhythms of agricultural production. As the economy shifted from one based on domestic production – the household as a near-independent economic unit – to one based first on retail trade and then on industry, a new model of family life emerged. This model defined itself first in terms of a gendered division of labor, then in the doctrine of separate spheres: that system in which women were confined to the home but granted near-tyrannical powers over matters of family, culture, and reproduction while males were sent bustling into the world under the injunction to be self-made. Ryan's description of this process is not unique; but what makes it influential is her understanding of how changes in religious practice, economic organization, and ethnic composition helped create the middle-class model of the privatized family – and how in turn the private family shaped the mindset of a maturing middle class:

> By midcentury, five years after the erection of Utica's [the industrial city at the center of Oneida County] first steam-powered factories . . . responsibility for maintaining purity, sobriety, and docility had been largely absorbed by the private family. . . . Homes [of the native-born middle class] had become shrines to temperate living, moral fortresses against the chaos of the streets, now inundated with a foreign population whose hallmarks from the middle class perspective were dirt and drink. . . . Sexual constraint, temperate habits, maternal socialization, and education, were productive of small families, conservative business policies, dogged work habits, and basic literacy skills – that is, the attributes required of small shops and stores and an increasing number of white-collar workers. . . . Thereafter the family itself became the cradle of middle class individuals. (238-9)

Now Ryan's Onieda County abutted directly on the county where Henry James's sternly Presbyterian grandfather, William James, Sr., made his fortune in real estate, capped by his acquisition of the property on which he helped build the city of Syracuse, a mere fifty miles west of Utica on the Erie Canal. And what is remarkable about this contiguity is that thereafter the James family of upstate New York comported itself to exactly *none* of the ideological lineaments that Ryan describes. Patriarchal the Jameses were to be sure: William's will effectively disinherited the novelist's father Henry James, Sr., on account of his lackadaisical approach to college and career; and although Henry Sr. effectively broke the will and assured himself of a solid $10,000 per annum (a princely sum in the nineteenth century), he was hardly less willful in the management of his family than his own father had been. Yet in both his vociferously expressed opinions and in the management of his own clan, Henry James, Sr., positioned the Jameses in conspicuous opposition to the emergent norms of the middle-class family. He praised free love – perhaps, as he later claimed, without understanding the implications of his own argument. Such a defense, however, could not possibly have been offered for his bold denunciation of the piety of family feeling, which, he argued, is of little use except insofar as it anticipates a more perfect union of mankind with itself. Out-Emersoning the Emerson of *Self-Reliance,* Henry thundered:

3

I love my father and mother, my brother and sister, but I deny their unconditional property in me. . . . I will be the property of no person, and I will accept
property in no person. I will be the son of my father, and the husband of my
wife, and the parent of my child, but I will be all these things in a thoroughly
divine way, or only as they involve no obloquy to my inward rightness, only
as they impose no injustice on me towards others.

(Matthiessen, 55–6; hereafter cited as *JF*)

Nothing could stand as more of an affront to the evangelically driven,
bourgeois family Ryan describes than this troping of the linchpin of the middle-class belief-system, the concept of private property. Nor, it might be
added, could any course of child-rearing be conducted on principles less suit-
ed to producing proper middle-class citizens than the eccentric education by
tutors and in a variety of private schools that the Jameses received, first in
America then in Europe. Henry Jr. described his father's principles of "sensuous education" in the following terms: "What we were to do . . . was just
to *be* something, something unconnected with specific doing." And to in-
culcate "being" rather than "doing" is to rear a Paterian aesthete, not a middle-class businessman (*JF*, 36).

The results of the James family experiment were various, to be sure. Recurrent bouts of depression to the point of breakdown afflicted all the
Jameses from Henry Senior on down, as did varieties of alcoholism, self-
balking or -defeating behavior, neurasthenia, business failure, and suicide.
On the other hand, the system did nurture three geniuses, producing America's greatest philosopher, one of America's greatest novelists, and in Alice
James a writer of such power that her diary has justifiably been placed next
to the work of two of her brothers. For our purposes, however, the main
point is that this experiment placed Henry James thoroughly outside of the
dominant cultural institution of his own moment in all of its attitudinal,
moral, and social dimensions at precisely the moment of its social institu-
tionalization. The results are reflected in his writing. There are families ga-
lore in James's fiction, to be sure, but there are few if any representatives of
the bunkered nuclear type that Ryan describes. Instead, we encounter families in every possible state of dissolution: orphaned girls wandering Europe,
like Isabel Archer of *Portrait of a Lady* or Milly Theale of *Wings of the Dove*;
motherless daughters writhing under the thumbs of their possessive fathers,
like Catherine Sloper of *Washington Square*; neglected children given over
to near-mad governesses, like Miles and Flora of *The Turn of the Screw*; neglected children used as a gruesome ploy in games of adultery and divorce,
like Maisie Farange in *What Maisie Knew*. And when we do encounter at the

apex of James's so-called Major Phase, a completed, successful family unit –
that of Prince Amerigo, his wife Maggie, and their child the Principino in
The Golden Bowl – it is a family like none other in fiction: cleansed from the
twin threats of an incestuous closeness between a daughter and her own father and of an adulterous relation between her husband and his former lover
only in the very last sentence of the very last paragraph of the very last page.

James's representations of "family," in other words, pose a remarkable affront to dominant domestic ideals; it is as if his own experience unmoored
him from the pietics of family relation, allowing him to regard it with eyes
at once clear and skeptical. As such, he takes his place as one of our very best
nineteenth- and early twentieth-century analysts of the twists and turns of
those relations. The gusts of perverse emotion, the impulses toward posses-
siveness, the overtones of sexual compulsion that pervade the vicissitudes of
courtship, the institution of marriage, the raising of children: these are as fully registered in James as in any other novelist of his era, if not more so. As
is something else: the relation between intimacy and economy, the way that
private relations, particularly those involving women and children, always
involve the transmission of property. The words of his father – "I will be the
property of no person" – ring ironically in the fates of Milly Theale and Isabel Archer, women who are transformed into just that, first by the social
world in which they are embedded, then by the men they choose to fall in
love with. And at the end of each of these texts, these characters, like all of
James's greatest characters, take up Henry James Sr.'s words and give them
(mutatis mutandis) a meaning all their own: "I will be the son of my father,
and the husband of my wife, and the parent of my child, but I will be all these
things in a thoroughly divine way."

James, I am suggesting, was endowed by his own family and his particular education with the virtues as well as the burdens of a thoroughgoing marginality. Indeed, he possessed the ability to see to the core of arrangements
naturalized by his culture, and to write fictions that enforce upon the reader the deep strangeness abiding in them. In his recognition of the essential
oddity of the familial, James stands with equal oddity alongside those figures
against which his reputation has historically been plotted, the nineteenth-
century "domestic" or female novelists whose novels of family life combined
a treacly rhetoric with a hard-eyed vision of domestic dysfunctionality. What
Mrs. E.D.E.N. Southworth or Susan Warner expounded on the level of mass
or popular culture, in other words, James articulated on that of high or elite
culture – often in plots and language as ostentatiously "sentimental" as that
of his female contemporaries. When the dying Ralph Touchett in *Portrait of*

a Lady turns to declare his love for Isabel, or the dying Milly Theale, as her last living act, endows Merton so that he may marry his lover, one is not above feeling a tug on the tearducts as powerful (and as manipulative) as that offered by any of the female contemporaries whom James and his fellow high-culture critics condescended to, reviled, or ignored.

Some critics – Alfred Habegger is chief among them – have taken this congruence as the sign that James invidiously appropriated the constructions of female culture, rewriting these plots with intentions and in idioms that enforced feminine weakness and ratified masculine power. Perhaps this is so; but it would take a longer argument than there is space for here to explore the full ramifications of James's involvement with the mass market fictions of his era (for a beginning, see the third section of this essay). For now, I would point to only one of the many distinctive uses that James makes of the plot of family dissolution that was circulating so powerfully throughout the various cultural arenas of mid- to late-nineteenth-century culture, one that placed him at odds not only with the "literary domestics," to use a somewhat unfortunate phrase of Mary Kelley's, but also the high-culture littérateurs of his own moment, like George Eliot or Anthony Trollope, who turned to the same theme. To James, finally, the point of that plot is to enforce upon his reader the thoroughly subversive lesson (very close to his father's) that relations contained in the family can be best understood as an adumbration of more fulfilled relations between people undertaken through the channeling of desire in all its manifestations: social, sexual, acquisitive, emulative. In other words, James's persistent use of the family plot, even or especially at his most sentimental, directs us to the recognition that human beings must not only reckon with the relations that construct them, but also work to build new, more efficacious ones. And it is in these new relations, formed out of the contingencies of social encounter – Millie's endowment of Densher and Kate, and Merton's subsequent moral transformation; Isabel's decision to return to her marriage to rescue her step-daughter; even Maggie's decision to reconstruct her marriage and the Prince's decision to follow her will – that bonds between people are given value and meaning as if for the first time. The contingency of human relations concealed by the bourgeois family and enforced in its frequently cruel patterns of courtship and child-rearing thus become for James the grounds of their reconstruction. As horrifyingly tragic as the entanglements of human intimacy often turn out to be, it is their very fragility that allows for their remaking. And that remaking, for James, is the utopian point of the exercise – one that projects the making of social value through and well beyond the nineteenth-century nuclear family in all its splendid dysfunctionality, and hence foreshadows new possibilities of relation whose lineaments we are only now beginning to discover.

JAMES AND NATION

The position that James's upbringing allowed him to assume vis-à-vis family, education, and reproduction also placed him outside of another dominant social form of the later years of the nineteenth and early years of the twentieth century: that of the nation. Or, to be more accurate, James the American expatriate was uniquely positioned both inside and outside this configuration at the moment of its full consolidation; and here too his distinctive position allowed him to perceive possibilities whose importance has become clearer only over the rest of the century.

To James the question of national identity was both crucial and ramified. His fictions play a remarkable number of changes on a plot critics once referred to as "the International Theme," in which naive Americans encounter a Europe that seemed both endowed with cultural wonders and suffused with a sinister, often sexual, knowledge of the world. At times, this encounter is tragic. Daisy Miller wanders into the Roman Forum, an area well known to be miasmal, and dies of consumption; Isabel Archer wanders into an English country-house and ends up, after a number of plot turns, making a disastrous marriage with a pestiferous aesthete. At others, it is comic: Lambert Strether, sent to Europe by his patron to retrieve her son from a dangerous liaison, ends up misconstruing every single relation he so encounters and returns to America with his mission undone and his own affections thoroughly called into question. At yet other times, the encounter is melodramatic, even hokey: in *The American* the resonantly named Christopher Newman falls in love with a European and ends up enmeshed in a plot involving mysterious family secrets, fatal duels, and a lover locked away in a prisonlike convent. Sometimes it is so laden with thematic richness as to bear the weight of world-historical import: in *The Golden Bowl* when the millionaire Adam Verver carries the cultural riches of Europe to a palace of art in American City, America (James is painting with a very broad brush late in his career), the novel is clear to note that this act of appreciative appropriation places him, and the booming American capital he represents, in the position of the imperial projects that preceded him – those of Greece, Rome, and England. The translation of empire, in other words, is one with the transmission of culture: the matter of Americans in Europe is not simply a case of the innocents abroad, but also one of the remaking of cultural power at the moment of modernity.

The "International Theme" might, therefore, better be known as the national theme – or what happens to an identity conceived of as national at the moment when capital, communications, and culture began to circulate more freely across boundaries both geographical and imaginative. To be sure, whatever his own willed expatriation – James left America in 1874, returned only briefly thereafter, and ended his life as a British subject – there are relatively few non-Americans in his fictions, and fewer as finely imagined and fully wrought as his dazed and confused Americans searching for a purchase on their own identity in a foreign clime. But if what he called "the complex fate" of being American is at the center of James's concern with the national question, this fate is not interrogated in isolation. What remains at stake throughout is the *relationality* of national feeling at the moment of international intermingling. It is only when they travel to Europe, after all, that James's Americans are able to define their own national identity. And James's Englishmen and Europeans are by that very same process forced to recognize their own transmutation: their transformation into objects of exotic touristical interest (such is the fate of the Englishmen that Isabel Archer's friend Henrietta Stackpole encounters – even, James broadly hints, of the one she marries); into stereotypes (the lascivious Roman Giovanelli of *Daisy Miller* is as much a stock character as the innocent American girl who encounters him); into commodities (this is the fate of Prince Amerigo, whose bemusement at his own acquisition by an American millionaire we watch with a sense of horrified detachment all our own). At the moment when identities start to circulate across and through national borders and boundaries, when financial and cultural capital are being exported wholesale from an attenuating British empire or a vitiated Europe to a new kind of world power, what it is to be "English" or "Italian" or "French" is as much up for grabs as it what it is to be "American."

James understands, then, that national identity is an increasingly powerful force in the world at precisely the moment of, and through precisely the logic of, the increasing ease of international exchange; and that, in such a context, the idea of the nation could do powerfully complex work. After all, in James's lifetime, the force of nationalism wielded together a welter of independent monarchies under the guise of a common language and culture, as was the case with James's beloved Italy or his far-from-beloved Germany. He hoped that both language and culture might do the same for the United States itself, which had in his youth been rent asunder in the Civil War and was struggling in his middle years to reconstruct itself on a new, imperial model. But this resurgence of national feeling, as James also sees with extraordinary clarity, was itself called into question by migrations of culture and language across national boundaries under the impact of such forces as technological change, like the steamships that carried James across the Atlantic; the diasporas of population registered by the Jews and Italians and Irishmen who James increasingly sees in the teeming slums of England or America; the rise of a mass culture that was to create wholesale histories, identities, vivid "senses of the past" – or, in the words of Eric Hobsbawm, "invented traditions."

To devote myself fully to all of these three (and the other myriad factors in "becoming national" that James anatomizes) would take a volume in itself. Let me advert only to one, James's description of the invention of national tradition in his 1904 memoir of a visit to the United States, *The American Scene:*

> No long time is required, in the States, to make vivid for the visitor the truth that the nation is almost feverishly engaged in producing, with the greatest possible activity and expedition, an "intellectual" pabulum after its own heart, and that not only the arts and the ingenuities of the draftsman . . . pay their extravagant tribute, but those of the journalist, the novelist, the dramatist, the genealogist, the historian, are pressed for dear life into the service. The illustrators of the magazines improvise, largely – that is when not labouring in the cause of the rural dialects – improvise a field of action, full of features at any price . . . ; the novelists improvise, with the aid of historians, a romantic local past of costume and compliment and sword play and gallantry and passion; the dramatists build up, of a thousand pieces, the airy fiction that the life of the people in the world among whom the elements of clash and contrast are simplest and most superficial abounds in the subjects and situations and effects of the theater; while the genealogists touch up the picture with their pleasant hint of the number, over the land, of families of royal blood. All this constitutes a vast home-grown provision for entertainment, rapidly superseding any that may be borrowed or imported, and that indeed already begins, not invisibly, to press for exportation. . . . It is the public these appearances refer us to that becomes thus again the more attaching subject; the public so placidly uncritical that the whitest thread of the deceptive switch never makes it blink, and sentimental at once with such inveteracy and such simplicity that, finding everything everywhere perfectly splendid, it fairly goes down on its knees to be humbuggingly humbugged. It proves ever, by the ironic measure, quite incalculably young. (*AS*, 458–9)

This selection is a remarkable performance indeed; not only does it give a flavor of the baroque prose style that was to mark the later Henry James –

9

to the chagrin of William, contemporary audiences, and most readers of our day – but it also suggests his remarkable understanding of the reciprocal role played by the institutions of mass culture and the "public" they address in the creation of national identity. What James is writing about here is the way that a romantic past for the American South got invented in a frankly Hobsbawmian way, the way that narratives of "local color" work to generate a sense of the hoary historical past of that region for the consumption of a national audience. Or, to be more precise, he is noting the way that that national audience is created by the very act of consuming fictions of exoticized regionalism. James's argument turns on the many uses of the word "subject" in that remarkably vague phrase, "the more attaching subject": it refers at once to the rapturous audience; the subject matter they perceive; and the varied members of a national collective – a national subject created by witnessing these fictions of home-grown exoticism – organized here not by the rituals of state power but rather by their own desire for bewitchment-by-entertainment (the desire to be "humbuggingly humbugged"). But James's analysis does not stop here. He goes on to suggest that these texts form the materials of not only an American romance but a cultural commodity vendable on the world stage, a national narrative "that begins, not invisibly, to press for exportation" onto a world market, there to compete on equal terms with narratives that have previously been imported to make the American one. "Quite incalculably young" as the American national subject may be, it becomes the very type of what we might want to call modernity (or even postmodernity). Transnational, even global, its various varieties are created willy-nilly out of organic, native traditions via a booming mass culture and create in their turn a collective, mass identity through the consumption of precisely these fictions of exoticism.

There is much in this passage to remind us of the work of contemporary critics like Homi Bhabha and Frederic Jameson – not least the deliberate use of an abstruse vocabulary in cultural analysis: James, like these critics, seeks to oppose the political work of mass culture in its most banalizing sense by writing a prose that cannot be consumed easily or digested at will. (And he is like Jameson, in particular, in another way: just as Jameson declared the Hotel Bonaventure in Los Angeles the very prototype of postmodernity, so too James described the hermetic environments of "the hotel world" as the very cynosure of the American leisure class of the Gilded Age). Needless to say, the comparison reminds us that James did not display attitudes we might call progressive as he faced these new possibilities. Indeed, he possessed more than the usual prejudices of his class and moment, in distinct contrast with his brother William, who forthrightly opposed the Philippine War, fought for the racial integration of Boston trolley cars, and vigorously protested the closing of hotels and resorts to Jews in the 1880s. And, as we have seen, Henry was invested in a vision of traditional high culture as providing the necessary social glue in a world where ethnic minorities and women were entering the body politic in increasing numbers, a vision many recent readers have found demeaning and oppressive.

For these reasons (among others), critics of the 1980s like Jameson, or Mark Seltzer, or Caroline Porter, were particularly hard on James, discerning in him the very type of the ahistorical aesthete enforcing the privilege of his class or cunningly deploying the tactics of an "art of power" dismayingly continuous with the policing institutions of modernity like the asylum, the prison, and the police themselves. More recent critics, focusing on passages like the ones I have cited above, have discerned in James a more complex cultural politics: an openness to the noncarceral elements of modernity, a critique of thinking in narrow and reductive categories, a receptiveness to fluid, transformative models of identity. Whatever position one adopts here – I myself adhere to the latter – one thing is clear: when considered under the sign of the national–international interrelation, James is a more cunning analyst than he is given credit for under the rubrics of class or racial analysis alone. Despite the force of his local prejudices, he speaks for an understanding of national identity that is as progressive as any of his day: one thoroughly situated locally yet standing stubbornly free of any one national appellation or identity. In his globe-trotting Americans or his bemused Europeans or even his own critical comprehension of the American scene, James depicts a world where national and cultural identity exists (as does identity generated in the context of the family) as something to be made, not something given, in a world where new possibilities of identity-formation are being conjured forth by an internationalizing economy organized by leisure, travel, and mass culture. In this endeavor, many of his characters succeed, many fail; some fail by succeeding and others still succeed by failing: there is a good deal of doubt, moreover, as to whether James is to be classified with any one of these (my own view is that he can be grouped with any of the four). But what is undeniable is that he faces the imperative with both a hard-headed prescience about its more problematic dimensions and a refreshing openness to its utopian possibilities. The man whose adolescence was marked by the American Civil War and who died at the height of the first war to be described with the modifier "World" understood all too well the forces that went into the creation of the modern nation state, forces that bring people together in common projects as benign as the endowing of art museums and as horrific as the slaughter of millions in the trenches of Manassas – or the Somme. And at a moment when nationalism in its most oppressive guises continues to bedevil the efforts to create a more just and tolerant world, the shrewdness and utopian potential of James's project of redefining identity transactionally, relationally – one might even say cosmopolitanally – ought neither to be denied or discounted.

JAMES AND LITERARY CULTURES

The Henry James I have been trying to sketch here is thoroughly embedded in the social, cultural, and familial politics of his own moment, but in such a way as to suggest richer, more complex possibilities in them: affectional bonds that stand within and outside those of the family; identities rooted in national histories but finally transcending nationalist particularisms. The same is true of James's place in literary context. Few writers have been so fully and brilliantly versed in the literary traditions of their own moment; fewer have been so influential in transforming them into forms we have only recently come to appreciate.

To begin with James's place in the tradition of his own moment, what is most remarkable is the breadth of James's literary acquaintanceship. A list of writers who influenced James (according to critics and/or James himself) would include Americans (especially Hawthorne and Emerson); English writers (Austen, Dickens, Eliot, Trollope); Frenchmen (especially Balzac, de Maupassant, and Zola); even Russians like Turgenev. Every movement of the time – realism, naturalism, aestheticism, symbolism – was reflected upon in James's criticism and frequently found its reflection in his own writing. And James was friends with many of the most important writers of his day: Edith Wharton was a close companion (and James kept guard while she undertook liaisons with her lover, Morton Fullerton, whom he later immortalized as Merton Densher in *The Wings of the Dove*), as was the novelist and editor William Dean Howells. So were eminent British literati like the editor and author Edmund Gosse. Even James's literary antagonisms speak volumes about his centrality to the literary scene. When James's disastrous attempt at a theatrical success, *Guy Domville,* closed at the St. James's Theater in London (one of its few good reviews, by the way, was provided by George Bernard Shaw, then just beginning his career), it was succeeded the next week by Oscar Wilde's *Importance of Being Earnest,* which proceeded to run for a solid year, accompanied by the gnashing of James's teeth.

Here too we can see James interacting with the conditions of his moment in such a way as to anticipate possibilities that got developed only in the years after his death. Consider, for example, one of the most hallowed commonplaces of James criticism: the powerful influence exerted on James by his great American predecessor Nathaniel Hawthorne. This line of analysis was more or less initiated by James himself, with a series of essays on Hawthorne that fairly quivered with what contemporary critic Harold Bloom calls "the anxiety of influence." In the most famous, for example, he uses his analysis of Hawthorne to anatomize all the things that American culture (and by extension Hawthorne) was missing, then adds a dismissive comparison of Hawthorne's most famous novel, *The Scarlet Letter,* to an obscure British romance, *Adam Blair* – a comparison of such stunning inaptness that most James scholars have found it unnecessary to refer to that text ever again. Yet, as critics have long argued – Richard Brodhead is the latest and most convincing of them – Hawthorne is everywhere in James. The power of Hawthorne can be glimpsed in thematic concerns like the fate of the American art-lover abroad, which Hawthorne memorably first explored in *The Marble Faun,* and upon which James rings so many memorable changes thereafter. It can be seen in plot-devices: Merton Densher's self-punishing discovery of a moral sense at the end of *Wings* owes everything to Donatello's similar recognition in the *Faun;* so does the Prince's at the end of *The Golden Bowl.* It can be seen in what one might want to call a moral recognition or sensibility: Isabel's decision to return to Osmond at the end of *Portrait* resembles nothing so much as Hester's decision to stay in Boston after Dimmesdale's death in *The Scarlet Letter.* More generally, it can be glimpsed in James's thematics of vicariousness – a quirk first encountered in Hawthorne's relentless Chillingworth, expanded into a narrative device in his remarkable *Blithedale Romance,* then carried forth in such memorable Jamesian versions as Ralph Touchett or Lambert Strether. It is extended in his very representational mode itself: with that admixture of realistic plots and character descriptions with the machinery of sheer romance that defines Hawthorne; often precipitated into names that chime with allegorical significance (*Daisy* Miller, *Adam* Verver); often elaborated into the strikingly romance-laden metaphors that increasingly govern James's narrative method. Descriptions of Gilbert Osmond's character may be perfectly well motivated in a traditional mimetic sense; but Isabel's figurative understandings of him in language reminiscent of Hawthorne's "Rappaccini's Daughter" invokes a world of good and evil that the urbane surface of the narrative would seem to disavow.

Yet it is important to remember that, for all Hawthorne does *for* James, James does a good deal *to* Hawthorne, placing the distinctive Hawthornean methods in a frame all his own. Consider the ways that James takes Hawthorne's experiment with the principle of vicariousness in *The Blithedale Romance* further in such texts as *The Ambassadors*. Hawthorne's novel gives us a narrator who is fascinated by, but stands resolutely outside of, the demands of intimacy; as he witnesses the figures he encounters in a Brook Farm-like commune in New England, he conceals from himself what is quite obvious to the reader: the erotic dimensions of his interest in a young woman named Priscilla, whose entanglement with the reformer Hollingsworth he has been winsomely regarding. Looking back at the end of the novel on the course his life has taken since his time in Blithedale, the narrator ends with a confession that is about as anticlimactic as any in American literature:

> Life . . . has come to a rather idle pass with me. Would my friends like to know what brought it thither? There is one secret, – I have concealed it all along, and never meant to let the least glimpse of it escape, – one foolish little secret, which may possibly have something to do with these inactive years of meridian manhood, with my bachelorship, with the unsatisfied retrospect that I fling back on life, and my listless glance towards the future. Shall I reveal it? . . .
> I – I myself – was in love – with – PRISCILLA! (247)

When James turns his eyes some fifty years later to the same plot, he sets out to recast the Hawthornean scene with an added spin all his own. James's bachelor, Lambert Strether, too, has found that his life has come to an "idle pass." He travels to Europe in the throes of a midlife crisis precipitated by his possible marriage to the oppressive Mrs. Newsome on a mission to save her son Chad from European dissolution, and, as he discovers, the affections of a beautiful European lady, M. de Vionnet. He is assured by one and all that theirs is a "virtuous relation" and chooses to believe this rather transparent social lie. When he happens to see these two together on a boat in the French countryside acting with an ease that bespeaks their deep "intimacy revealed," he discovers his self-deception with a shock that is positively Coverdalean in its anticlimactic force. But James goes Hawthorne one better in raising delicately, through this all-too-unsurprising discovery, another open secret – a secret within a secret: that the intensity of this revelation may lie as much in Strether's interest in Chad as in the facts of intimacy itself. These implications are not unknown to Hawthorne's text, since Coverdale is as obsessed with Hollingworth's opinion as he is with his bride-to-be; but they are strikingly accentuated by James in his staging of this primal scene. And James adds one more thing to the Hawthornean example: far from being an example of attenuation and loss, Strether embraces the consolations that come with "meridian manhood" lived on the bachelor plan. Somehow, it seems, merely seeing is enough: he can return to America not so much with a knowledge of his own, but with a knowledge of what knowledge looks like, with a greater intimacy with intimacy itself.

The point is not only that James does unto his precursor what great writers do to their predecessors – steal; it is that James makes it impossible for us to read *Blithedale* the same way again. He makes us aware of the multidirectional nature of the feelings that Hawthorne has anatomized, and of the visionary possibilities as well as the deep melancholia built into the model of the vicarious bachelor. A similar operation can be seen in James's encounters with any of his great contemporaries and precursors. George Eliot's Grandcourt, the pestiferous villain of *Daniel Deronda,* for example, provides the model for James's Gilbert Osmond; yet the thoroughly bourgeois, tasteless Osmond critiques the grandiloquent villainy of his predecessor, and reminds us, in a phrase that James would have liked, of the banality of evil.

What is important about this kind of relation, for our purposes, is not its specific dynamics, but what they tell us about James's role in literary and cultural history. James serves as a great conduit between the nineteenth- and the twentieth-century traditions of narrative. He participated fully and vigorously in the great formal traditions of the nineteenth century, yet experimented with them, accentuated those elements in them that, when pushed one step further, led in the direction of the destabilized, the epistemologically vertiginous. James takes up the interest in narrative perspective that Hawthorne and George Eliot and Flaubert all played with and writes *The Sacred Fount,* a text in which a monomaniacal obsessive spends a weekend in the country hypothesizing who is involved with whom, and ends up being told by a confidant that he is quite mad, a judgment the reader is by that point more than inclined to share. Or he takes up the interplay between romance and realism that is the hallmark of the nineteenth-century novel and comes up with *The Wings of the Dove,* a text that constructs its meaning through symbols so resonant that they pass well beyond any known register of realistic representation. Or he takes up the problem of literary interpretation itself by writing "The Figure in the Carpet" – a story whose central point seems to be that the ability to interpret a literary text is indistinguishable from a disastrous monomania. In responding to and revising the fictional work of the nineteenth century, in other words James prophesies the directions it would take in the twentieth. And he foretells not only the moment of modernism but that of its recessive, self-parodic, fiction whose main action often seems to be the undoing of the process of fabulation itself. In short, James helps invent the postmodern.

But James's Janus-faced engagement with literary culture does not stop there. James is important not only as a practitioner but as an example of the cultural conditions that make possible the literary career; and here too his example is remarkably Janus-faced. On the one hand James was – made himself into – a figure upon whom we look back with some nostalgia: the man of letters. It's important to remember that James was perceived, by his detractors as well as his admirers, not only as the preeminent novelist of his time (so significant in his native America, for example, that an apartment building was named after him; so important in England that he is buried in the Poet's Corner at Westminster Abbey) but also as one of the great critics, fully the equal of contemporaries like Gosse in England or Howells in America. He played a particularly crucial role in both England and America, moreover, as both a mediator and a theoretician. He was one of the first to explicate fully and crucially the European tradition for an Anglo-American audience; the author of one of the most important and interesting essays defending the proposition that fiction was indeed an art; the author, in the prefaces to the New York Edition, of some of the most important reflections on that newly defined art. No wonder, then, that not only audiences of his own time, but also a number of writers in the years thereafter, treated James as a kind of a literary polymath, one who challenged the specialization that has increasingly marked both the literary and the critical world. The surest sign of this, it seems to me, is the breadth of admiration for James among those figures who have sought most intensely to keep the tradition of the man of letters current throughout an age of increasing specialization. T. S. Eliot, Edmund Wilson, Lionel Trilling, Irving Howe, and more recently Cynthia Ozick, have all argued for the nineteenth-century ideal of the broadly read sensibility extending itself over the literary and cultural field and, in so doing, have turned at crucial moments to the example of James.

But lest we consign James too quickly to just the status of benign anachronism from which I have been trying to rescue him, it's important to keep in mind that he was a thoroughly up-to-date practitioner of the literary trade. James was the first major writer to employ a literary agent, for example; one of the first to have his work transcribed onto that newly perfected invention, the typewriter. His attitude toward business dealings was as thoroughly dis-enchanted as any I know; reading his correspondence with editors and pub-lishers, one senses his grandfather the wheeler-dealer lurking behind the mask of the Master of the literary world. James's attitudes toward the new-ly engorging mass audience, too, were more complex than we assume if we think of him as a stuffy man of letters. For one thing, it is crucial in reading James to remember that he was fascinated by mass culture from the very be-ginning – it was a viewing of a touring company of *Uncle Tom's Cabin* that first alerted an eight-year-old Henry James to the possibilities of dramatic art – and that, throughout his career, both the figurative resources and the plot devices of his fiction are frankly lifted from melodrama, Gothic fiction, and sentimental novels. When Charlotte Stant turns to Prince Amerigo early on in *The Golden Bowl,* the reader should think of Judith Krantz or Sidney Shel-don, not Hawthorne or George Eliot:

> "Well, now, I must tell you, for I want to be absolutely honest." So Char-lotte spoke, a little ominously, after they had gotten into the Park. "I don't want to pretend, and I can't pretend a moment longer. You may think of me what you will, but I don't care. I knew I shouldn't and I find now how little. I came back for this. Not really for anything else. For this . . . To have one hour alone with you."
> (23:89)

James's engagement with the booming mass culture of the later nineteenth and earlier twentieth centuries is perhaps less significant, however, than James's attempt to find a place for himself in that sphere. These efforts are not quite as laughable as they might seem. James, it is important to remem-ber, made his name with a vast popular success, that of *Daisy Miller,* which was an international sensation when it was published in 1879 (and from which, for complicated reasons, James realized practically nothing); *Portrait of a Lady,* too, was immensely successful with both the critics and James's readership alike. As tastes changed throughout the 1880s, James tried to re-capture his earlier success, writing fictions like *The Bostonians* and *The Princess Casamassima* that attempted to ride the waves of realism and nat-uralism, respectively. After their failure, James's attempts to court this new-er audience turned to the theater, where, as we have seen, he was an equal-ly spectacular failure. Thereafter followed the so-called Major Phase, that period during which James's writing became increasingly hermetic, elabo-rate, mannerist; but even here James attempted to capitalize on those in his audience who found the very difficulty of this work a sign of its distinction. Such, at least, is the idea behind his New York Edition, a monumental revised edition of his works, with new (and unbelievably abstruse) introductions by James himself. For that edition was intended to allow the self-proclaimed Master to achieve, late in life, some financial security. That it did not financially succeed – James realized only $221 from its proceeds – is less important, for our purposes, than the fact that James was still conceiving of his writing as a means of doing so, still searching for his niche in the increasingly segmented marketplace of the later years of the nineteenth century and early years of the twentieth.

Striking the stances of the Flaubertian aesthete and the avid businessman; searching high cultural distinction and a financially remunerative popular success; incorporating mass cultural topoi into his texts and yet at the same time proclaiming his distaste for its overt manifestations: these define a distinctive position of the Jamesian artist standing both inside and outside the literary marketplace at one and the same time. And, it might be argued, these various impulses define precisely the conditions of possibility for the generations of artists, writers, and poets who were to follow in James's path. If James, as I have been arguing, is to be read as the first great modern writer, he is most fully that in his unstable negotiation between artistic vocation and professionalism, devotion to the highest sense of the aesthetic and an equally intense yearning for popular success. Indeed, we might put it that James is the first figure to merge these two impulses: to discover that to strike a stance of superiority to the forces of the marketplace is to find a distinctive niche within it. It is a discovery that poets and novelists have been exploring – and exploiting – ever since.

OUR HENRY JAMES?

The James I have been describing here is one, I hope, that readers will both recognize and feel alienated from. At moments, he explores issues and problems in a way that feels vibrantly alive; at others, his vision feels irrevocably other. Paradoxically, what I have discovered in teaching James is that readers respond vividly to precisely his oddity, his alienation, his (to use James's own sense of the term) queerness: for these, after all, ring with a sense of estrangement that is thoroughly, archetypally modern (if not postmodern). We miss the real importance of James, however, if we attempt to turn him into one of our contemporaries – even if, as I have tried to suggest here, James gives a range of subversive or alternative readings to the dominant cultural commonplaces of his moment in such a way as to offer our hypercritical age a critical leverage on those perceptions. But James's chief usefulness for the contemporary reader is not to identify subversive potentials in his own culture for our complacent approval. Rather, it is that he foregrounds the sheer range of possibilities that circulated through his own time, and suggests the difficulty of navigating among them. Like Spencer Brydon, the protagonist of "The Jolly Corner" who comes back to New York to encounter a ghostly vision of the self he might have been had he stayed, James returns us to familiar territory to see things there we did not think we knew. And in so doing, he challenges us to make similar journeys, to face equally destabilizing recognitions. If, to cite but one example, in his metafictional works, James stages a crisis of interpretation, he also challenges the disenchanted literary idiom of our time. Reading *The Sacred Fount*, it is difficult to be unsuspicious of *anything* – even the hermeneutics of suspicion itself.

James, I am arguing, is profoundly of moment at the current moment not because he deals with issues that matter to us in a way that we find pleasing or powerful (although often he does that), or because he offers us a chance to diagnose the ideological tendencies of his own moment (although often he does that, too). Rather, James is crucial to the contemporary reader because he challenges us continually to rethink our own sense of the relation between past and present, of the possibilities of familial or national or literary life, without ever ceasing to understand that this process is a process, not a dogma. It is telling, I think, that the only one of James's major fictions to achieve fully formal and thematic closure, *The Golden Bowl*, was his last completed novel, as if the achievement of a resolution were coterminous with the cessation of the process of rethinking, revising, and reworking that *The Golden Bowl* epitomizes. And it is even more telling that immediately upon finishing a novel that itself intensely revisits the rest of his work, James should have written a series of prefaces which re-read his own achievement, including one for *The Golden Bowl* that revisits the notion of revision itself.

Some may cite this self-revising tendency as an example of the very worst of the narcissistic self-concern and grandiosity that define our very worst image of Henry James: that of a figure who, in the words of his brother William, chewed more than he bit off. It would be senseless to deny that James can irritate as well as enliven: after sixteen years of reading, reflecting upon, and teaching James, I still find some paragraphs so irritating that I vow never to read another one again. And yet I do; and when I do, I find his work a constantly renewing challenge, not only to my re-reading of it, but also to the very ways in which I have gotten used to thinking about reading itself, to its range of interpretive possibilities, its set of cultural ramifications. It is in just this wary but respectful spirit that I seek to introduce the essays that follow in this "Companion" to James: one which, I think, mirrors the kinds of companionship James offers us. James was a famously loyal friend; but in his works he increasingly abjured the charms of companionship for a persistent challenge to his readers' more sanguine self-conceptions. My hope is that the essays which follow will do likewise: that they will not only offer useful contexts and glosses but that they will also send the reader back out to James, there more fully to reconstruct her own relation to the fascinatingly complex, wildly excessive, rapidly metamorphosing culture – familial, national, literary – of our own moment: a moment that increasingly looks, for all the world, like the moment of Henry James.

WORKS CITED

Brodhead, Richard. *The School of Hawthorne.* New York: Oxford University Press, 1986.

Eley, Geoff, and Suny, Ronald. *Becoming National: A Reader.* New York: Oxford University Press, 1996.

Habegger, Alfred. *Henry James and the "Woman Business."* Cambridge University Press, 1993.

Hawthorne, Nathaniel. *The Blithedale Romance* and *Fanshawe.* The Centennial Edition of the Works of Nathaniel Hawthorne, Vol. 3. Columbus: Ohio State University Press, 1965.

Hobsbawm, Eric, and Ranger, Terence. *Invented Traditions.* Cambridge University Press, 1983.

Matthiessen, F. O. *The James Family: A Group Biography.* New York: Oxford University Press, 1947.

Ryan, Mary. *Cradle of the Middle Class: The Family in Oneida County, New York, 1790–1865.* Cambridge University Press, 1991.

I

MARTHA BANTA

Men, Women, and the American Way

There is little or nothing going on in Henry James's mind that is *not* about social relations between women and men; every issue is ultimately gendered. Thus to think about gender in James is to think of just about everything he said and wrote. It is necessary, therefore, to draw some lines in this essay, to single out certain aspects and particular moments in time for specific consideration, with the understanding that all those other things are left unattended. The focus here is upon James's long novel, *The Golden Bowl,* published in 1905, and *The American Scene* of 1907, compiled from notes James gathered in 1904 and 1905 while roaming the America of President Theodore Roosevelt after an absence of twenty years. These two specimens cut loose from the living flesh of his extensive career are not anomalies. Both the fictive narrative and the text of social commentary forcefully represent the accumulative results of James's lifelong study of the self-limiting manner by which the gender-shaped society of his homeland imposed narrowly defined sexual, political, and cultural functions upon its men and its women.

First (James recollecting the hard lines drawn in the sand on what was right and proper behavior for males and for females in the days of his youth prior to the Civil War, during the war years, and in its aftermath) and last (James responding to the gender classifications he encountered upon his return visit to the States in 1904), James's reactions stand in awkward opposition to the received wisdom vouchsafed by his male contemporaries. As shall be seen, this is especially the case in regard to the views expressed by one of the most publicly vocal of his compatriots, Theodore Roosevelt, twenty-sixth president of the United States whose Progressivist administration energetically commanded the years between 1901 and 1909. To get at the nub of arguments that absorbed James's generation in the opening years of the twentieth century (and that continue to absorb ours), James's observations are set against Roosevelt's pronouncements on the duties expected of all males aspiring to be true Americans that conflate social, biological, and national identity. Then it comes clear where the Rooseveltian position slots a man like Henry James, who could claim to be neither authentically male nor authentically American. But hold fast to the realization that what either man has to say about what it means to be male and masculine has everything to do with what it signifies to be female and feminine, as well as what is implied by the ultimately gendered definitions "the American" and "the cosmopolitan."

Of course, the United States has "males" and "females" – those biological entities distinguished solely by basic sexual differences – but has this nation a variety of persons in full possession of the complicating characteristics indicated by the gender terms "masculine" and "feminine"? In the name of "American Exceptionalism," some have argued that this is a land where the laws of man and nature are bent so that things happen (or do not happen) in ways unique to its society and history.[1] But could America be *that* exceptional that it denies differences of "gender" altogether? There were times when Henry James thought so, and it concerned him greatly.

"There were the two sexes, I think, and the range of age, but, once the one comprehensive type was embraced, no other signs of differentiation" (*AS* 224). There were times when it appeared to his enquiring mind that even sexual distinctions had been eliminated. "There are no 'kinds' of people, there are simply people, very, very few, and all of one kind" (*AS* 27).

Nullity of differentiation naturally worries a novelist, for think what this fuzziness does either to the making of traditional plots based on gendered conflicts over money, sex, and marriage, or to the *un*making of novelistic formulas through efforts to introduce new developments in the writing of prose fiction. Surely, a great deal was at stake for James if America offered no gender distinctions as stimuli for his imagination.

As a much-traveled cosmopolitan who had been in and out of Europe since childhood and who lived abroad from 1883 to 1904, James appreciated the plenitude of stories available to writers working the international circuit. Any eager story-teller at work in England and on the Continent could count on copious examples of the intricate negotiations taking place between men and women whose complex destinies are dramatically heightened at every twist and turn by the fact that each contains both masculine and feminine elements in their nature; across the Atlantic the writer's imagination was further enriched by those nuances of class, race-nationality, and manners that make individuals fascinatingly at variance from one another. So what was an American-born author – self-described as "the restless analyst" – to do when faced by the seeming absence of gender distinctions as he wandered about gathering impressions for *The American Scene?* Ever grateful for small favors in the midst of a culture barren of the variations provided by "Europe," it was a godsend for James to realize that America at least admits the existence of two gender types: men who are in business, women who tend to whatever forms the nation's "society" takes.

Growing up in the 1840s and 1850s, James learned early that being demonstrably "masculine" in America was mainly associated with the making of money. Two other possibilities were also allowed the male sex in America: being a Daniel Webster (the politician) or being tipsy (the idler living on inherited wealth). If the tippling clubman was viewed with some contempt in comparison with the man of public affairs, at least both shared recognized forms of male behavior. Since women were denied access to Wall Street and the marketplace, and since statecraft and the gentlemen's club life were also off limits, members of the female sex – together with males for whom "femininity" was the ruling attribute of their gendered nature – were left with the leavings; their designated fate was to rattle around in that limited area of social and cultural affairs lying well outside the arenas of money, politics, and power.

Through his early decision to devote his life to the vocation of authorship, James automatically placed himself within the "feminine" sphere; in the eyes of the True American Male he was neither recognizably masculine nor American. But one must recognize that although James was shunted, and shunted himself, across the gender-line where his female compatriots held forth, James never identified himself fully with what it means to be a woman. He always held himself to be male as a biological fact and a man as a social entity, however much he recognized the feminine sensibilities that governed his inner life, his creative impulses, and his slant on the wide world of cultural affairs.

It will not do to think of James as a proto-feminist. One should know better than to go to his writings for brilliant insights into the lives of working-class women, of women of color, or of the female members of the "new alien" hordes. He cannot be expected to respond with either sympathy or understanding to the New Woman as she attempts to enter the corridors of political power as a turn-of-the-century Daniel Webster or to achieve recognition within the professional world. See James for what he is: author of tales mainly about upper-class unmarried women involved in various courtship rituals and marriage rites with upper-class men at the private level, and recorder of the social splits that separate males from females in the nation's public life. Value him for what he gives, which is a good deal, especially when compared with what Theodore Roosevelt and like-minded males had to offer.

To be a man or a woman in America was no happy state of affairs; this fact impressed itself upon Henry James with increasing pressure over the years. By the time he sent *The American Scene* to his publisher, its pages were filled with his anxiety over the ruinous effect upon American life when notice was granted to only two kinds of people: the man of business and the woman of society. "Character is developed to visible fineness only by friction and discipline on a large scale," he wrote, "only by its having to reckon with a complexity of forces" (*AS* 315). As James checked out the social landscape, his long-held fears were reconfirmed: lack of relational complexity between men and women stifled any chance for creative reciprocity between attributes of "masculinity" and "femininity"; marriage plots continued to follow patterns laid down by the martial arts, however carefully authors might hide the latent violence; national "history" defined itself in terms of money, brutal short-cuts, and aggressive acts, rather than of culture, continuity, and creative contemplation. For James to write about "The American Scene" committed him to talking in public about gender; this meant worrying in private about the consequences should Theodore Roosevelt's presidency reinforce rhetorical connections between the nation's "masculinity," its business activities, its moral and martial codes, and its race future.

In January 1905, Henry James attended a dinner at the White House. He could not bear the Roosevelt type (noisily adolescent, exhaustively intense, bitingly homophobic) nor Roosevelt's expansionist politics (militant, chauvinistic, self-righteous). Roosevelt's distaste for the Jamesian type (effeminate, Anglophiliac, the mere artist) was just as pronounced. On that occasion, energetic "masculinity" writ large shared the same table with unassertive "femininity," but the two men minded their manners and conversed amiably throughout the evening. On other occasions, however, both before and during his time as president, Theodore Roosevelt made resoundingly clear what he intended the American Way to be: one decisively bound to his belief in the gender functions universally exacted of males and females in all "civilized" countries that it was this nation's destiny to protect against infiltrations of "foreign" degeneracy.

As the ultimate Public Man, Roosevelt commanded the means to make his views known that James would never enjoy; he mounted the bully pulpit as New York Assemblyman, New York City's Police Commissioner, Assistant Secretary of the Navy, and Vice-President under William McKinley until the latter's assassination in 1901 projected him into the presidency. Ever skillful at choosing his audiences, Roosevelt saw to it that every public speech or printed essay added force to his campaign for the adoption of his packed agenda of Progressive policies. Amidst all the various calls to action he made regarding scores of political issues, he pounded his pulpit with particular vigor when expressing his unswerving belief that the nation's future greatness depended upon upholding two related ideals: the strenuous assertion of American masculinity demonstrated as will, work, and readiness for moral (and mortal) combat, and the patriotic support given by the American female who dedicates her life to mothering strong sons.

What actually did masculinity mean to Roosevelt? It was a matter of "character," he maintains in "Biological Analogies in History." In turn, "character" depends as much on inborn qualities available only to legatees of the "right blood" as it does upon having been properly trained in American mores. Weakness of character – viewed as lack of virility, the tendency to shy away from war, and self-indulgence in effete luxuries – is effected by weakness of "blood," which is why it is crucial to keep members of the "civilized" races safe from a declining birthrate and from the encroachment of the "barbaric" races.[2]

Roosevelt equated "manhood" with "statehood" when speaking on one of his favorite topics, "the winning of the West" – the "great epic feat in the history of our race" – that proves America allows "scant room for the coward and the weakling."[3] Even though the blessed "old iron days have gone" and we live "in softer times," "there is small space indeed for the idler, for the luxury loving man who prizes ease more than hard, triumph-crowned effort" (324–5). The American male possesses "the positive virtues of resolution, of courage, of indomitable will, of power to do without shrinking the rough work that must always be done" (326). He will never show the "least touch of flabbiness, of unhealthy softness," of "self-seeking ambition," and of "contempt for the moral law" (ibid.). And beside every right man, there stands the right woman. America remains safe for its supreme role in the world's politics as long as it rests upon "the individual manliness and womanliness, using the words in their widest and fullest meaning" (327).

Whenever Roosevelt calls upon both sexes to uphold as their mutual aim "to be a good husband or good wife, a good neighbor and friend, to be hardworking and upright in business and social relations, to bring up many healthy children," it is the male to whom he speaks directly, as when he calls upon him to do "not only his duty to himself, his family, and his neighbors, but his duty to the State" (ibid). It is assumed the women will learn from their men what is expected of them to do for their country.

Although Roosevelt's rhetoric and tone rings with self-confidence, that confidence stems from real anxieties. Challenges to America's national greatness through the sapping of American masculine force come from two impinging types: 1) the unassimilable immigrant who defiles native purity with his bad "blood" and bad "character"; 2) the expatriated American who may have the right "blood" but who possesses the wrong "character." Now, Henry James came from Irish Protestant stock, and the large family sired by his grandfather William (who wrote Big Business in capital letters) had fully assimilated to the native culture; but James forfeited his right to be a true American when he left the States to take up residence in the "foreign" literary world.

"The man," writes Roosevelt, "who becomes Europeanized, who loses his power of doing good work on this side of the water, and who loses his love for his native land, is not a traitor; but he is a silly and undesirable citizen."[4] Accordingly, James is the type who forms "a noxious element in our body politic" through "that flaccid habit of mind which its possessors style cosmopolitanism" (ibid.). One should disdain men who have "some organic weakness in their moral or mental make-up" and praise those "who are robustly patriotic, and who have sound healthy minds" (21). By becoming "a second-rate European" – "over-civilized, oversensitive, over-refined" – the Jamesian type "has lost the hardihood and manly courage by which alone he can conquer in the keen struggle of our national life" (22). Warming up to his attack, Roosevelt concludes, "Thus it is with the undersized man of letters, who flees his country because he, with his delicate, effeminate sensitiveness, . . . finds he cannot play a man's part among men, and so goes where he will be sheltered from the winds that harden stouter souls" (23). A special doom awaits men who choose expatriation; they stop being men altogether and collapse into a state of "nothingness." If the European comes to America and fails to assimilate while failing "to remain a European," he "becomes nothing at all" (26). If American-born, "this same being does not really become a European; he only ceases being an American, and becomes nothing" (22).

Roosevelt assails the scandal of failed masculinity on several fronts. The male who does not stay in America denies his manhood; anyone who lives abroad is classified as "feminine" whatever his or her biological status. The male who stays but does not work is also condemned to be a man without a country. Since what artists do is not considered real work, the man who takes up the literary life abroad is doubly damned. As for women (dropped in by Roosevelt as a bit of an afterthought, since it is Man speaking to Men that energizes his rhetoric): they forgo their intended sex role and their status as good citizens if they neither marry nor bear healthy children.

In the middle of these assertions – many of which attack the very basis by which James defines his worth, his individuality, and his status as a citizen of the world – there appears a point at which James's questions begin to overlap with Roosevelt's answers. Both men eye the impact made upon the nation's strenuous life by the man of business; both analyze the role held by those (male and female) who neither toil nor spin in the marketplace; both, that is, debate the nature of the "proper" division of labor between the sexes. Having established this intersection of common concern, one sees better just where James starts to veer away from Roosevelt when it comes to the lives of Americans of either sex who create culture, not nations; who make conversation, not money.

In 1899 Roosevelt delivered one of his signature statements, "The Strenuous Life." Addressing his words to a receptive audience of strenuous Chicagoans – "men who pre-eminently and distinctly embody all that is most American in the American character" – he announced that he wished

> to preach, not the doctrine of ignoble ease, but the doctrine of the strenuous life, the life of toil and effort, of labor and strife; to preach that highest form of success which comes, not to the man who desires mere easy peace, but to the man who does not shrink from danger, from hardship, or from bitter toil, and who out of these wins the splendid ultimate triumph.[5]

On almost every public occasion Roosevelt would return to making connections between the individual act and its consequences to the national good, between what is expected of the manly male and the womanly female, for "as it is with the individual, so it is with the nation" (269). "In the last analysis a healthy state can exist only when the men and women who make it up lead clean, vigorous, healthy lives" (ibid.). "The man must be glad to do a man's work, to dare and endure and to labor. . . . The woman must be the housewife, the helpmeet of the homemaker, the wise and fearless mother of many healthy children" (ibid.). This is no little matter; if these efforts should fail, a form of cultural genocide will result.

> When men fear work or fear righteous war, when women fear motherhood, they tremble on the brink of doom; and well it is that they should vanish from the earth, where they are fit subjects for the scorn of all men and women who are themselves strong and brave and high-minded.　　　　　　　(ibid.)

What exactly does Roosevelt have in mind when he speaks in ringing tones about the "work" American males must not shirk? What *kind* of work exactly is expected of real men? Elsewhere he extols the frontiersman bearing axe and rifle who "won the West" away from "barbaric tribes"; elsewhere he acknowledges the importance in times past of the medieval knight; elsewhere he allocates glory for men who are willing to leap into the battle fray during the nation's current military ventures abroad; and everywhere he chooses for himself the role of Daniel Webster through dedication to a life of politics and statecraft. But these are heroes of whom he speaks. What of ordinary men caught up in day-to-day activities?

Roosevelt honors the part commonly played by men in the commercial world. Since there are today "great branches of industry which call forth in those that follow them more hardihood, manliness, and courage than any industry of ancient times," he is willing to elevate some to the heroic level of the Man of Business.[6] Still, Roosevelt distrusts the moral and civic ravages caused when the business instinct goes uncurbed. The businessman, *the* signifier for American masculinity throughout James's youth, is viewed by Roosevelt as a potential threat to true masculinity and true Americanism. As the nation moves into the twentieth century, newly responsible for exerting power along a global plane, the placement of too much emphasis upon business success may portend less rather than more vigor; it might lead to those habits of slothfulness Roosevelt associates with the indolent artist. This, then, is the danger:

> If we lose the virile, manly qualities, and sink into a nation of mere hucksters, putting gain above national honor, and subordinating everything to mere ease of life; then we shall indeed reach a condition worse than that of the ancient civilizations in the years of their decay. (150)

What had James to say as he compiled notes for *The American Scene* about the gendering of the ethos of business and politics that effaced the presence of persons who reside beyond the shadows cast by the towers of Wall Street or the capitol domes of political power? Several things not on the mind of Theodore Roosevelt, that is for certain.

In his continuing campaign against the arrogant power of the Trusts, Roosevelt busily worked to cut big business down to size. Through his support of antitrust legislation, he made it clear to the nation's industrialists that the government had the ability to rein in excessive profit-making. Like Hercules cleansing the Augean stables, Roosevelt intended to end the pollution of the business scene and to restore moral rectitude and stability to the economy. Responding to major social crises is precisely what activist statesmen are in the position to do, and Roosevelt had the energy, the intelligence, and the will to correct the Big Picture of Big Business by pitting his ideals of manly, moral militancy against forces threatening to negate the American Way. These public accomplishments are not possible for quiet literary persons who touch down briefly on belated visits to the States, clearly not possible for one of the effete expatriate idlers Roosevelt denounced for being "nothing at all."

As James assessed the ruinous effects of unleashed "pecuniary power" that marred the face of every urban center he visited in 1904 and 1905, he concluded that money was lord and master in America; he was appalled by the stupidity by which it was made and the stupidity of how it was spent. However, the conclusions to which James came about the social implications of this situation differ markedly from those reached by Roosevelt. What separates the two positions is not the fact that Roosevelt, as president, was able to write, speak, and act with jeremiad anger against the Trusts; it is not the difference in effective power at each man's command. Rather, it is a matter of what each believed is most at stake for society once selfish business interests are in the saddle.

Roosevelt thundered against the monopolists (the sector of the business enterprise he singled out for reform) because of his conviction that unless the big industrialists were brought to heel the nation's political base – and with it the nation's manhood – was in danger. That is, Roosevelt as the leading statesman of his day took up the strong man's duty to protect the rights of decent American males in the workplace. Always in opposition to Roosevelt's relentlessly single-sex perspective, James as the artist ("out of it" in every way recognized by masculine America) assessed the mortal damage being done to the lives of the nation's women as well as to its men. With business (males making money as their only public activity) defining what America "meant" before the world, then culture (what women were delegated to do by default of male participation) had no worth on the American scene.

At stake for Roosevelt were good business practices as opposed to bad business dealings for the sake of a society that let good men work hard and good women mother children. At stake for James was culture in general for having to contend with any form of business activity; women, abandoned by men focused single-mindedly upon making money in a nation where "the imagination at once embraces" "the appearance of a queer deep split or chasm between the two stages of personal polish, the two levels of the conversible state, at which the sexes have arrived"; a nation where "the unmitigated 'business man' face" assaults the social scene in contrast to "the women over the land . . . [who] appear to be of a markedly finer texture than the men" by being "less narrowly specialized" and "less commercialized" (51).

The accounting *The American Scene* makes of a national gender crisis comes to us by way of the mind of an author who represents the "feminine" side of the male sex. James acknowledges he cannot dissect the intricacies of the business climate or follow the ins and outs of political battles carried out in the public arena. This is, he apologizes, "a line of research closed to me, alas, by my fatally uninitiated state" (88). But if Roosevelt is everything James is not, James is much more than Roosevelt. As "the painter of life," James holds a privileged perspective. Who can match the writer's capacity to wonder whether, "for pure drama, the drama of manners, anything any- where else touches it" (51)? In truth, James knows that whatever social scene he tests, he is in "danger of seeing, in comparison, almost nothing else in it – nothing, that is, so characteristic as this apparent privation, for the man, of his right kind of woman, and this apparent privation, for the woman, of her right kind of man" (ibid.). Because of his feminine instincts, James smells something rotten in the state of American society. Because he senses that the balance of power between the sexes is askew and that labor's value is divid- ed along gender lines, he can declare that Americans are inflicted with "a so- ciety of women 'located' in a world of men, . . . the men supplying, as it were, all the canvas, and the women all the embroidery" (52).

New York and Washington, D.C., are the sites for two extended medita- tions by James upon the harm done to the nation's chances for creating a civ- ilized society to which both sexes contribute equally; each city provides him with a different kind of corroborating evidence that complicates the nature of the central problem. New York City represents Business rampant; it dra- matizes the means by which the money-making process is made visible in a country that largely forgoes signs of "a visible Church, a visible State, a vis- ible Society, a visible Past" (102). First off, James finds that the cityscape is divided into two parts: Downtown, the location of Wall Street and the mer- cantile area; Uptown, the place where a man's success in making money is advertised by means of the "palaces" he erects along Upper Fifth Avenue and by the jewels he drapes upon the trophy woman he marries so she may serve as a window display for his masculine achievements.[7] The schism between male activity and female dependency is at its crudest in New York City. Washington, D.C., supplies James with a different venue; it lets him check the validity of his initial impression that America manufactures only two kinds of people: men who do business, and women who (like himself) are "nothing at all."

The nation's capital is Roosevelt territory, the field where politics is busi- ness and only the right kind of male (stringently defined by race, class, and masculine energy) may apply to play the big game. Men like Henry James can never hope to be members of that team – but then James holds no such aspirations; his wish is to observe, to analyze, and to conclude what the city of white domes and wide avenues might signify. James, on the prowl around Washington, surprises himself by finding another city hidden to the general public: the City of Conversation, where an astonishing social phenomenon is at work. In these secluded enclaves, men and women, working in unison, create a life of the mind and the imagination through good talk that centers on topics other than strategies of political power or the enhancement of material gain. What pleases James most about this special world is that it endows a saving completeness upon each sex. Elsewhere women are limited to only half of life (usually the smaller half); here they possess the fullness of self-expression. Elsewhere men are solely "businessmen," only partially intact; here they are "men of the world" interested in everything, which means they are interested in what interests women. *This* is what James likes most: men stepping over the boundaries of male action to join in the lively cultural life created by women and, by doing so, closing the unnatural gap that separates masculine from feminine, the very gap Roosevelt's national ethic is dedicated to sustain.

What are horrors to Roosevelt are joy to James. From James's perspective, the American male has everything to lose if he continues to ignore the gains that would come to him if the way of the City of Conversation became the model for the American Way. If, however, the male stays trapped within the dominant formula that ascribes value to masculine labor alone, he may "with no matter what dim struggles, groupings, yearning, never hope to be anything but a business-man" (254). By adhering to gender-blindness, he abdicates his rights to "the boundless gaping void of 'society'; which is but a rough name for all the *other* so numerous relations with the world he lives in that are imputable to the civilized being" (254–5).

As for deprivations suffered by the American female when shunted off to the side, it depends on where she appears in *The American Scene:* whether in the passages where James muses on the situation in New York City or in those on Washington, D.C. The women of New York's Upper Fifth Avenue appear on James's pages as passive victims, sealed away in ornate mansions, wearing elaborate tiaras, bereft of any means for self-expression through the neglect and indifference of their men Downtown. Once James arrives in Washington, he puts things differently since he glimpses an ideal society shared alike by men and by women. He seizes this occasion, however, to return to what disturbs him about the general cultural situation that besets the woman in America. The achievements of the American woman (upper-class, backed by money and by social status, to be sure) are both loss and gain. She is no helpless victim or inconsequential idler. By means of her intelligence, taste, and vigor, she has seized the opportunity given her by the man's "default" to make American life "over in her image" (255). Nor is she invisible. In fact, it is the male who disappears from the nation's social scene, while the woman is "two-thirds of the apparent life – which means that she is absolutely all of the social" (ibid.). Still the losses each sex suffers are great under the abnormal conditions imposed by the Rooseveltian view of the American Way.

When the man deserts the woman's side and leaves the task of creating an American culture to her, he makes of her "a new human convenience, not unlike fifty of the others, of a slightly different order, the ingenious mechanical appliances, stoves, refrigerators, sewing-machines, type-writers, cash-registers, that have done so much, in the household and the place of business, for the American name" (256). Wretched males; in their rage to imprint "business" across the face of the nation, they do not even let cultural work alone; they convert it and its makers into yet other utilitarian objects of commerce.

The American woman is no fool. Cannot she see, James asks, that she has been duped into holding down an impossible position? Making use of the language of the business contract, James reinforces his belief that a bad bargain has been made once the woman accepts the man's "agreement signed and sealed" without listening to a saving instinct that would tell her, "No, this is too unnatural; there must be a trap in it somewhere – it's addressed really, in the long run, to making a fool of me" (257).

How different the contract between the lively women and men of Washington's City of Conversation, one that brings profit to both parties once "Man is solidly, vividly present and the presence of Woman has consequently, for the proposed intensity, to reckon with it" (ibid.). Note this: the male does not enter the female domain in order to diminish the woman's role.

> Nowhere more than in Washington, positively, were the women to have struck me as naturally and harmoniously in the social picture . . . the way being their assent to the truth that the abdication of the Man proves ever (after the first flush of their triumph) as bad really for their function as for his.   (259)

The pleasure that comes to Henry James in the opening years of the twentieth century through his vision of an American culture of conversation shared equally by men and women does not necessarily promise full pleasure to us as we close out this century. James welcomes the expression of the "feminine" in the man's life, but he does not consider it imperative that women fully express their nature's "masculine" attributes. He wishes men to become more than money-makers and power-brokers in the manly world outlined by Theodore Roosevelt, but he would be dismayed if women moved into the worlds of business or politics. Nor can James have much to offer women or men positioned in class or ethnic categories other than those of Caucasian, upper-class, urban; he does not act in ways we might readily recognize to dissolve race and class boundaries. The bridges he wants built between the sexes entail letting men into the world of women's cultural work, rather than encouraging access for women into the male business world. But given his time and his place, and factoring in the obstreperous, strenuous presence of Theodore Roosevelt, who takes it upon himself to define how good Americans should line up with the two allowable types – male and female, the observations James makes as a social critic in *The American Scene* are hardly negligible; they are, in fact, astonishing.

What of Henry James the novelist? What did he have to say, and how did he say it, when he left off the discourse patented by "the restless analyst" in *The American Scene* and took to writing prose fiction narratives? Well, there is *The Golden Bowl*, the long novel published in 1905 while James was wandering across the United States. What a marvelous test-case it provides for the debate over gender expectations carried on by Roosevelt and James! In setting up this elaborate fictive narrative about the consequences of a strange set of marital arrangements, James was freed from the constraints placed upon his imagination when it was necessary for him to stay true to the mix of social reportage and impressionistic speculations he brought to *The American Scene*. By locating his story about the fates of three expatriate Americans in England, beyond the immediate reach of Roosevelt's strenuous rhetoric, he was able to "let himself go" even further. He could place on show Adam Verver, the Princess Maggie, née Verver, and Charlotte Verver, née Stant, within the relatively open society of Edwardian England that includes more than the two kinds of people allowed by the American Way: Adam the Big Businessman, presently retired, currently loafing in his role as Expatriate Connoisseur of beautiful objects (whether male or female); Maggie the Daughter to the Father who is also, as it were, her Husband; Charlotte the Trophy Wife of the Big Businessman, the Society Entrepreneur, and the Adulteress.

Ah, what a relief for James to get to write the story of an adulterous affair in a country like England, which beautifully provides the location for *that* kind of woman with *that* kind of man. And consider the possibilities for human drama (hardly encouraged by Downtown New York or the environs of Capitol Hill) offered by Charlotte's lover in the form of the Italian Prince – the Personage collected by the Big Businessman to be the Daughter's Husband, who is left with nothing to do or to be except to fill the function of the Adulterer joined in passionate, duplicitous union with the Adulteress.

In writing *The American Scene* James made canny use of the literary tradition of the allegorical type, a tactical approach that supplies further irony to his depiction of a nation that forces its men and women into two narrow slots: the Man of Business and the Woman of Society. In *The Golden Bowl* he plays, first, with the fact that outside of the United States a large number of gender categories exist; next, he takes these formalized types and runs with them. Now, free to particularize madly, James demonstrates that Adam as the Father is a certain kind of paternal figure; that Maggie as the Daughter is a unique individual; that Charlotte's dual role as Wife and Adulteress dissolves any notions suggested by such limited categories.

In addition to Adam, Maggie, Charlotte, and Prince Amerigo (characters certain to people Theodore Roosevelt's worst nightmare), there are Fanny Assingham and her husband, Colonel Bob, two more gender types who would have difficulty passing through American Customs. Colonel Bob comes closest to qualifying as the manly man favored by Roosevelt; he has been an army man who logged many years as an astute business manager of military affairs. But he is retired now, and appears to be an indolent lounge-about with nothing to do but to frequent his London club and trail after his wife to various society functions. Why, he actually spends hours talking with Fanny, or rather, listening to her, just as if they had created their own private City of Conversation! As for Fanny, she seems the worst type of American female: childless, expatriated from her native New York, with the look of "a daughter of the South, or still more of the East, a creature formed by hammocks and divans, fed upon sherbets and waited upon by slaves."[8] In fact, Fanny is a "doer," as are Charlotte and – eventually – Maggie. It is this quality of making important things happen that most upsets the Rooseveltian gender formula, for James's women perform while his men stand about as spectators and beneficiaries of women's work.

Charlotte (in everyone's view, always "magnificent") is the novel's most vivid example of a woman at work doing "it." James does not explicitly specify what "it" might be, but that hardly matters. What matters is that she *does* and does brilliantly anything to which she turns her energy, her will, and her intelligence. It was "the doing by the woman of the thing that gave her away.

She did it, ever, inevitably, infallibly – she couldn't possibly not do it. It was her nature, it was her life, and the man could always expect it without lifting a finger" (vol. 23, 49). But as James's reading of this gendered action points out, the woman's work brings profit to the man. "This was *his*, the man's, any man's position and strength – that he had necessarily the advantage, that he only had to wait" to have his own position made "right" (ibid.).

Examine the case of the men in James's accounting of the gender (and sexual) dynamics by which *The Golden Bowl* presents a world filled with more than two biological types (male and female) and two social types (Businessman and Society Woman). Adam Verver is the American male who, having made his millions, chooses to abandon the world of business affairs and his native shores. During his States-side career accumulating money, he could well have been one of the monopolists Roosevelt's antitrust activities were intended to curb, but his job of building business nonetheless made him the dominant male American type recognized by Roosevelt and James, however differently they responded to his presence on the public scene. But now Verver is retired, expatriated, collecting art, idling as if "sitting about on divans, with pigtails, smoking opium and seeing visions," while others cry, "Let us then be up and doing" (vol. 24, 92). From Roosevelt's perspective Verver is that detestable person, the useless dilettante incapable even in his second marriage to an astonishingly healthy female to sire good American sons. To James, Adam Verver's function as a male is far more complicated, and much more interesting, than that of a husband whose inertia has made him a cuckold, whose failure to father sons signifies sexual impotence, and whose collection of art objects for the purpose of importing "culture" to American City proves he has given himself over to woman's work.

Adam Verver turns "feminine" in Europe, as Roosevelt might expect when the American male allows himself "to go native" and to forget his duties as the manly American citizen. But James's narrative gives Verver a cultural leg to stand on and a richly gendered role to play. Not that James lets Verver off easily. Everything about his actions (and lack of action) – as father, husband, and especially as collector – is scrutinized, analyzed, questioned. But the force of James's story insists that Verver as the type of the expatriate who fulfills the role of the female is not to be condemned out of hand; just as James places no a priori judgments upon the complex activities of Charlotte, Fanny, and Maggie when they appropriate the masculine role as movers and shakers and the makers of profit – for others, if not for themselves.

It is the figure of Prince Amerigo that most intriguingly tests the entrenched gender formulas James is out to challenge. Here is a titled but impoverished

Italian, named for a has-been explorer of the New World, who lives neither in the United States nor in his native land. "Bought" as a suitable mate for Maggie, the Prince brings as his dowry a deep, dark, dense Old World record of violence and magnificence. He promptly proves his male sexuality by siring the Principesso (hardly likely to grow up as the solid American citizen, however much American money and American blood the child will inherit). But what function is left for the Prince to take? Is it his fate to be that perpetually useful commodity, the Married Man? But an odd thing happens in regard to the relation between real time and a conjugal relation that is more an allegory than reality. "Less of [time] was required for the state of being married than he had, on the whole, expected, less, strangely, for the state of being married even as he was married" (vol. 23, 291–2). Nor can Amerigo hope to be a Man of Affairs, even in the management of his own time. This is taken out of his hands by Maggie through her "homely work" and by Charlotte through "her brilliant efficiency" (vol. 23, 318–19). Colonel Bob puts his finger on the central problem when Fanny is alarmed that the Prince will by default take up that most questionable of male roles from an American perspective, that of the Adulterer. "What in the world did you ever suppose was going to happen? The man's in a position in which he has nothing in life to do" (vol. 23, 278).

There is a masterful passage in *The Golden Bowl* that captures the particular plight of the man in "modern" society who has found no way to use all of himself, neither his masculine nor feminine qualities, neither the public nor the private self. It describes what the Prince feels during the long weekend he spends at Matcham, the English country house where the needs and appetites of bodies (both male and female) are well attended to, but not the mind nor the imagination. The Matcham experience highlights the consequences of Maggie's having ignored what the Prince told her on the eve of their marriage, when he cautioned her by saying, "There are two parts of me": the history of his family and his race (the collectibles Adam and Maggie have eagerly purchased), and "my single self, the unknown, unimportant – unimportant save to *you* – personal quantity" (vol. 23, 9). In the brief years of their marriage, Maggie has disregarded her husband's "personal quantity," so absorbed is she in nurturing her father's "single self." As a result, by the time the Prince arrives at Matcham, he has assumed the one role left to him: lover of his wife's father's wife. In the following description, the Prince places the rest of his "self" on hold while making use of his splendid body. The schizoid situation traditionally imposed upon women is here experienced by the man cast into the female role.

By exerting a high degree of detachment, the Prince enjoys

the amusement of a certain inward critical, life; the determined need, while apparently all participant, of returning upon himself, of backing noiselessly in, far in again, and rejoining there, as it were, that part of his mind that was not engaged at the front. His body, very constantly, was engaged at the front – in shooting, in riding, in golfing, in walking over the fine diagonals of meadow-paths or round the pocketed corners of billiard-tables; it sufficiently, on the whole, in fact, bore the brunt of bridge-playing, of breakfasting, lunching, tea-drinking, dining, and of the nightly climax over the *bottigliera* [wine cellar], as he called it, of the bristling tray; it met, finally, to the extent of the limited tax on lip, on gesture, on wit, most of the demands of conversation and expression. Therefore something of him, he often felt at these times, was left out; it was much more when he was alone, or when he was with his own people, or when he was, say, with Mrs. Verver and nobody else – that he moved, that he talked, that he listened, that he felt, as a congruous whole. (vol. 23, 327–8)

And where does James take this man who has been reduced to the sum of his public parts – and the women who have had equal damage done to them through their complicity in the greater social plot that threatens to turn human beings of either gender into nothingness? The Prince is last glimpsed, enclosing Maggie within the embrace of his powerfully sexual bodily presence, saying, "I see nothing but *you*" (vol. 24, 369). The mistress has been discarded; the father has gone away; the wife and the husband are reunited. The story's ending seems to snap shut; all looks as it should according to the conventional wisdom of the American Way defined by Theodore Roosevelt – a man who would not have allowed this messy situation to commence in the first place and who would never sanction the telling of such a lurid tale if it had. But *The Golden Bowl* obeys no such conventions, reaches no soothing conclusions, grants no stability to its gender relationships. That the Prince insists that nothing exists beyond Maggie's presence is no happy thought; that Maggie accepts the "force" of his words with "pity and dread of them" makes mock of the traditional felicitous (ibid).

Henry James's fictive accounts of how men and women react complexly to themselves and to others forever resisted the American Way imposed by Theodore Roosevelt. How could *that* vision of a strong national morality accommodate the dual awareness possessed by Maggie and the Prince: "I see it's *always* terrible for women" – "Everything's terrible, *cara* – in the heart of man" (vol. 24, 149)? Progressivist reform policies must refute such insights; a nation self-limited to only two gender types – the manly male and the mothering female – dare not harbor such thoughts.

37

Roosevelt writes old-style narratives whose endings are settled before the story begins; James creates new-style narratives without conclusions or solutions that raise questions about the infinite variety of *persons* each sex can offer. But at one point James's gender ethics starts to coincide with Roosevelt's. Like Roosevelt, James is haunted by the fear that life may prove to be "nothing at all"; both pour their energies into a commitment to "do" – Roosevelt as the American statesman, James as the cosmopolite artist.

It was a pity Roosevelt was unable to honor the strenuous life chosen by James; a pity this man of vigorous intelligence and powerful public presence was limited to a single-sex view of consequential (that is, "masculine") action. Nonetheless, James pressed forward on his own terms as "that queer monster, the artist, an obstinate finality, an inexhaustible sensibility. . . . It all takes doing – and I *do*. I believe I shall do yet again – it is still an act of life."[9]

What an "act of life" may entail cannot be dictated before the fact by biological or social classifications. Only careful attention to the telling of gendered lives can express what it is like for masculine and feminine versions of "that queer monster" – that "inexhaustible sensibility" harbored within the personality of either sex – to do all they can to stave off the dread fate imposed by the American Way of "being nothing at all."

NOTES

1 In *The American Scene* James notes that one must wait to see what happens to the relation of the sexes, but "the thing is happening, or will have to happen, in the American way – that American way which is more different from all other native ways." Whatever the consequences, by means of "the certainty of the *determined* American effect," "the American way will see it through." (*The American Scene*, ed. John F. Sears [New York: Penguin Books, 1994], p. 263; henceforth abbreviated as *AS*, with page references cited parenthetically in the text.)

2 See Roosevelt's running argument in "Biological Analogies in History," Romanes Lecture delivered at Oxford University, England, June 7, 1910; printed in *Literary Essays, Works of Theodore Roosevelt, Memorial Edition,* Vol. 14, pp. 65–106 (New York: Scribner's, 1924).

3 "Manhood and Statehood," address at the Quarter-centennial of Statehood, Colorado Springs, August 2, 1901; printed in *The Strenuous Life,* in *Works of Theodore Roosevelt,* Vol. 15, p. 323. Page references cited parenthetically in the text.

4 "True Americanism" (essay in *The Forum,* April 1894); printed in *American Ideals,* in *Works of Theodore Roosevelt,* Vol. 15, p. 20. Page references cited parenthetically in the text.

5 "The Strenuous Life," speech before the Hamilton Club, April 10, 1899; printed in *The Strenuous Life,* in *Works of Theodore Roosevelt,* Vol. 15, p. 267. Page references cited parenthetically in the text.

6   Review of "The Law of Civilization and Decay" by Brooks Adams in *The Forum*, January 1897; printed in *Literary Essays,* Vol. 14, p. 149. Page references cited parenthetically in the text.

7   This follows the line of argument set by Thorstein Veblen in 1899. See *The Theory of the Leisure Class: An Economic Study in the Evolution of Institutions,* chapters 3–4 (New York: Macmillan, 1899).

8   *The Golden Bowl* in two volumes; in *Novels and Tales of Henry James* (New York: Scribner's, 1909), Vol. 23, p. 24. Page and volume references cited parenthetically in the text.

9   *Henry James Letters,* ed. Leon Edel, in 4 vols. (Cambridge, Mass.: Harvard University Press, 1974–1984), Vol. 4, p. 706.

2

FRANCES WILSON

The James Family Theatricals: Behind the Scenes

Within the last year [Henry] has published *The Tragic Muse*, brought out *The American*, and written a play, *Mrs Vibert* (which Hare has accepted) and his admirable comedy: combined with William's *Psychology*, not a bad show for one family! especially if I get myself dead, the hardest job of all.

> *The Diary of Alice James*, 1890

With that work [Howells's *Hazard of New Fortunes*], your *tragic muse*, and last *but by no means least*, my *psychology*, all appearing in it, the year 1890 will be known as the great epochal year in American literature.

> Letter from William James to Henry James, 1890

I like to think it open to me to establish speculative and imaginative connections.

> Henry James, "Is There a Life after Death?", 1910

He waited, Henry James, until 1890 to realize his dream of writing for the stage. While the desire to be a dramatist had haunted him "from the first," James had for some reason stalled. Contemplating the years of "waiting, of obstruction," he sensed a certain resistance in his delayed start, as if realizing that it is in the nature of desire to postpone its satisfaction: "It is strange nevertheless that I should never have done anything – and to a certain extent it is ominous. I wonder at times that the dream should not have faded away" (James, *Complete Notebooks* [hereafter cited as *Notebooks*], 226). The melodramatic excess of this statement is balanced against a contrasting version of events: "When I was younger [the drama] was really a very dear dream with me – but it has faded away with the mere increase of observation" (quoted in James, *Complete Plays*, 44).

This essay does not consider whether James's dream of writing drama faded or did not fade away. Instead, it examines James's own desire to fade away during his dramatic years, both with embarrassment at the failure of his plays and in a fantasy of self-effacement. Dorriforth, in James's meditation on the future of the theater, "After the Play," argued that "We go to the theatre to be absorbed . . . to give ourselves up," in the theater we "lose ourselves" (James, *Scenic Art*, 228). James's literary ambition, his "long cherished dream," was not, as he overstated, to *find* himself as a dramatist, but in fact to lose himself as one, and it is this that was "ominous" about his scenic fantasy. The theater allowed James to explore the self as performance, to give himself up to what he called "different experiences of consciousness" (James, "Is There a Life after Death?" [hereafter cited as "Life?"], 226).

This exploration of the limits of consciousness took place with greater effect behind the scenes of James's drama than on the stage itself. The dramatic impulse – "the impulse towards dramatisation, heightening, expression, acting out," as Eric Bentley describes it – also describes the James family relations during James's dramatic years (Brooks, *The Melodramatic Imagination*, i). If melodrama can be characterized as a theater of excess in which "characters represent extremes and they undergo extremes, passing from heights to depths, or the reverse, almost instantaneously" (Brooks, 36), then James's relations to both drama and family can be called melodramatic. For the drama of extremes also describes what Alice James called the "family show," the melodramatic obsessions and relations of Alice, William, and Henry James between 1890, when *The American* was first performed in Southport, and 1895, when *Guy Domville* was jeered in London.

In these years the James siblings would each fulfill their long-awaited ambition to realize "different experiences of consciousness," in both their professional interests and their personal relations. What speculative and imaginative connections can be made between William's explorations into ghosts, mediums, and telepathy, and the final completion of his *Principles of Psychology* (1890), Alice's long suspension between living and dying which finally terminated with her getting herself dead in 1892, and Henry's writing for the stage? And what light might these connections throw on James's failure as a dramatist, the fact that there was something in his writing that was unstageable? At the same time that James's plays were seen as over-literary, written in a language that nobody spoke, the James family were writing one another's lines and acting one another's roles in a drama that had done with speech altogether. The foundations of this drama were laid long before the 1890s, and this particular theatrical dynamic extends beyond the intricate relations of William, Henry, and Alice alone. Each member of the James circle struggled with the problem of how to experience, express, and efface the self and how to maintain the barrier between audience and actor in the family scenes.

Any description of the James family history leads back to the vocabulary of the theater, and in presenting the full family group as a cast of players "suffused and united and interlocked" – as Henry James put it at the start of *A Small Boy and Others* ([hereafter cited as *SB*] 4) – before focusing on the specifically dramatic relations of William, Henry, and Alice, I am taking my cue from the Jameses themselves as well as from their biographers. The James family formed what Henry called a "company of characters," and as he reminisced on the scene and the figures of his childhood James wrote that he could still "see the actors move again through the high, rather bedimmed rooms" (*Notes of a Son and Brother* [hereafter cited as *NB*], 4, 73). Henry James describes himself here as a spectator for whom the "figures distribute themselves"; he is a voyeur who pauses to "catch myself in the act" (*NB* 7, 17), and it is in thus "dawdling and gaping" that he famously remembers his cousin Marie being told by her mother to stop making a scene. This was an event that "told me so much about life. Life at these intensities clearly became scenes; but the great thing, the immense illumination, was that we could make them or not as we chose" (*NB,* 106–7). This anecdote nicely links the beginnings of Henry James's life-long preoccupation with the scenic art with the act of observing his theatrical relations while obscuring himself in the shadows, and thus it shows how closely involved his relations with the family and with the theater were to be for him. F. O. Matthiessen repeats this motif by describing his book, *The James Family,* not as the work of a writer but as a theatrical event:

> My own role has been something like that of a director of a play. I have tried to see to it that the actors were assembled in a series of significant and representative scenes, that the various scripts – in many cases the two halves of a hitherto separated correspondence – were dovetailed together, that any necessary cuts and foreshortenings should be made, and that the cues should fall pat. Then I have sat back and enjoyed the performance, without the usual nervousness as to how my extraordinary cast would acquit itself.
>
> (Matthiessen, vi)

Dissassociating himself from his drama in this way, Matthiessen is echoing James's own hope as a dramatist, that plays will write themselves and therefore free the author from responsibility for the work – but this is looking ahead.

If, as Matthiessen suggests of the Jameses, their "drama . . . finds its center in what happened in that family circle" (Matthiessen, vi), an account needs to be given of the *dramatis personae* who were on the scene from the beginning. For if James always felt *at home* with the scenic art, it was a feeling that involved all of the uncanny strangeness and familiarity that being at home entails. And in James's home life there was a drama onstage as well as backstage; a drama in which richer lines and more entrances were given to William and Henry, the two eldest sons, than to Wilkie and Robertson, the two younger sons, who have nothing more than walk-on parts and early exits in traditional accounts of James family life. William and Henry were placed at the footlights; they had more interesting public roles than those assumed for their mother, Mary, or her sister, the ever-present Aunt Kate, or for Alice, the youngest of the five children. Henry James Sr. saw the world as a stage and his children as an experiment in self-expression; they were to all find characters for themselves, whether they would occupy center-stage or wait in the wings. For Henry Sr. insisted that no matter what they chose to do with their lives, his children should cultivate individualism and be *extraordinary*: "What we were to do . . . was just to *be* something, something unconnected with specific doing" (*SB*, 50–1), Henry James recalled. Henry Sr.'s motif had been to "Convert, convert, convert!" (123); to recycle waste into valuable material; to dramatize experience, however dull or ephemeral; to change base metal into gold: "we breathed an air in which waste, for us at least, couldn't and didn't live, so certain were aberrations and discussions, adventures, discursions, alarms of whatever sort, to wind up in a 'transformation scene'" (123). This motif would return to haunt Henry James after the failure of *Guy Domville*, when his notebooks were preoccupied with the idea of wasted years and with his relief at the realization that the scenic method of composition need not be discarded but could be transformed into another medium, as it fitted "the complicated chambers of *both* the dramatic and the narrative lock." Therefore, James concluded, "my infinite little loss is converted into an almost infinite little gain" (*Notebooks*, 115, 116).

The process of conversion in the James family had begun in the early nineteenth century by William James, the grandfather of the novelist. As a poor Irish émigré aged eighteen, William James had left County Cavan in 1789 to settle in Albany, New York, amassing the second largest fortune in the state. His death in 1832 provided the means for Henry James, Sr., the fourth of his ten children by his third wife, to pursue a life dedicated to nonconformist theological thought and study. This had not, however, been William James's intention: a strict Presbyterian, he disapproved of the effects of unearned money on the minds of the young and idle. In an episode that Henry Sr. would repeat fifty years later in relation to Wilkie and Robertson, William James deliberately left his bookish son next to nothing. Henry Sr. fulfilled his father's worst expectations by successfully challenging the terms of his will and securing for himself a $10,000 annual income, which ensured that he never did a day's conventional work in his life. Instead, he immersed himself in the cosmopolitan upbringing of his children while he struggled with the question that was to absorb him intellectually and to become the subject of ten now-forgotten works: the nature of God's relation to man. When his children asked their father what they could say that he "did," Henry James records his replying: "Say I'm a philosopher, say I'm a seeker for truth, say I'm a lover of my kind, say I'm an author of books if you like; or, best of all, just say I'm a Student" (*NB, 65*).

The restlessness of Henry Sr.'s intellectual and spiritual pursuit is reflected in the education he chose for his children, which his son Henry described as being driven by an "incorrigible vagueness of current" (*NB*, 1). Between 1855 and 1860 Henry Sr. moved his young family from New York, where he felt that nothing extraordinary could happen to them, to schools in England, France, Switzerland, and Germany. Apart from Henry, the James children all felt that their European experience had left them uneducated and adrift. They had managed, as their father had hoped, to "absorb French and German" in this "sensuous education" (*NB*, 183), but at the cost of acquiring a sense of community or roots. This stay in Europe not only provided the young Henry James with the galleries and cities that would haunt his fiction; it introduced Henry to the Théâtre Français, which served as his model for the ideal drama whose standard and success he sought to emulate in his own plays. But William – who was to become one of America's most important psychologists and philosophers – was keen to study in a more rigorously scientific and systematic manner and felt, with hindsight, the educational experiment to have been a waste that he could not convert into value.

While William and Henry had at least been old enough to appreciate the variety of places they visited, Wilkie, Robertson, and Alice had been ten, nine, and seven respectively when they had left for Europe, young enough to make the continual traveling and sight-seeking irksome and onerous. Not having a settled home-life or schooling that would provide them with friends of their own, the James children were solely dependent on each other for the sharing of games, ideas, and interests. It was at this stage that they also learned to share experiences and symptoms, both conscious and unconscious, to "see with the same sensibilities and the same imagination, vibrate with the same nerves, suffer with the same suffering: have, in a word, the same experience of life," as James was to write in a story he planned in 1895 about a brother and sister who understood each other "too well" (*Notebooks*, 111).

Mary James, who accompanied her husband without complaint, complemented his excited idealism with her own solidity and stringent parsimony. Accounts of their mother's character from the James children stress her goodness, her quietness, her central position in family life and leave unmentioned any descriptions of humor, imagination, warmth, or empathy. Both Mary James and her sister, Catherine Walsh or "Aunt Kate," were unquestioning in their support of Henry Sr.'s unconventional beliefs – "Your father's *ideas*, you know – !" – had been Mary James's refrain (*NB*, 151) – and he, in turn, never questioned their instinctive moral virtue. Women in the James family are described as natural embodiments of the state of selflessness toward which the men are intellectually struggling. Henry James recalled his mother as possessing "a selflessness so consistently and unabatedly active" that he was forced to wonder whether it had "anything ever left *acutely* to offer." (*SB*, 167). Alice's observation of Aunt Kate, likewise, suggests that her urge to immerse herself in others had more to do with her femininity than her spirituality: "the truth was, as her long life showed, that she had but one *motif*, the intense longing to absorb herself in a few individuals" (Yeazell, 162). The James family were all to share this longing for absorption and desire for selflessness, and Henry's developing fascination with the drama surely had its roots in the idea of one character converting into, being absorbed into, another.

The only woman who was to challenge this idealized and contradictory perception of femininity as an identity both solidly at the core of the home and yet fluidly merging into others, without a core itself, was Wilkie's adored wife Carrie, who was disliked intensely by her brother's family for what was seen as her unnatural greed and selfishness. William's own wife, also called Alice, fitted well the family conception of womanhood: she was both a devoted mother and a constant support to her husband in the long years of writer's block and despair that accompanied his pioneering and brilliant works on psychology and philosophy. Robertson, meanwhile, was to try the devotion of his wife, also named Mary, by leaving her and their children and requesting a legal separation to which she would never agree. While Mary waited patiently for her husband to return home to her, Robertson's own troubled life was to trap itself in a cycle of alcoholism and unemployment.

Alice never married. She shared her life with her parents in New York and later, with her constant companion, Katherine Loring, whom she met in 1873, she moved to London to be with Henry. She had the first of three terrible breakdowns when she was nineteen, after which she underwent "motorpathy" in the Winter of 1866–7. "I have longed and longed for some pal-

45

pable disease," Alice wrote in her diary, for the conditions she suffered from were vaguely called "nervous hyperaesthesia," "spinal neurosis," and "suppressed gout" (*Diary,* 206). She had her second breakdown in the "hideous summer of '78," at the same time as Robertson was collapsing into a state of profound depression and drunkenness. Alice's role as the only recognized patient in the family is confirmed by Henry Sr., who firmly reminded Robertson, when he wrote to report on Alice's condition, that "any other care upon our hands, while this absorbing state of things endures, would be intolerable." His father went on to tell Robertson about the extraordinary exchange he had had with Alice, in which she had asked him if he thought her contemplation of suicide was "a sin" and he had replied that "so far as I was concerned she had my full permission to end her life whenever she pleased" (Yeazell, 15). Alice would continue this dispassionate discussion of her death until she eventually died of breast cancer in 1892, aged forty-four. She had been bedridden for the best part of thirty years, and during the last three years of her life had secretly kept a diary in which she recorded, with great irony, her surprise at her continued existence, her political opinions – particularly those concerning Ireland – and her vicarious involvement in Henry's venture into the theater.

Henry James Sr. and Mary James were both to die in 1882, within eleven months of each other: William noted that his father had "culminated his life by this drama of complete detachment from it" (W. James, *Correspondence,* 343–4), a performance Alice would repeat ten years later. Henry James dealt with the loss of his mother by converting it, like his scenic method, into "an infinite little gain," and rather than painfully detaching from her he instead incorporated her into himself: he told Charles Eliot Norton that "our lives are so full of her still that we scarcely yet seem to have lost her" (James, *Letters* [Lubbock], 92). The James children became graveyards for their parents and for each other, and the family ideal of self-detachment became indistinguishable from the stranger idea that the self was the harborage of others.

Alice was by no means the only member of the family to be ill, physically or mentally. Her father had lost a leg as a result of a childhood injury and later, in 1842, on his first visit to Europe with his two eldest children, he experienced a serious nervous collapse that left him with the conviction that "the curse of mankind is its sense of selfhood." His subsequent belief in the "nothingness of selfhood" led him to find solace in the teachings of Swedenborg. This debilitating awareness of the self would characterize the crises of all the James children, and it became the defining feature of Henry James's dramatic years, which resulted in his own breakdown in 1895. William was to suffer from a "physical and nervous frailty . . . which later manifested it-self so seriously as to interfere with his studies" and which prevented him from enlisting, with Wilkie and Robertson, in the Federal armies during the Civil War (*Letters,* ed. Lubbock, 47). In the 1870s, at the same time as Al-ice's second breakdown and Robertson's depression, William had also gone through a suicidal crisis that Perry describes as a "pathological seizure" (Per-ry, 322). William wrote that at this time he had "about touched bottom" (Per-ry, 322), but his collapse, like his father's, proved to be an intellectual turn-ing point in which he began to look for a "philosophy to save him" (Perry, 324). His long depression ended in 1873 with his acceptance of a permanent appointment as Instructor in Anatomy and Physiology at Harvard, where for the next thirty-five years he taught physiology, psychology, and philoso-phy. After twelve years of writing and research, William James's first major work, *Principles of Psychology,* was published in 1890, and he was subse-quently established as America's foremost psychologist. It was at this time that William began to explore the possibilities of life after death and telepa-thy, and his subsequent involvement in psychical research led him to devel-op friendships with the spiritualists Frederick Myers and Henry Sidgwick.

The fruitless search for self-expression was to cause Robertson years of crippling unhappiness. After fighting in the Civil War, Robertson had found no means of converting his imagination and experience into something valu-able and lasting; he lost his wife and family, his ambition, and his money. In 1866, together with Wilkie, he invested in an unsuccessful attempt to set up a cotton plantation in Florida run by freed slaves from the South, and in 1868 the two brothers had then both traveled west to work on the railroads, af-ter which they were each to marry. Wilkie, in another failed business ven-ture, lost $5,000 of his father's money and as a result, to his bitter disap-pointment and anger, he was excluded from Henry Sr.'s will. Robertson, while not excluded, was left a token gesture by his father. Wilkie died a year after his parents, aged thirty-eight, of Bright's disease of the kidney, leaving behind him a complex web of debt. His widow was to have no more contact with the James family. In the 1890s, Robertson began to look for solace in his father's work, *The Secret of Swedenborg,* in which he became, he wrote in true Jamesian style, "nearly wholly absorbed" (Strouse, 19). But, as William Dean Howells remarked in his reading of that book, the secret re-mained elusive (he "kept it"), and when Robertson died alone of heart fail-ure after a drinking bout on July 3, 1910 – six weeks before William – noth-ing in "the turbid sea of his life" (*NB,* 39) had been resolved.

The fact that there was no audience for Robertson's death is glaringly at odds with the dynamic of the rest of the James family, as William, Henry, and Alice had all shared a preoccupation with death scenes. As Alice wrote to William on Aunt Kate's death in 1889, "Death at a distance from the scene is much more shocking. . . . This experience has given me a renewed sense of sorrow and regret that you and Harry were not spectators at the last hours of dear mother and father" (Yeazell, 162). Alice went on to note, "thank Heaven," that Aunt Kate's attempts to "absorb herself" in her family were met by "the individuals" with resistance (Yeazell, 162), which is an unexpected remark because, while resistance would play a great part in Alice's, William's, and Henry's relations to one another's writing, otherwise the correspondence between the Jameses suggests that they did not attempt to resist aborption in each other. On the contrary, a letter Henry Sr. wrote to Henry Jr. in 1873 emphasizes the degree to which the family were involved in each other:

> My paternal feeling grows so much . . . as I grow older, becomes so much more intense and absorbing, that I am compelled in self-defense to keep it under, lest its pains (so inevitable in the present disjointed state) should come to exceed its pleasures. . . . Your long sickness, and Alice's, and now Willy's have been an immense discipline for me, in gradually teaching me to universalize my sympathies. (Strouse, 19)

Absorption in one another's pains and ideas and the universalization of sympathy or, as Alice put it, an "exaggerated sympathy for suffering" (Strouse, 208), is something that Alice, William, and Henry would perform in a private theatrical all their lives. The letters and diaries that these three Jameses left indicate that they related both through and for one another, and that communication between them took the form of an extreme identification. Dying and drama therefore became interchangeable activities: "Our absorbing interest just now is of course Harry's dramatic debut at the end of the month," Alice wrote to William's wife in 1890; meanwhile, she continued, "I am working away to get myself dead as soon as possible . . . but this play of Harry's makes a sad complication, as I don't want to immerse him in a deathbed scene on his 'first night,' too much of an aesthetic incongruity!" (Yeazell, 184–5).

So, when Henry James embraced the theater in 1890 with his dramatic adaptation of *The American,* he was not acting alone. What the writings of Henry, William, and Alice show during the period of 1890–5 is that they were *all* obsessed with the theatrical in terms of performance, staging and the scenic, participating in what James called "the intense desire of being to get itself personally shared" ("Life?" 224). The success of their family dramatics is caught in what James believed was the "best formula for the fabrication [of] a dramatic piece. . . . Action which is never dialogue and dialogue which is always action" (*Notebooks*, 54); for the family relations were performed either in scenes of unspoken empathy and understanding – in action that *exceeds* dialogue – or in scenes of intellectual dialogue that were sublimated into action. The "dialogue which is always action" can be found in the relations between Henry's drama, William's psychologizing, and Alice's dying.

"Relations," as James famously noted, "stop nowhere," and the relations between Henry's and William's ideas continued into their work, where William agreed that "the feelings of relations are everything." In his *Principles of Psychology*, William argued that human consciousness flowed in a continuum, like a stream, and that this stream of consciousness was analogous to the life of a bird, made up of flights and intervals:

> The places of flight are filled with thoughts of relations [which] for the most part [are obtained] between the matters contemplated in the periods of comparative rest. . . . The only images intrinsically important are the halting places. . . . Throughout the rest of the stream, *the feelings of relations are everything.*
>
> (W. James, *Principles of Psychology* [hereafter cited as *Principles*], 243)

William's description of the stream of consciousness fits both Henry's description of the scenic art – his conviction that life was composed of scenes – and Alice's description of her own deathbed scenarios. All three describe a structure consisting of scenes of action and intervals of contemplation. Alice saw her life as one long interval before the final curtain, which was a scene she awaited with the same trepidation and excitement that Henry described in his long years of waiting to become a dramatist: "But after an interval, a long one, the vision has revived" (*Notebooks*, 52). The relation between the ideas here is one of many suggestions that for Henry the scenic ideal was less a personal ambition than part of the family show; Alice's diaries record the staging of *The American* as "The great family event, over which I have been palpitating for the last 18 months" (A. James, *Diary*, 161).

If the feelings of relations between the Jameses were "everything," their ideas about relations connect both because ideas and thoughts in the James family were in continual circulation and also because members of the family seemed to share a consciousness. As William wrote to Henry, 21 months after Alice's death: "I confess now that I 'realise' you in your loneliness. . . .

I feel as if we formed a part of a unity more than I ever have before" (W. James, *Correspondence*, 290). The James family "realised" one another with such powerful empathy that consciousness often appeared as an out-of-body experience, and it is in this context that I want to place Henry James's obsession with writing drama and its relation to Alice's and William's obsessions with death, for James's dramatic years were also preoccupied with ideas of the living dead.

Strangely, when Henry addressed William's notion of "realising" another, of bringing the self and others into being, it was in the context of his essay "Is There a Life after Death?" and he referred to it here as the idea of renewed being through another, of "enjoying another state of being" ("Life?" 211). Published in 1910, the year in which both William and Robertson died, this opaque and anxious meditation is haunted by thoughts of (and by) his siblings. James is not concerned with death and the "afterlife" in any orthodox sense, but with the *limits of consciousness experienced by the living* – "there are so many different experiences of consciousness possible" (226) – and his writing snags on the fraught issue of "independence of thought and more especially this assault of the boundlessly multiplied personal relation (my own)" (223). James subsequently buckles under the strain of his endeavor to define the self that is speaking as independent and empirical, as speaking *for* itself. He writes as if "speaking for myself only and keeping to the facts of my experience" (223) were the most difficult state for consciousness to achieve, but "I had best do so simply for myself, since it is only for one's self that one can positively answer" (216). Detaching oneself from others and realizing their difference is the problem: "The question is of the *personal* experience, of course, of another existence; of its being I my very self, and you, definitively, and he and she, who resume and go on, and not of unthinkable substitutes and metamorphoses" (204). An individual, personalized life existing after death is hard to conceive, James argues, only because consciousness when alive is in an undifferentiated state, compounded with unthinkable substitutes and metamorphoses: "How can there be a personal and a differentiated life 'after' . . . for those for whom there has been so little of one before?" (201). James's thoughts in this essay bear witness both to his mourning of William and Alice and to his struggle to free himself from them while expressing himself through them, as his mediums. In his relations with William as a child, Henry noted that "what I probably most did, all the while, was but to pick up, and to the effect not a bit of starving but quite of filling myself, the crumbs of his feast and the echoes of his life" (*NB*, 13). It is little wonder then if James held that writing drama, and thus orchestrating the filling of the self with another consciousness, was his salvation as a writer: "The very provocation offered to the artist by the universe, the provocation to him to *be* . . . what do I take that for but the intense desire of being to get itself personally shared, to show itself for personally sharable" ("Life?" 224).

While James had claimed since childhood that writing for the stage would save him, his interest in drama as a medium was not so straightforward and his attitude toward it is characterized by melodramatic irrationality. If drama was his "salvation," it was also his "sacrifice"; it was both the highest and the lowest form of representation, both vulgar and sublime, something he wanted to do both for "fortune's sake" and for the sake of art (*Notebooks,* 52). And while James wrote that he had "cherished" his "project" of writing for the stage "from the first," and stressed that he saw drama as his natural medium, it was a kind of writing that he curiously couldn't begin and, once he had begun, he couldn't leave safely alone. He insisted on repeating the dismal experience of *Guy Domville* over and over again: "you must spare my going over again that horrid hour, or those of disappointment or depression that have followed it," he apologized to William (W. James, *Correspondence,* 337). After the failure of *Guy Domville* James "swore" to himself "an oath never again to have anything to do with a business which lets one into such traps, abysses and heartbreak" (Edel, 77), and yet the next week he became involved in writing a play for Ellen Terry that would itself be abortive. This "trap" seemed to be self-imposed, for again and again he insisted that his only salvation, his only hope for the future, lay in *self-release:* "I only have to let myself *go!* So I have said to myself all my life. . . . Yet I have never fully done it . . . it seems the formula of my salvation, of what remains to me of a future" (*Notebooks,* 57). William's involvement with the Society for Psychical Research involved monitoring the dead, selves that had already been let go, and so his research, Henry's writing and Alice's wasting body all desired the same end: an escape from the narrow and restrictive confines of – and limited understandings of – the unshared self.

In a diary entry two years after Alice's death, Henry described himself as the spectator of his own tragedy, as the observer of his own death, and as caught between living and dying:

> The idea of *death* both checked and caught me; for if on the one side it means the termination of the consciousness, it means on the other the beginning of the drama in any case in which the consciousness survives. In what cases

may the consciousness be said to survive – so that the man is the spectator of
his own tragedy?   (*Notebooks*, 83)

James became the spectator of his own tragedy – in both senses of the word
– when he watched the first night of *Guy Domville*. Both here and in "Is There
a Life after Death?" his discussion of death becomes a discussion of drama,
with James expressing the same attractions and resistances to both. Death,
like the drama, is a suspended state between termination and beginning. The
termination of consciousness, like the scenic art, is a subject with which he
is fascinated – "I confess at the outset that I think it the most interesting question in the world" – and to which he is deeply resistant: "I began, I may accordingly say, with a distinct sense that our question didn't appeal to me"
("Life?" 217). James describes himself as passive in the face of each: just as
"death both checked and caught" *him*, the ideas of life after death and of drama each sought *him* out: "The question [of life after death] subtly took care
of itself for me – waking up as I did . . . to its facing me with a 'mild but firm'
refusal to be settled" ("Life?" 219), and "the theatre has sought me out," he
wrote of the drama (*Notebooks*, 52). Although the question of consciousness
after death leads James to wonder if there is, in the life before death, a self to
speak of, the merit of the performed play is its autonomy – at least it "would,
for better or worse, have spoken for itself" (James, *Theatricals*, v).

James no sooner establishes the self as something to be shared, to be "realised" and spoken for in others, than he writes the self out of the act altogether. If a play speaks for itself, how can it then speak for the author? These
scenarios of being confronted by, rather than of confronting, death and drama suggest that James saw himself less as the performer than as the outside
observer of his life; even in his autobiography James took himself out of the
spotlight, referring to himself only with caution and often in the third person, giving it, as F. O. Matthiessen wrote, the curious status of being "one
of the least self-centered autobiographies on record" (Matthiessen, 72). This
erasure of himself from the scene of his own action is caught again in his description of his state of mind one month after the trauma of *Guy Domville*:
"it is rapidly growing to seem to have belonged to the history of someone
else" (Edel, *Treacherous Years*, 101). Similarly, Alice complained in her diary that the only drawback to her longed-for death was that she would probably not be there to observe it, that "it will probably be in my sleep so that
I shall not be one of the audience . . . a creature who has been denied all dramatic episodes might be allowed, I think, to exist at her extinction" (A.
James, *Diary*, 135). If the thrill of drama for Henry was its invitation to lose

52

the self, and the thrill of the séance for William was its dramatization of the lost self, the loss of the self for Alice also became a dramatic experience. Alice had been "rehearsing" for her "curtain" to "roll down" all her adult life, and she dramatized it in the form of a diary so that she might, as she put it, "pose to myself before the footlights of my last obscure little scene" (129, 135, 222).

The drama of Alice's dying should not be looked at outside her brothers' own relations with drama and with death. For all three staged scenes in which the body becomes a medium for other voices. In the séances that William was organizing, the dead communicated through the body of the living so that the medium acted the part of the ghost. In the plays that Henry was writing, forewarned by Elizabeth Robins's remark that the actor should "let Ibsen play you rather than you play Ibsen," his lines were speaking the players (Edel, 38). Alice, meanwhile, was experimenting with hypnosis, with getting her body into the trance-like state that would enable her unconscious to break through the medium of consciousness; and this at the same time that Henry was discussing with George Du Maurier the plot for *Trilby*. In his notes, James reveals a fascination with the idea of the body as a medium and records how Svengali's talent had taken over Trilby, had "played in her and through her." James himself then planned a story about "the idea of the *hypnotization* of a weak character by a stronger" (*Notebooks*, 62), just when Alice was being hypnotized by Katherine Loring, to whom she also dictated the last 14 months of her diary. Loring was Alice's medium to her unconscious life, her writing, and the outside world. She acted Alice's part for her. Similarly mediated were Henry's relations with his father; he wrote in his autobiography that he had felt his father most completely through the medium of his mother. He related to his father's ideas "indirectly" and recalled "assisting at intellectual 'scenes'" between Henry Sr. and William (*NB*, 150) "just as though," Matthiessen comments, "he had been watching a play" (190).

The question of self-erasure and of the "personally shareable" self is particularly germane to the relation of the James family to one another's work. Writing, for William, was a process of hollowing out the self while reading was a process of filling the self up with the author, which he often found indigestible: "You seem to me so *constitutionally* unable to 'enjoy' [reading anything of mine]," Henry complained to his brother (Perry, 425). William wrote to Henry that "I *hunger* and *thirst* for more of those stories. . . . I don't see how you can produce at such a rate. . . . I should think you'd feel all *hollowed* out inwardly, and absolutely need to fill up" (408, italics added). Henry responded that, although he was not utterly emptied, "At times I do read almost as much as my wretched little *stomach* for it literally will allow"

(409). Meanwhile, Alice was learning to "assimilate the apparantly indigestible mass" of Henry's drama (A. James, *Diary*, 224), and her filling up with excitement about *The American* – "I have to thank the beautiful play for all the interest and expectancy with which it has filled the last two years" (224) – was preventing her from being able to fill up on William's writing. William wrote to Alice of "the *interest in the play* which Katherine says you now feel to have prevented you from getting the 'full good of' *me*" (Perry, 420). In his letters to Henry in 1890, William describes his experience of his brother's writing as carnal; reading *The Tragic Muse* "leaves a good taste in one's mouth" (Perry, 413). Alice's illness is put down to a kind of intellectual constipation: "I am entirely certain that you've got a *book inside you* about England, which will come out yet. Perhaps it's the source of all your recent trouble" (418, italics added). To be unable to write makes one fade away; William writes of his own "starving condition" (Perry, 15). But so too does the act of writing itself: William describes finishing the *Psychology* as "hard on the digestive organs" (Perry, 415).

The James family fed upon each another, filling up on each other's writing. Each measured the limits of their consciousness against the borders of the body, and this vocabulary of filling up and emptying is echoed in the language of excess and waste that James employed to describe his relations to both drama and death. James had his father to thank for "the interest he shed for us on the whole side of the human scene usually held least interesting – the element, the appearance, of *waste*" (*NB*, 105). Yet, for James, excess and waste are less what the body *converts*, as Henry Sr. had taught his children, than what the subject *abjects* in order to define himself, in order to ensure that we are "abjectly and inveterably shut up in our material organs," as James wrote in "Is There a Life after Death?" (205) The James family felt trapped in their material bodies at the same time as they felt excessive to them, and when he wrote in one of his prefaces that his dramatic style demanded "an anxious *excess* of simplicity," James captured both the melodrama of his writing and of his relations. For, while James's desire as a writer was to "let myself go," Alice described her body as a frail structure held together by the will. She wrote of a body whose borders were continually threatened by the violent internal expulsion of her own excess, the release of which would render her abject:

> Conceive of never being without the sense that if you let yourself go for a moment your mechanism will fall into pie and that at some given moment you must abandon it all, let the dykes break and the flood sweep in, acknowledging yourself abjectly impotent before the immutable laws.
>
> (A. James, *Diary*, 149)

Alice felt that her body wasted and grew excessive against her own volition: "Ah woe, woe is me! I have not only stopped thinning but am taking unto myself gross fat" (142). Keeping Henry's secret about embarking on the drama makes her want to "explode" and leads her to wonder about her infinite capacity to retain excess and the lack of "receptacles for my overflow" (105).

The time he spent dreaming about drama James described as wasted. Again and again he despaired over what he called "my long tribulation, my wasted years" and he questioned the value of the dramatic enterprise: "Has a *part* of all this wasted passion and squandered time (of the last 5 years) been simply the precious lesson . . . of the . . . divine principle of the Scenario?" (*Notebooks*, 115). Wasting time and accumulating waste as the body decays: these issues are recycled in James's thought on "renewed being" and "personal decay" in "Is There a Life after Death?" For if the body is "such obvious and offensive matter for decay and putrescence," we are left wondering "what there is for renewal to take hold of" ("Life?" 208). He suggests that by redefining what we know as waste we can redefine the limits of the self: "The probability is, in fact, that what we dimly discern as waste the wisdom of the universe may know as a very different matter. We don't think of slugs and jellyfish as the waste, but rather as the amusement, the attestation of wealth and variety" (203). Hating waste of any sort, the Jameses were all concerned with the process of "conversion" and they created an ecosystem of their own. In 1869, Henry wrote home from Europe to say that his ill health was "the result of Alice and Willy getting better and locating some of their diseases on me" (quoted in Strouse, 111).

The members of the James family were continually losing themselves in one another, asking each other to take one another's parts. Henry's play *The American* was so identified with Alice that he called it "the other invalid" and Alice wrote in her diary of renaming her brother "Henry the patient" ("I have never seen an impatient look upon his face" (A. James, *Diary*, 104). During the first night of *Guy Donville*, Henry asked William to send him a telepathic message, as he was counting on "psychical intervention from you – this really is the time to show your stuff." This kind of thought transference would be pure drama for James – a perfect example of "action which is never dialogue and dialogue which is always action," for the telepathic exchange reaches beyond linguistic and physical mediums. Although Henry asked William to telepathically energize his nerves, Alice noted that it was *her* body and not his that was experiencing stage fright: "H seems to be cheerful about his play and to be unable to grasp my flutterations about it" (105).

If the James family realized themselves only in each other, their relations to their own material beings would necessarily be distanced. William observed that Alice's death, like their father's, was strangely disembodied: "In her relations to her disease, her mind did not succumb. She never whined or complained or did anything but spurn it. She thus kept it from invading the tone of her soul" (W. James, *Correspondence*, 205). It was Henry who was feeling her physical pain for her, as Alice noted: "He comes at my slightest sign and hangs on to whatever organ may be in eruption and gives me calm and solace by assuring me that my nerves are his nerves and my stomach his stomach" (A. James, *Diary*, 104). In his notes for a short story one month after the failure of *Guy Domville*, Henry called this kind of identification the "Pain of Sympathy." Of course, Alice's disengaged relations to her body conformed entirely to William's own theories of "split-up-selves" and "supernatural phenomena" (W. James, *Letters*, 311; *Principles* I, 210). In his 1890 paper "The Hidden Self," William described this letting go that Henry and Alice both dreamed of, as "abandonment." "The nervous victim," as Alice paraphrased his argument, "abandons certain portions of his consciousness" (*Diary*, 148), which to Alice, who complained that she had never been able to leave her consciousness for more than five minutes, seemed like a blissful idea. Apart from the effects of hypnosis and morphine, the only time that Alice had ever left her consciousness was to lose herself in the drama: "It has been so thrilling to have that terra incognita, the stage, opened up to us, and to be able to project ourselves into the consciousness of the playwright," she wrote in 1891 (196). For William, death was merely the will's abandonment of the body; Alice was then living-on according to William's definition of life, and it was in this state that she lost herself in Henry's drama and Henry found himself hanging on to her body.

Although it is too easy to say that Alice died because her brothers and her father wrote, it could be argued that Alice was literally dying to write. Her diary, written in the last three years of her life, was kept up until her last moments, as if her life had become a drama in which she had to write herself out. After Alice's death, Katherine Loring continued to write Alice's diary herself and she added as a final entry that Alice had died writing:

All through Saturday the 5th and even in the night, Alice was making sentences. One of the last things she said to me was to make a correction in the sentence of March 4th "moral discords and nervous horrors."

    This dictation of March 4th was rushing around in her brain all day, and although she was very weak and it tired her much to dictate, she could not get her head quiet until she had had it written. (232)

On hearing of her imminent death, William wrote to Alice with great excitement that, "when that which is *you* passes out of the body, I am sure there will be an explosion of liberated force" (W. James, *Letters,* 311), and here William's anticipation of the death-bed scene relates to Henry's description of his ideal scene of writing. For this "explosion of liberated force" was what Henry sought all his writing life, and the continual refrain of his notebooks between 1890–5 is the desire to lose himself in his writing, to pass out of his body in the hope that his work would take on an energy of its own. So here the familiar Jamesian restraint, the capacity to maintain a masterful distance from his work, is complicated by his insistent desire to immerse himself into it. There is a sense, therefore, in which Henry was also dying to write.

James's relation to writing drama can be characterized as one of repetition and resistance. This took the form of a compulsion to return to the scenic art all his writing life: "my plan is to . . . return repeatedly," he wrote (*Notebooks,* 52), "in a state of abject, lonely fear . . . trying again, again and yet again" (*Letters* 3 [Edel], 318). The repetition of the "memories and pains" that the "utterance of that word" – scenario – "pressed" upon James "with an extraordinary tenderness of embrace" strangely harbored his resistance to them (*Notebooks,* 115). For repetition is a kind of suspense, a resistance to moving on, "both the recall of an earlier moment and a variation of it: the concept of repetition hovers ambiguously between the idea of reproduction and that of change, forward and backward movement" (Brooks, *Reading for the Plot,* 99–100). Repetition is also a kind of remembering, ritualistically keeping alive what it is you want to forget, and James found himself, years later, reenacting the same tragic scenario:

> I come back yet again and again, to my only seeing it in the dramatic way. . . .
> I come back, as I say, I all throbbingly and yearningly and passionately, oh,
> *mon bon,* come back to this way that is clearly the only one in which I can do
> anything now.   (*Notebooks,* p. 261)

James's resistance to drama is similiar to his relation to reading William's work. This he also resisted while claiming to relish, and he immersed himself in William's writing as opposed to maintaining his intellectual distance: "I can read you with rapture," he wrote, disingenuously (Perry, 424). His reading of William's *The Pluralistic Universe* was calculated to nourish his brother and to offer to him Henry's own self: "It may *sustain* and inspire you a little to know that I'm *with* you, all along the line" line (Perry, first italics added). And again, James wrote to William that "philosophically, in short, I am 'with' you, almost completely" (Perry, 425), as if reading involved the handing over of one's consciousness. The identification with William that Henry made on the occasions that he read his brother's work, an identification so intense as to make impossible any genuine criticism or appreciation, bears no relation to the thorough and critical readings that William gave of Henry's work, which included telling his brother that he found his plays "unsympathetic," depending entirely as they did on characters' misreadings of each other. Not only was Henry unable to read William's writing critically, he was unable to read him at all while he was writing drama, precisely because of his sensed frailty of self: "I blush to say that I haven't had freedom of mind or cerebral freshness (I find the drama much more *obsedant* than the novel) to tackle . . . your mighty and magnificent book, which requires . . . an absence of 'crisis' in one's own egotistical little existence" (*Letters* 3 [Edel], 330). It is curious then that William's letters to Henry at the end of the 1880s are full of anxieties about his *own* resistances and full of attacks on Henry's perceived *lack* of resistance, Henry's fluid capacity to let himself loose into endless writing:

> It must seem amusing to you, who can throw off a 'chef d'ouevre' every three months, to hear of my slowness. But my time is altogether taken up by other things, and almost every page of this book of mine is against a resistance which you know nothing of in your resistless air of romance.　　　(Perry, 396)

William resisted recognizing Henry's very real resistances to both novel writing – resistances that provide the subject matter for his voluminous notebooks – and to writing drama. He also resisted recognizing Henry's own resistance to *him,* Henry's resistance to reading his brother, and his resistance to William's influence.

　　Both brothers were to resist reading Alice. When, after Alice's death, Katherine Loring had four copies of the diary privately printed, as Alice had wished, and sent a copy each to Henry and William, she recalled that William "never thanked me for his copy, simply acknowledged receipt of it and certainly never made any suggestion as to its being read or not" (A. James, *Diary,* vii). Henry, meanwhile, destroyed his copy, less because, as he claimed, it was indiscreet than because he felt *unable to read it* due to seeing here his own script and to hearing his lines repeated by his sister. James felt himself "caught in the act": "When I see that I say that Augustine Birrell has a self-satisfied smirk after he speaks . . . I feel very unhappy and wonder at the strangeness of destiny" (A. James, *Diary,* viii). Resistance was a family affair and extended beyond relations with Aunt Kate. William noted in his introduction to his father's *Literary Remains* that for Henry James Sr., "a mere resistless 'bang' is no creative process at all. A *real* creation means nothing short of a real *bringing to life* of the essential nothingness." (21).

Bringing William and Alice to life in himself comes close to what Henry was trying to do in his dramatic years, and in late 1891 James's notes and stories were also preoccupied with narratives of living deaths, with having one's dead self 'galvanised' in the form of another. Yet the galvanizing in the family circulated, and if Henry replaced a critical and dispassionate reading of William's writing with an empathetic telepathy ("I am 'with' you"), then in 1890 he had the perfect "creative" reading experience and the ideal occasion in which to galvanize his brother. Frederick Myers, prominent in the Society for Psychical Research, wrote to Henry asking him to read to the Society William's letter on the celebrated medium, Mrs. Piper, who would later be a courier between Henry and his mother. Reading William thus would make Henry a medium for his brother, whom he begged to "imagine me at 4.00 on that day, performing in your name." William replied to Henry that he would "*think of you* on the 31st at about 11.00 am to make up for the difference of longitude," the whole episode echoing Henry's request on the first night of *The American* for 'psychical intervention' from William (153). (This would again be repeated five years later when, before the first performance of *Guy Domville*, Henry asked William "to unite in family prayer for me on Saturday 5, at 8.30." [335]) Referring to this reading of his paper, William added in a postscript to Henry that he had "*melted* over" his "most beautiful and devoted brotherly act" (Perry, 416), recalling Alice's comment in her diary that Henry's over-identification with her physical pain displayed a "pitch of brotherly devotion never before approached by the race" (A. James, *Diary*, 104).

So when William was given cause to blend into his brother he lost himself not in a reading of Henry but in Henry's reading of him. Henry responded to William that his paper had gone down well and that "you were very easy to read and altogether the 'feature' of the entertainment" (Perry, 417). The same could not be said of the reading of the parts in *The American*, the observation of which James found personally alienating, as if it were not his drama at all: "I sat in the stalls watching and listening as to the work of another," he told William before asking him to send him a telepathic message on his opening night: "spend *you* the terrible hours [between 8 and 11] in fasting, silence and supplication!" (*Letters* 3 [Edel], 318). When resistances broke down, the brothers achieved pure telepathy and it becomes unclear who wrote whose part, or who was the audience and who the performer.

If writing and reading constituted for the Jameses an out-of-body experience, Henry's reactions to his drama resemble Alice's relations to her body during breakdowns, when it became for her "something alien, powerful, terrifying, bad" (Strouse, 119). And yet this kind of alienated consciousness is what Henry defined to William as being the best, found only in "the individual so capable as I am of the uncanniest self-effacement in the active exercise of the passion of observation" (quoted in James, *Complete Plays*, 37). Is this why James described the drama as his "salvation" – because the real drama lay, like Alice's death and William's séances, in the desire to stage his own effacement while looking on? For drama even dispenses with the writer himself; James wrote to William that "the authorship (in any sense worthy of the name) of a play only *begins* when it is written" (W. James, *Correspondence,* 55), as if it were the actors and the audience who wrote the play and therefore carried the responsibility for its success, usefully erasing the anxious body of the author. But alienation from one's own consciousness was easier to come by for William and Alice, who saw complete projection as just an act, an experiment with the self. William realized and mourned the ultimate *isolation* of subjectivity, suggesting that "nothing can fuse together thoughts which are sundered by the barrier of belonging to different personal minds. The breeches between such thoughts are the most absolute breeches in nature" (*Principles* 226), and Alice humorously noted in her diary "the immutable law that however great we seem to our consciousness no human being would exchange his for ours" (A. James, *Diary,* 48). For Henry, on the other hand, the drama of "abandonment," of "self-effacement" in the exercise of "observation," was an urgent aspiration, a way of dealing with the terrible burden of consciousness.

"What is there in the idea of Too Late," James mused in February 1895, weeks after the experience of *Guy Domville* (*Notebooks,* 112), as if he were haunted by the idea of waiting so long that you miss the main event. In James's descriptions of drama he is never *on time,* as if his fantasy of self-effacement were enacted in his having come to the drama either too early or too late. Authorship couldn't begin or could never end: "The play was not over when the curtain fell, four months ago: it was continued in a supplementary act or epilogue which took place immediately afterwards" ("After the Play," 226). Similarly, drama was alternatively higher or lower than writing itself, leaving James suspended between having neither started nor finished with the theater, which was itself both above and beneath him. Whichever way he turned, James's accounts of the drama describe a scene in which he is absent; establishing himself as a dramatist he realized himself in the very act of erasing himself. Alice shared this fascination with staging her own absence, with finding herself precisely where she was not, and her body, like Henry's drama, was in a state of suspense, continually being, as she said, "neither dead nor recovered" (A. James, *Diary* 142).

Were James's theatrical years a waste of time? What value is there in waste? These were the questions that were to preoccupy him after 1895. The Jameses defined themselves by endlessly expelling and converting the wastes and excesses of the body and the self, be they ideas, illnesses, or relations, and from within the closed economy of the family theatricals James attempted to write dramas in which no word was wasted and no gesture without weighty significance. In James's plays, as in his family relations, an excess of meaning strains communication to breaking point; language itself becomes onerous and excessive and meaning starts to show in hints and gazes, in what is unsaid but deeply understood between characters. In "After the Play" James speculates on a telepathic theater, in which language and character are each excessive, so the actors "won't even go through the form of speech." This sublimated drama describes the theater of the James family, in which bodies showed what language could not tell and each was constituted by the reading of the other's part. James's vision of the theater of the future is a dreamlike landscape in which figures have faded out altogether and the costumes stand in for "the interpretation of character": "Therefore, the theatre, inevitably accommodating itself, will be at last a landscape without figures. . . . There will be little illustrations of costume stuck about – dressed manikins; but they'll have nothing to say; they won't even go through the form of speech" ("After the Play," 233). This prospect is bearable only because by then, James twice stresses, as if to convince himself, "we shall, as I say, have buried our dead" (232, 233). Once the dead are buried the fact of being alive is confirmed, and yet neither William, Alice, nor Henry James could bury their dead nor keep them buried. In "After the Play" James was envisioning a future in which refuse and corpses can be properly cast aside and the self need no longer be found at the border of other selves. This is Kristeva's theater of abjection: "No, as in true theater, without makeup or masks, refuse and corpses *show me* what I permanently cast aside in order to live. . . . There, I am at the border of my condition as a living being" (Kristeva, 3).

What had James learned from his dramatic years, from the years of waiting and the years of repetition? Perhaps it was this: that the self never can coincide with himself, is always Too Late in relation to his desires. This was the theme of many of James's subsequent short stories, and in "The Beast in the Jungle," John Marcher puts it thus: "It was the truth, vivid and monstrous, that all the while he had waited, the wait itself was the portion" (New York Edition, v. 17, p. 125).

WORKS CITED

Brooks, Peter. *The Melodramatic Imagination: Balzac, James, Melodrama and the Mode of Excess*. New Haven and London: Yale University Press, 1976.

Brooks, Peter. *Reading for the Plot*. London and Cambridge: Harvard University Press, 1992.

Edel, Leon. *The Treacherous Years: 1895–1901*. London: Rupert Hart-Davis, 1969.

James, Alice. *The Diary of Alice James,* Leon Edel, ed. Harmondsworth: Penguin, 1964. Cited in text as *Diary*.

James, Henry. "After the Play." In Allan Wade (ed.), *The Scenic Art: Notes on Acting and the Drama*. London: Rupert Hart-Davis, 1949.

James, Henry. *A Small Boy and Others*. In *Autobiography*. New York: Criterion, 1956.

James, Henry. *The Complete Notebooks of Henry James,* Leon Edel and Lyall H. Powers (eds.). New York and Oxford: Oxford University Press, 1987. Cited in text as *Notebooks*.

James, Henry. *The Complete Plays of Henry James,* Leon Edel, ed. London: Rupert Hart Davis, 1949.

James, Henry. "Is There a Life after Death?" In W. D. Howells et al., *In After Days: Thoughts on the Future Life*. London: Harper, 1910. Cited in text as "Life?"

James, Henry. *Letters*. Percy Lubbock, ed. London: Macmillan, 1920.

James, Henry. *Letters, Vol. 3,* 1883–95, Leon Edel, ed. London: Macmillan, 1980.

James, Henry. *Notes of a Son and Brother*. London: Macmillan, 1914. Cited in text as *NB*.

James, Henry. *Theatricals: Second Series*. London: Osgood, McIlvine and Co., 1895.

James, Henry, Sr. *Literary Remains of the Late Henry James*. Boston: Osgood, 1885.

James, William. *Letters*. Henry James III, ed. 2 vols. Boston: Little, Brown, 1926.

James, William. *The Correspondence of William James,* Ignas K. Skrupskelis, and Elizabeth, M. Berkeley, eds. Vol. 2. Charlottesville and London: University Press of Virginia, 1993.

James, William. *Principles of Psychology*. London: Macmillan, 1910 (originally published 1890). Cited in text as *Principles*.

Kristeva, Julia. *Powers of Horror: An Essay on Abjection*. New York: Columbia University Press, 1982.

Matthiessen, F. O. *The James Family*. New York: Alfred A. Knopf, 1947.

Perry, Ralph Barton. *The Thought and Character of William James,* Vol. 1. Boston: Little, Brown, 1936.

Strouse, Jean. *Alice James*. London: Harper Collins, 1980.

Yeazell, Ruth Bernard. *The Death and Letters of Alice James*. Berkeley, Los Angeles, London: University of California Press, 1981.

3

PHILIP HORNE

Henry James at Work: The Question of Our Texts

A bright, excited student reads Henry James's story *Daisy Miller* for an assignment. She especially likes one phrase, used by the wilful heroine's Italian companion, explaining Daisy's fatal exposure of herself to Roman fever in the moonlit Coliseum: "*she* – she did what she liked." The quotation is going to be part of the title of her paper. But she leaves her copy of the book at home, and has to consult another edition in the library. In this other edition, for all her efforts, she can't locate the phrase she tagged; when she finds the relevant scene, it's different. There the Italian companion less resonantly says, "she wanted to go." Our student thought, too, that she remembered the story's hero, Winterbourne, answering with a look down at the ground and a meditative echo of the missing phrase: "She did what she liked!" But here she finds the character behaving quite differently – querulous rather than thoughtful. To the Italian's "she wanted to go" comes back bluntly, "'That was no reason!' Winterbourne declared." If our poor baffled student casts the book aside in sheer frustration at this betrayal, who can blame her? All she wanted was "the text" of the story.

But she persists, determined to find an explanation of the anomaly. And she may be led to some useful discoveries, with far-reaching implications; about the story, about James, about history, and about literature. The edition she first read was that in the Oxford University Press World's Classics, edited by Jean Gooder;[1] the one she first picked up in the library was a little 1974 Penguin, whose cover bears a photograph of Cybill Shepherd in the Peter Bogdanovich film of the story. Skimming the shelves, she now comes across three official-looking volumes, also from Oxford University Press, called *The Tales of Henry James*, edited by Maqbool Aziz, covering James's stories from 1864 to 1879, with "Daisy Miller" in the last volume. Aziz gives the tale a headnote that helps illuminate her puzzle.

First appeared in the *Cornhill Magazine*, vols. xxxvii–xxxviii (June–July 1878), pp. 678–98, 44–67. This first publication was followed by two unauthorized periodical appearances. . . . The tale received book status first in

America where the *Cornhill* text was reprinted as No. 28 of Harper's Half-Hour Series (New York: Harper and Brothers, 1878). The first revised version came when the tale appeared in book form in England, in volume i of *Daisy Miller: A Study* (1879). This text was later reproduced in volume xiii of James's first "Collective Edition" (1883). Using the text of 1879, James finally revised the tale for the New York Edition, where it appears in volume xviii (*Daisy Miller, Etc.*, 1909). During James's lifetime, the final text was reprinted in *The Uniform Tales of Henry James* (London: Martin Secker, 1915–20).[2]

Flicking through the back pages of Aziz she sees that he records the substantive differences between all these texts in his heroic section of "Textual Variants." This buzz of detail might make it seem she's opened a Pandora's box here; but with careful unpacking she can evade the sting (of confusion and despair) and extract the honey. As she summons selected guides from the shelves (and we put in a supplementary word over her shoulder here and there), she can see what R. P. Blackmur called "the story of a story"[3] unfold. The field termed by Jerome McGann a literary work's "bibliographical environment"[4] opens up before her and – when she reflects on it in the right light – offers rich pickings. The case is, like all cases, particular; but much of its interest is representative.

"First appeared in the *Cornhill Magazine* . . . "

In this James's novella is like many nineteenth-century novels, American and English, that made their first appearance in serial form, in magazines, or (as in Dickens's case) through monthly part-issue. "Daisy Miller" is most often taught in American literature courses and treated as an archetypally American work; but as the *Oxford Companion to English Literature* reveals, the *Cornhill Magazine* (1860–1975) was English: a "literary periodical of consistently high quality,"[5] founded by Thackeray, and edited in 1878 by James's friend Leslie Stephen, soon to become the father of Virginia Woolf. Henry James's own 1909 Preface to the story, reprinted in the invaluable Library of America volumes of James's *Literary Criticism*, gives an explanation for this unusual place of publication (James's first ever appearance in a British magazine; 336 items by him had previously appeared in American journals). James sent it

> to the editor of a magazine that had its seat of publication at Philadelphia and had lately appeared to appreciate my contributions. That gentleman however (an historian of some repute) promptly returned my missive, and with an absence of comment that struck me at the time as rather grim – as, given the circumstances, requiring indeed some explanation: till a friend to whom I ap-

pealed for light, giving him the thing to read, declared it could only have passed with the Philadelphian critic for "an outrage on American girlhood."[6]

John Foster Kirk, the editor of *Lippincott's Magazine,* thus passed up America's chance to be first with this notoriously American work. Pulling down *A Bibliography of Henry James: Third Edition,* a crucial reference guide listing details of all James's publications, by Leon Edel, James's most prominent critic and biographer, and Dan H. Laurence, our intrepid student can work out that there were several other American magazines which might have taken "Daisy Miller." The most hospitable, however, the *Atlantic Monthly,* under the editorship of James's supportive friend, novelist William Dean Howells, was to serialize his new short novel *The Europeans* in July 1878.[7] Moreover, James may well have wanted to make a special impression, and as a writer of fiction, in England, where he had recently settled and where in February 1878 he had a book published for the first time (by Macmillan, a volume of essays: *French Poets and Novelists*). The *Cornhill* was an illustrious frame for a début: it had published novels by Trollope, Mrs. Gaskell, and George Eliot.

"Two Unauthorized Periodical Appearances . . . "

James's Preface wryly notes that the immediate success of the story was attested by its being "promptly pirated in Boston – a sweet tribute I hadn't yet received and was never again to know" (*LC II,* p. 1270). The complexities of international copyright law, until 1891, protected works first published in the U.S. from piracy in Britain, but only originally American copyright was recognized in the U.S. (though in fact James's *The American* was pirated in Britain in 1877).[8] When James began publishing periodically in both countries he had to make special arrangements for simultaneous publication to guarantee copyright protection. At any rate, the piracy of *Daisy Miller* in Boston and New York, was in periodicals and didn't affect his book copyright.

"No. 28 of Harper's Half-Hour Series . . . "

Thus he was able to arrange with the House of Harper for the tale to come out in the "Half-Hour Series," where within weeks it sold a remarkable 20,000 copies.[9] Big sales, but this Harper first book edition has its own moral. James signed for a 10 percent royalty, and might thus have hoped for a high return. But with the exceptional degree of controversy about the story – "society almost divided itself into Daisy Millerites and anti-Daisy Millerites," said Howells[10] – the Harpers chose to cash in by issuing it in what Michael Anesko in his authoritative *"Friction with the Market": Henry James and the Profession of Authorship* calls "the cheapest possible format,"[11] paperbound at twenty cents or clothbound at thirty-five. In spite of the high sales figure, then, James was saying to Howells in June 1879 that "I have made $200 by the whole American career of D.M."[12]

The whole question of the contractual and other publishing arrangements the author makes or finds imposed, of timing and publicity and pricing and critical reception and so forth, can be crucial in determining the fate of the finished work. The literary critic and historian John Sutherland suggestively calls this force "the shaping power of contract."[13] Henry James did not write *primarily* for money, and in a sense he was in this case prepared to sacrifice the highest immediate returns in the interest of making his name, hoping for larger profits down the road; but he was bitter by 1879. As he told Howells, probably with some tactical exaggeration for a friend who was also a powerful editor, "I am a very bad bargainer and I was born to be victimized by the pitiless race of publishers." The story *did* make him famous, at any rate.

"The First Revised Version . . . "

Maqbool Aziz's useful headnote only now gets to the first English book edition of 1879, two volumes from Macmillan, where *Daisy Miller* was put together with "Four Meetings" and "An International Episode," a *nouvelle* James had consciously written as "a *pendant* or counterpart" to his hit (*Henry James Letters* II, p. 183). If our student looks closely at the Penguin in the library, she will find that its text is taken from this edition. So how is she to account for the variation between the texts she has read? Is the Oxford World's Classics text she first looked at then the *un*revised version? On the contrary, when she looks at the "Note on the text" in that edition, it transpires that it reprints the even further revised text of the New York Edition.

"The New York Edition . . . "

The "New York Edition of the Novels and Tales of Henry James," to give it its full title, appeared near the end of James's career in 1907–9 in 24 volumes. It was a huge undertaking, and occupied James for a number of years in writing Prefaces for all the fictions he included (there were striking omissions, like *Washington Square* and *The Europeans* and *The Bostonians*), in closely revising their texts (some very heavily), in supervising the taking of photographs for the frontispieces, and in generally attempting to ensure an "absolutely supreme impeccability"[14] for the enterprise. Like many other authors toward the end of their lives, James embarked on a project of self-reordering, self-recollection, and self-representation, extending his artistic control, as it were, so that he gave a shape to his whole oeuvre. The revised texts of the New York Edition, especially of earlier works like *The American* and *Daisy Miller,* where James has cut and pasted the original pages on larger sheets and filled the margins with ballooning alterations to almost every sentence, have been described as constituting different works from the originals, and have provoked increasing critical attention, stimulated partly by the brilliant, tantalizing accounts of the complex psychology and the creative intricacies of the revision process in the final Preface, that to *The Golden Bowl.*[15]

In *The Tales of Henry James* Aziz himself reprints the serial version of the tale from the *Cornhill,* but giving variants from the subsequent editions. The other two texts are later and represent to different degrees James's further thoughts. The unsuspecting reader – like our student-detective – may be surprised, or startled, or even outraged, to find out that significant critical decisions have been preemptively enforced in an edition to the extent of determining which words she reads, which text she is to respond to.

Some special reflection on the editor's role seems indeed salutary here, for there is now a widespread anxiety or unease in the literary and academic community about the sources and processes that select and filter for us the texts we read, the texts through which we explore many of our important ideas. For years the bibliographical world, or the sphere of textual criticism, was mostly acknowledged by others as a necessary evil, left to its own experts, and asked simply to provide "definitive," reliable editions for critics to work with and readers to read. But in our self-conscious era people are becoming properly suspicious of all sorts of products and services that formerly, for the most part, were swallowed without blinking. We scrutinize with increasing skepticism claims to authority or definitiveness, we disbelieve the hyperbole of blurbs, we deconstruct the ideology of the cover design on our paperbacks. Though the world of books is to be valued as a relative place of intellectual and emotional liberty, where freedom of expression nurtures freedom of belief, it has its own codes and power structures and is governed by its own institutions, though also riven by its own internal divisions, which we need to understand and be aware of at least partially if we are to be good literary citizens, responsible readers and writers.

Even as American society in 1878 seemed split into Daisy Millerites and anti-Daisy Millerites, so feelings run high in the scholarly world – bewilderingly to the noninitiate – on the question of the choice and composition of "copy-text" for an edition of a given literary work. There are good reasons for the differences of opinion. Authors go through all sorts of agonizing and complex processes while creating literary works, and the result can be a proliferation of different drafts or versions. Sometimes there are many manuscript drafts before first publication, as with Wordsworth's *The Prelude,* first drafted in 1799 and first published as a whole, posthumously, in 1850; but sometimes the author publishes and then takes the opportunity of a new edition to rethink and rewrite in a more or less radical way. W. H. Auden did this to put into effect changes in his moral and political outlook; W. B. Yeats to ensure that his printed poems embody his present self; the sensitive Tennyson partly to eliminate faults pointed out by reviewers. How is an editor to choose? And if there survives only a scrappy dossier of notebooks and papers, can and should the editor cut-and-paste into existence (as was done posthumously with Hemingway's *Garden of Eden*), what is known as a "reading text"?

The usual understanding, though it has come under some challenge in the wake of theoretical dismantlements of the authority of "the author," is that the editor's task is to reconstruct as closely as possible the author's original intentions for the form of a work. But in many cases – indeed, in that of Shakespeare, usually thought of as the "author" par excellence – the original intention cannot be ascertained with any certainty, and there is no unproblematically "authentic" text. Shakespearian scholars lack printed versions with clear authorial sanction and are compelled to speculate, often elaborately. The Shakespearians end up cultivating complicated family trees of ramifying conjecture, on which, say, a Quarto text of a play might have a bafflingly complex provenance, supposedly representing one actor's script patched together with the scribbled notes of a rather deaf spy in the audience and put into print years later by a team of compositors of markedly different reliability and variable sensitivity to Shakespeare's versification.

In the case of most modern authors, and certainly James, editors fortunately escape the need for such extravagance of reconstructive conjecture. Although there are comparatively few surviving manuscripts, we know that in most cases James closely monitored the transmission of his works into print. In fact, he often oversaw more than one printing of a given work: the editor of a fiction by James may have to cope with a dazzling spectrum of printed authorities, all with some degree of authorial supervision and thus presumably sanction: a first serial publication, a first English book edition and first American book edition, usually both revised from the serial, then often second and third editions with further authorial revisions, and last the large-scale revision of the New York Edition. The problem with recovering "the author's original intentions for the form of a work" in such circumstances, where we have a surplus of intentions dating from different moments, is to know to *which* "author" – the first creator, the mature or senile reviser, some other incarnation? – we should assign creative authority.

To put it briefly, an editor choosing a copy-text (one who is not in a position to produce a parallel text) needs to decide on the determining consideration for an edition: respect for the author's last known lifetime wish for the state of the text, which sometimes, as in James's case, can be very strongly expressed, and here would lead to the use of the 1909 New York Edition; or on the other hand respect for the literary-historical moment of first (or early) publication, a course that might seem appropriate in the case of *Daisy Miller,* which was an "event" in 1878 in a certain textual form. Both choices have advantages. Use of the last lifetime edition avoids the appearance of violating the known last textual wishes of the author concerned for the profile of a life's achievement, and works on the not-unreasonable assumption that the maturely accruing artistic judgment of the writer late in the career is likely to produce the best text. Use of the first published text, however, or the first book edition, can yield a more precise sense of what the work meant at the time it first appeared: we are better able to understand its reception, to see what faults or controversial qualities it may have had (if they were subsequently revised out), to think about its influences and its influence on other works of the period.

To list the advantages of both practices is to become a pluralist, reluctant to see either abandoned in favor of the other,[16] With major authors and works, where the market will support rival editions, this need not be a balloon debate, with the losing party hurled unceremoniously down to oblivion. Surely in taking the intentions of authors so seriously as to devote so much time to reading them, we will do well to show respect to what, on mature reflection, they expressly intend for the appearance of their works. In most cases it does not seem that they felt first publication terminated their intimate relation with, or their property in, the work; and who is any critic to decide that the reading public should be deprived of the author's final thoughts? On the other hand, we would be naively partisan fans, false to the wisdom for which we honor them, if we were not prepared to take account of the human, emotional, ideological, political, economic, and other contingencies that mitigated and gave body to their imaginative achievements. That is, if we are striving for truth, we should see the authors in and of their time as well as above or ahead of it. The raw impact of a new author's first appearance on the literary scene, the sense of live potentiality, may be lost on us if we read only a later text that has been brought into line with a developed technique and refined by an established figure who has left certain paths untaken and is covering his tracks.

Let us hope, then, that after going into the matter a little our student feels positively *glad* that available paperbacks give her the chance to read both the 1879 and 1909 versions of *Daisy Miller,* to balance the claims of "freshness" and "maturity." If she has unusual stamina she could even read the story, also in the original serial form, as reprinted by Aziz (in fact there are only a few tiny differences between the *Cornhill* and 1879 texts). Unmentioned in Aziz's headnote quoted above, just to add a "special" to this menu of versions, is that his edition reprints in an Appendix James's 1883 *Daisy Miller: A Comedy in Three Acts,* a never-produced adaptation commercialized to the point of a strained happy ending in which Daisy recovers from her illness and the Europeanized Winterbourne successfully rehabituates himself to "the American tone" (*Tales* III, p. 161).

> WINTERBOURNE. . . . We shall be married the same day. (*To Daisy.*) Shan't we, Daisy – in America?
> DAISY, *who has risen to her feet, leaning on his arm.* Oh, yes; you ought to go home!   (*Tales* III, p. 596 [Act Three, Scene Nine])

To read this artistically not-so-happy twist on his delicately tuned ironic tragedy of cultural and sexual misunderstanding may not add to the student's list of James masterpieces. But it may certainly focus, by contrast, her sense of the formal and technical choices that shape the way the story works; as, for instance, when Winterbourne's thoughts in the play have to be conveyed to the audience in a clumsy aside. In the first, flirtatious meeting between Winterbourne and Daisy, the story can "go behind" Winterbourne, can clearly sketch his sense of the situation:

> In Geneva, as he had been perfectly aware, a young man was not at liberty to speak to a young unmarried girl except under certain rarely-occurring conditions; but here at Vevey, what conditions could be better than these? – a pretty American girl coming and standing in front of you in a garden.
>   (*Tales* III, p. 157)

What goes unspoken in the story's dialogue has to be enunciated somehow in the play, lest it pass unnoticed by the spectators:

> WINTERBOURNE, *aside.* Does she accept my acquaintance or not? It's rather sudden, and it wouldn't do at Geneva. But why else did she come and plant

herself in front of me? She is the prettiest of the pretty, and, I declare, I'll risk
it!   (*Tales* III, p. 534 [Act One, Scene Four])

In effect, James is confessing here his failure in the kind of lateral thinking between artistic forms that might have found a true dramatic equivalent for the effect in the story. It is scarcely plausible that Winterbourne would *formulate* all of this for his own benefit; he is twisted by James into becoming himself the blunt explainer ("it wouldn't do at Geneva") of situations and social codes that in the story can be conveyed unobtrusively through the nuanced narration. Reading the play with its comparative crudities can bring home, in its heightened colors, the tricky position of James as a professional writer attempting to please a mass audience (by fitting in with the unsubtle tones of the Anglo-Saxon theater of the 1880s).

Looked at in another way, the dramatic version can also be understood, in Aziz's phrase, as "an interesting commentary on the novella" (*Tales* III, p. 522), as a piece of indirect criticism. The same would be true of the 1891 dramatic version(s) of *The American,* or the play versions of *The Other House* or *The Outcry* or "Owen Wingrave" (entitled "The Saloon").[17] Along similar lines, it is not only in the explicitly self-critical Prefaces that the New York Edition constitutes an act of artistic self-reevaluation for James; the revisions themselves, with their manifold inflections of the approach to the action and occasional alterations of the action itself, also amount to a practical criticism of the original version, even while the effort James puts in is a mark of the value he continues to attach to the works concerned. This is hardly surprising in an author whose creative impulses are so inextricable from his critical responses; in whom, for example, to read another fiction like Maupassant's "La Parure" is to imagine a different kind of ironic construction and write his own story, "Paste."

We have considered some of the editorial questions about works that exist in multiple versions, the kinds of thinking that can inform the choice of a copy-text, but sometimes the adversarial ways of argument into which such discussions tend to fall – youthful freshness versus stale mannerism, mature mastery or manipulation versus experimental groping or edge – can seem aridly circular. As students of literature we are not compelled to make such choices, only to locate and articulate kinds of interest that enlarge our understanding. The indisputable fact is that James put an enormous imaginative effort into revising and representing a huge body of his own earlier work for the New York Edition, and the process is a subject for study in itself. Comparing versions of a work offers a lively interpretative stimulus by showing us the author actually at work, or literary history in the making, and the detective work involved in collating versions leads us into attempting to construct a satisfactory understanding of the process, provoking our curiosity and seeming – almost – to show us the writer's verbal imagination in the act.

When we say "Daisy Miller" to each other, then, we may strictly speaking not be referring to the same work. Not just in the philosophical sense, whereby my reading of it will always be different from yours. Our experience of the work may also differ because, in a literal, textual sense, we're not talking about quite the same work. We may be disagreeing about the characterization of Daisy because, for instance, your version – the New York Edition – gives importance to the phrase, "she did what she liked," generalizing Daisy's wilfulness, whereas in mine – the 1879 – it doesn't figure, and, more flatly but with a certain eloquence, Giovanelli just says, "she wanted to go."

If we go into print without checking our textual ground, we risk ending up with egg on our face. The great English critic F. R. Leavis, who prized the early and middle James over the late James of F. O. Matthiessen's "Major Phase," in 1947 was on the point of taking advantage of a new edition of *Roderick Hudson* (1875) to draw attention to the freshness, vigor, and vividness of the young James's writing. Unfortunately for his argument, as he ruefully conceded, the Chiltern edition reprinted not an early edition, but the 1907 New York Edition text, and the passages Leavis chose to pick out as particularly fine turned out to have been introduced by the very same older James he was alleging had become fatally mannered and detached from life. Leavis was forced to make a grudging acknowledgment even while holding to his central claim: "It is true that what particularly strike one as characteristic felicities in the writing turn out again and again to have come in with the late revision, yet it didn't need this to make the writing wonderfully intelligent, brilliant and sensitive."[18] Poor Leavis's candor here made him the subject of misrepresentation later: "We may recall the misapprehension of Dr. Leavis, who was led to make certain claims for Henry James's early manner on the assumption that the reprint he used of *Roderick Hudson* used the text of 1874 [sic], though in fact it was derived from the much revised text of 1907."[19]

We've just had a brief dip in some of the murky depths that lurk beneath the feet of the reader who stops skating and pauses to test the thin ice of the textual surface. For some, perhaps, this momentary immersion may merely give an unwelcome glimpse of the troglodytic workforce slaving to provide "pure" texts in the dark underworld below the bright, would-be untroubled landscape of hermeneutics. For others, though, and especially given the wealth of angles from which new historical connections are entering literary studies, it may suggest ways in which the concerns of editors, bibliographers, and publishing historians can intersect fruitfully with those of criticism. The serious critic of a fiction by James not only needs to know about its main recent critics, I would argue, but also its early critical history, its critical reception, and James's own remarks about it in Prefaces and letters. As I have suggested, James's revisions and adaptations can be seen as part of the critical dossier.

But, then, to adapt James himself in the Preface to *Roderick Hudson,* "Really, universally, relations stop nowhere, and the exquisite problem of the [critic] is eternally but to draw, by a geometry of his own, the circle within which they shall *appear* to do so." Which means in this case that criticism should be informed – as far as is practicable – by a sense of the ethos and history and affiliations of the sources of fact and opinion it deals with or draws on, both past and present. Thus, for a small example, in the case of *Daisy Miller,* as I have suggested, we may make interest of various kinds from the seemingly bland fact that its first publication is in the *Cornhill.* After the copious reviewing James had done as an apprentice writer on his native American scene, it was a grand step in the great British footprints of Thackeray and Trollope, both specialists in their own blend of satire and tenderness. It was at the same time an extension of James's *American* connections, in the sense that he had met Leslie Stephen in 1869 – or even before – through their common friend Charles Eliot Norton, the American follower of Ruskin's social and artistic thought and founder of *The Nation,* to which both James and Stephen were contributors. Early perceptions of the story as snobbishly anti-American, moreover, and attacks on James's expatriation as treachery, may well have been fueled by the apparently pointed planting of his journalistic flag atop the British Establishment and far from American soil – which was in fact a result of the *Lippincott's* rejection.

Our alertness will properly extend, of course, to the modern mediators of James to us – and to ourselves: it is sensible, and interesting, to be aware of the variety of ideological traditions and emphases, as well as of personal interests, that can shape critical, historical, biographical, bibliographical, editorial, and other representations. "Authorities" should be prepared to *earn* our trust; and we should be prepared to put in some work before bestowing it. Henry James's posthumous career, as might be expected of the author of "The Aspern Papers," has not been without incident – when the author and his literary agent are no longer on the scene, executors and "experts" quickly take over – and much cultural–historical interest inheres in the successive dealings of, among others, Percy Lubbock (1879–1965, the English first editor of James's letters [1920]), Leon Edel (1907–1997, James's grand Canadian biographer [in five volumes, 1953–72] and re-editor and selector of his letters [in four volumes, 1974–84]), and F. O. Matthiessen (1902–50, author–editor of the influential biography–anthology *The James Family* [1947] and first editor [with Kenneth Murdock] of *The Notebooks of Henry James* [1947]).[20]

The selection of works by James that is readily available to be read and taught, as these days of booming canon-studies make us highly aware, affects our sense of him; and in so huge an oeuvre – it might take a year to read all his published works, and nowadays time is short – there is more room for variation of emphasis than with a compact six-pack like Jane Austen's. At the level of teaching, changing or enlarging the body of material that is commonly referred to can take a long time; generations of opinion-forming writers and academics may lag behind the latest developments, may continue to think of James *as,* in effect, the few works they read in their student days. Certain notable features can drop out of sight in the landscape. Considerable but less central works like *The Tragic Muse* or *The Sacred Fount* cannot easily be taught if they are out of print or very expensive; recent Penguin editions may bring them back into focus.

The serious student, critic, or scholar can go to a good library for a fuller sampling of James. Even then, we do well to be aware of the omissions, inadvertent or intentional, that result in the absolute or practical nonavailability of certain shorter texts even for pretty enterprising readers. Frederick Wegener has compared the Edel–Laurence *Bibliography,* for instance, with the splendid pair of 1984 Library of America Edel–Wilson volumes of James's *Literary Criticism* and discovered troubling inconsistencies (compounded by some obscurity about plans for other volumes): the memorial essays on James Payn and Charles Eliot Norton are inexplicably omitted, for instance, as is the 1900 introduction to Goldsmith's *Vicar of Wakefield.*[21] In the same edition's 1993 pair of Richard Howard volumes of James's *Collected Travel Writings,* one can look in vain for the essays of 1907 on the speech and manners of American women, or for the extraordinary lecture of 1905 on "The Question of Our Speech," all companion-pieces to the investigations of American culture in *The American Scene* – which *is* included.[22] There is also no sign in the British volume of James's August 1878 essay on "The British Soldier" (in *Lippincott's Magazine*), or of his 1878 reports on

Parliamentary debates for *The Nation*. It seems these works, dropping out of otherwise wonderfully useful and entertaining volumes, have – prejudicially – missed their chance of being regularly looked at, as have James tales happening to be omitted from the selections published by the major houses like Penguin and Oxford.

Proper consideration of James's letters would take a chapter, or a book. But it should be said that the situation is confusing and unsatisfactory; and here too some warnings are due. The main recent edition is Leon Edel's majestic four-volume *Henry James Letters*, but we cannot rely on it alone. It is thought that there are over 12,000 letters by James, scattered in libraries and private collections; if we take Leon Edel's own figure of 15,000 as a working total, the nearly 1,100 in his four volumes make just over 7 percent of that total. On the whole, too, as one would expect, they bear out the image of James projected in Edel's biography. Percy Lubbock's two volumes of 1920, constrained though he was by the necessity of tactfully avoiding the franker references to those still living, contain 230 letters later omitted by Edel. Edel has published two single-volume selections, each of which contains letters unavailable elsewhere. And many more of James's individual correspondences have become separately available, either complete or substantially so. Many of them adjust our sense of James's knowledge and experience, his social range, and his literary career. We can now read James's correspondences with, for instance, William James, W. D. Howells, R. L. Stevenson, H. G. Wells, Ford Madox Ford, Edith Wharton, Edmund Gosse, Henry Adams, T. S. Perry, John Hay, William Roughead, Elizabeth Robins, Macmillan's, the Daniel Curtises, and others. A calendar of all traceable James letters, which will alter the world of James scholarship, is presently being completed by Steven Jobe, whose checklist of published letters in the *Henry James Review* in 1990 is already a crucial research tool.[23]

James's playfully fantasticating "Private Life" (1891) offers a haunting image of the fetishized "author," discovered in a darkened room, unresponsive to outside sounds: "his back was half-turned to me and he bent over the table in the attitude of writing" (New York Edition, v. 17, p. 237). In our attempts to get a full-face look at James the author, to see "how he wrote," we can track down and read all his own thousands of letters, all his fictions, essays, plays, travel-sketches, reviews, biographical works, and so forth. We can dwell on intriguing glimpses into his practices in the study, sometimes from James's own lips, as when George Prothero, in 1888 a Cambridge don, asked him for details and recorded them abbreviatedly:

he told me ab*t* his way of work*g*, noth*g* unusual or eccentric ab*t* it – he just
plods on gener*ly*, day aft. day, doesn't work bef*re* bkt, means to stop at lunch,
but gen*ly* works on till ab*t* 4 p.m. never does anyth*g* after that; seldom has a
bad day, some*ts* one better *tn* usual, wh how*r* takes a lot out of him: Port*t* of
a Lady the last of his bks wh he wrote twice over, as he used to write *tm* all =
now he writes, slowly & deliber*ly*, but it stands as he writes it.[24]

In 1897, after much "plodding on," James's writing hand gave out – for the
long haul, at least – and he engaged William MacAlpine, the first of the typ-
ists to whom he was to dictate. This mechanical adjustment may have had
an aesthetic corollary, for the development of the involved but colloquial,
dramatically "spoken," later Jamesian style has been attributed by his last
typist, Theodora Bosanquet, to the dictatorial situation: "'It all seems,'" he
once explained, "to be so much more effectively and unceasingly *pulled* out
of me in speech than in writing."[25] Perhaps this insight is more intimate than
it seems.

We can seem, moreover, to catch flashes of James's authorial face in the
mirrors of his *Notebooks* and Prefaces, both documents of reflective self-
consciousness rare in the annals of fiction. Both show the logic of Jamesian
conception and readjustment with inspiring candor as well as with provoking concealments and silences.

But in spite of all these opportunities, the author's biographical back remains tantalizingly half-turned to us. It may after all be in his actual labor
over his texts, the choices we can sometimes trace him making in the process
from notebook sketch to magazine version to first edition to revised version,
that we most intimately see Henry James at work.

NOTES

1   Henry James, *Daisy Miller and Other Stories,* ed. and with an introduction by
    Jean Gooder (Oxford: Oxford University Press, 1985).
2   Aziz (ed.), *The Tales of Henry James* (Oxford: Oxford University Press, 1973 to
    date), Vol. III, p. 154 (hereafter cited as *Tales*).
3   Blackmur applies this phrase specifically to James's Prefaces in "The Critical Pref-
    aces of Henry James," in *Studies in Henry James,* Veronica A. Makowsky (New
    York: New Directions, 1983), 15–44, p. 17.
4   Jerome McGann, *The Beauty of Inflections: Literary Investigations in Histori-
    cal Method and Theory* (Oxford: Clarendon Press, 1985), p. 85.
5   *The Oxford Companion to English Literature: Fifth Edition,* ed. Margaret
    Drabble (Oxford: Oxford University Press, 1985), p. 230.
6   Henry James, Preface to "Daisy Miller &c," *Henry James: Literary Criticism:
    French Writers; Other European Writers; The Prefaces to the New York Edi-*

tion, ed. Leon Edel and Mark Wilson (New York: The Library of America, 1984), p. 1269 (hereafter cited as *LC II*).

7   See Ellery Sedgwick, "Henry James and the *Atlantic Monthly:* Editorial Perspectives on James' 'Friction with the Market.'" *Studies in Bibliography* 45 (1992), 311–32, for a very helpful and suggestive account of James's relations with the magazine that was in a sense the foundation of his literary career.

8   See Leon Edel and Dan H. Laurence, *A Bibliography of Henry James: Third Edition, Revised with the Assistance of James Rambeau* (Oxford: Oxford University Press, 1982), pp. 32–3.

9   See Michael Anesko. *"Friction with the Market": Henry James and the Profession of Authorship* (New York: Oxford University Press, 1986), pp. 43–4, for an excellent account of the international publishing situation at the time and James's strategy within it.

10 In a letter to J. R. Lowell, quoted in William T. Stafford, *James's "Daisy Miller": The Story, The Play, The Critics* (New York: Charles Scribner's Sons, Scribner Research Anthologies, 1963), p. 112.

11 Anesko, p. 43.

12 *Henry James Letters,* edited by Leon Edel (Cambridge, Mass.: Belknap Press of Harvard University Press, 1975), 4 vols., 1974–84; II, p. 243 (hereafter cited as *Henry James Letters*). (By my arithmetic, 10% of 20,000 × 20 cents would be $400; but publishers' accounting practices can be eccentric, and James may be misremembering.)

13 John Sutherland, *Victorian Novelists and Publishers* (Chicago: University of Chicago Press, 1976), p. 101.

14 Henry James to Charles Scribner, 12 May 1906 (quoted in Philip Horne, *Henry James and Revision: The New York Edition* [Oxford: Oxford University Press, 1990], p. 44).

15 See, for instance, Horne, *Henry James and Revision,* or David MacWhirter (ed.), *Henry James's New York Edition: The Construction of Authorship* (Palo Alto: Stanford University Press, 1995).

16 According to Aziz, "When an editor is confronted with a multiple-version work, he cannot afford to think of textual authority in any absolute term – even the so-called final version is a tentative final with a compulsive revisionist" (*Tales* II, 1978, p. xxv).

17 See Leon Edel (ed.), *The Complete Plays of Henry James* (Philadelphia and New York: Lippincott, 1949).

18 F. R. Leavis, "Henry James's First Novel" (review of *Roderick Hudson*), *Scrutiny* 14 (September 1947), pp. 295–301.

19 John Butt, "Editing a Nineteenth-Century Novelist (Proposals for an Edition of Dickens)," in *Art and Error: Modern Textual Editing,* ed. Ronald Gottesman and Scott Bennett (London: Methuen, 1970), pp. 155–66.

20 There are helpful and fascinating chapters on James's literary afterlife in two recent books: Ian Hamilton's *Keepers of the Flame: Literary Estates and the Rise of Biography* (London: Hutchinson, 1992), and Michael Millgate's *Testamentary Acts: Browning, Tennyson, James, Hardy* (Oxford: Oxford University Press, 1992).

21 See Frederick Wegener, "Henry James on James Payn: A Forgotten Critical Text," in *New England Quarterly* (March 1994), 67 (1), 115–31.

22 The three pieces in question can be found – in good libraries – in Henry James, *French Writers and American Women,* ed. and with an introduction by Peter Buitenhuis (Branford, Conn.: Compass Publishing Company, 1960). The volume that leaves them out is *Henry James: Collected Travel Writings: Great Britain and America: English Hours: The American Scene: Other Travels,* ed. Richard Howard (New York: The Library of America, 1993).

23 "A Calendar of the Published Letters of Henry James" (two parts), *Henry James Review* (Winter, Spring 1990), 11 (1,2), 1–29, 100. See, for a judicious review of Edel's last volume, Tamara Follini in *Essays in Criticism* (January 1986), 36 (1), 81–8; or, for a more general account, Philip Horne, "The Editing of James's Letters," *The Cambridge Quarterly* (Spring 1986), 126–41.

24 G. W. Prothero's journal, June 2, 1888. The manuscript is at King's Cambridge MS (Misc 77/3, entry fol 29 (verso)). Acknowledgment is due to the Provost and Fellows of King's College for permission to publish this extract here.

25 Theodora Bosanquet, *Henry James at Work* (London: The Hogarth Press, 1924), p. 7.

4

DOROTHY J. HALE

Henry James and the Invention of Novel Theory

Henry James's literary critical essays, especially the Prefaces that he wrote for the New York Edition of his fiction (1905–7), have generally been regarded as the foundational documents for Anglo-American novel theory. When we look at the series of major books devoted to James's criticism – works ranging from Joseph Beach's *The Method of Henry James* (1918) and R. P. Blackmur's *The Art of the Novel* (1934) to James E. Miller, Jr.'s *Theory of Fiction: Henry James* (1972) – we can understand why. James's discussion of novels seems qualitatively different from what had gone before: James dignified fiction by talking about it as art. Although consumed by a popular audience in search of entertainment and written by anyone who could pick up a pen, although often hurriedly composed to meet a deadline for magazine serialization, although *about* virtually anything at all, novels and short stories could, in the right hands, James declared, be as aesthetically significant as poetry, painting, or drama. But had James merely proclaimed fiction to be capable of artistic greatness, novel theory might still have had to wait to be born. James is credited with inventing a new discipline because he not only deemed the novel worthy of critical analysis but also helped establish the terms for that analysis. In collecting the eighteen Prefaces to the New York Edition into one volume, Blackmur was moved to call these essays "the most sustained and I think the most eloquent and original piece of literary criticism in existence" (*The Art of the Novel*, viii; hereafter cited as *Art*). And in his even more comprehensive collection of James's statements about fiction, Miller marvels that James "remained remarkably consistent in his views from the beginning to the end of his career" (xv).

Not every subsequent scholar has considered James to be so comprehensive or consistent, but whether they have attempted to collate, regularize or refine him, critics for more than half a century have found in James's fictional and critical writing both the inspiration for and the substance of a systematic description of the novel. The tradition most self-consciously derived from James effectively understood novel theory as a modern day anatomy;

the aim was to identify and classify what would eventually be called the "elements" of fiction. In the process, attention turned away from the comparatively unscientific remarks James made about art and artists, the muse and creative inspiration, life and experience, and focused on what seemed his more empirical observations about the literary object. Thus, while codifiers of James punctiliously include in their lists of Jamesian theoretical topics headings such as "The Writer and His Culture" or "The Relation of Art and Life," the bulk of their categorizations are devoted to a range of technical issues – including "Plots, Actions, Centers," "Narrative in the First Person," "The Dramatic Scene," and even "The Necessity of Fools."[1] Not surprisingly, in a work like *Understanding Fiction* (1943) by Cleanth Brooks and Robert Penn Warren, the theoretical enterprise became indistinguishable from an instruction manual. The theory of the novel inspired by James thus defined the "art" of the novel as, in Beach's approving term, a "mechanics" of fiction (xiv).

But if James inaugurated the era of the fiction-writing handbook and workshop, he is also credited – and blamed – for exerting a more general influence on the development of Anglo-American novel theory. The anatomies and handbooks that dissect fictional form are, on this view, symptoms of a more thoroughgoing literary formalism not exactly invented by James but certainly fostered by him and his followers. Critics of James claim that his study of fictional technique is embedded in a larger aesthetic theory that values artistic form to the exclusion of other sorts of meaning; especially in the Prefaces, James's detailed analysis of novelistic form implies that form is the highest "value" any art work can have – and he even suggests that what he calls "life" has, by comparison, no value at all until it becomes "formed" through art. As he famously writes in the Prefaces, "life [is] all inclusion and confusion, and art [is] all discrimination and selection" (*Art*, 120). What is included and why it is chosen are secondary concerns; the signal difference between life and art is the fact of selection. When James declares, "Really, universally, relations stop nowhere, and the exquisite problem of the artist is eternally but to draw, by a geometry of his own, the circle within which they shall happily *appear* to do so" (*Art*, 5), he suggests that art does not express the meaning of "relations" but rather enacts the formal illusion of life's limitability. For James, the project of raising the novel to a high art form is integrally connected to the belief that well-made works of art redeem "life" by giving it meaning – but it is difficult to say what this meaning is other than the contentless value of form itself.

By the 1980s Anglo-American critics dissatisfied with formalism of all kinds looked for a way to reconceptualize the relation between "art" and "life." For scholars interested in the novel, the recently translated Russian theorist M. M. Bakhtin provided a sociolinguistic theory that seemed a compelling alternative to the Jamesian tradition. Since Bakhtin's essays were composed primarily in the 1930s, the future of novel theory may appear to have been conceived along anachronistic lines; but Bakhtin's rejection of the Russian formalism of his own time worked to establish a sympathetic – if not exactly analogous – relation between distant cultural moments. Bakhtin's cultural difference added to his attraction in other ways. Working out of a Russian philosophical tradition informed by European thinkers like Kant and Marx, Bakhtin promised to rescue novel theory from the confines of lists and categories and restore criticism to a real world where aesthetics, literary history, cultural history, and the philosophy of language mattered. Bakhtin's definition of the novel as social discourse encouraged a generation of scholars to read novels not as a geometry of form but as cultural productions filled with social and political meaning:

> The novel can be defined as a diversity of social speech types (sometimes even diversity of languages) and a diversity of individual voices, artistically organized. The internal stratification of any single national language into social dialects, characteristic group behavior, professional jargons, generic languages, languages of generations and age groups, tendentious languages, languages of the authorities, of various circles and of passing fashions, languages that serve the specific sociopolitical purposes of the day, even of the hour . . . is the indispensable prerequisite for the novel as a genre.   (Bakhtin, 262–3)

Whereas James imagines that form gives meaning to life by giving life form, Bakhtin treats the novel's meaning as derived from the social languages that constitute it. For James, technique is diverse and form unified; for Bakhtin, any single novel is defined by its multiplicitous and heterogeneous social "voices." At the beginning of his influential essay, "Discourse in the Novel," Bakhtin explicitly signals his departure from formal definitions of the novel by criticizing the students of technique, the discipline that he calls "stylistics": "More often than not, stylistics defines itself as a stylistics of 'private craftsmanship' and ignores the social life of discourse outside the artist's studio, discourse in the open spaces of public squares, streets, cities and villages, of social groups, generations and epochs" (259).

The story of how Anglo-American novel theory developed is thus currently understood in superecessivist terms, as the escape of novel theory out of James's artificial circles to the social realities of the Bakhtinian public square. But now that the critics are no longer so invested in establishing James as either the fountainhead or nemesis of proper theoretical procedure, we may be better able to articulate the full philosophical problematic that informs his aesthetic theory. If it seems unsurprising that a retrospective reading of James allows us to see his work in a new light, it may be more remarkable to discover that rereading James rewrites our understanding of the development of novel theory. By attending to the "categories" that have been deemphasized in the systematization of James – specifically his account of how and why a novel gets created – we find at the heart of Jamesian aesthetics an ethical imperative that, in its untheorized reiteration in the Anglo-American tradition, becomes a significant counterplot in the progress of novel theory. This untheorized imperative is so enduring and pervasive that it constitutes a categorical assumption about the novel as a genre; theorists who are otherwise eminently self-conscious about the philosophical and methodological assumptions that divide them seem unaware of the significance of their agreement in this regard.

This ethical imperative, which even the Bakhtinian critics of James have taken for granted, might be called the appreciation of alterity. Following James, Anglo-American novel theorists have generally assumed that novels are conceived in and through an artist's desire to comprehend the identity of an "other"; a good novel, these theorists would have it, satisfies the artist's desire so fully that both the appreciation for the other and its alterity become objectified in the novel's form. I have elsewhere shown how, since James, theorists have insisted on characterizing this perceived dialectic between artist and other as a social relation – what I term "social formalism"[2] – but here I confine myself to demonstrating how the appreciation of alterity recurs as an ethical imperative in the work of three prominent Anglo-American theorists, all representative of different theoretical schools and yet all influenced by James: James's immediate disciple Percy Lubbock; the narratologist Dorrit Cohn; and the Neo-Aristotelian Wayne Booth. Booth's enthusiasm for the theory of the novel advanced by M. M. Bakhtin also gives us an opportunity to reconsider the reasons for Bakhtin's Anglo-American popularity. Bakhtin's swift induction into the Anglo-American tradition bespeaks, I hope to show, his real compatibility with the formalist theoretical tradition that is so influentially begun by James.

At first glance, nothing seems less committed to the value of alterity than James's radically subjectivist definition of the novel as the "authentic" expression of authorial point of view. What distinguishes the novel as a genre is, for James, a twinned mimetic task. On the one hand, the novel's generic purpose is to "reproduce life" in a way that will make it "interesting." On the other hand, this "interest" is itself a mimetic effect, derived from the author's ability to represent authentically his own particular experience of life:

> The question comes back thus, obviously, to the kind and the degree of the artist's prime sensibility, which is the soil out of which his subject springs. The quality and capacity of that soil, its ability to "grow" with due freshness and straightness any vision of life, represents, strongly or weakly, the projected morality. That element is but another name for the more or less close connexion of the subject with some mark made on the intelligence, with some sincere experience. *(Art, 45)*

Such talk of the artist's "prime sensibility" makes the character of the artist sound crucial to the novel's reproduction of life. Yet what in James's account distinguishes the artist from any ordinary person? His superior sensibility and intelligence do not mean that the artist enjoys feelings and knowledge that are unavailable to the ordinary person, nor does his special "quality and capacity," the "kind and degree" of his sensibility, result in the possession of specific virtues that would make him qualitatively better than others. What distinguishes the artist is, on the contrary, simply his ability to express his own point of view authentically. The "projected morality" of a novel is thus for James a function of the artist's sincerity, her fidelity first to her own perspective and second to the "mark" made on that perspective by "experience." In "The Art of Fiction" James declares that the sources of novelistic interest "are as various as the temperament of man, and they are successful in proportion as they reveal a particular mind, different from others. A novel is in its broadest definition a personal, a direct impression of life" (9). In his letter to the Deerfield Summer School (1889), James democratically assures the coed student body that "any point of view is interesting that is a direct impression of life. You each have an impression colored by your individual conditions; make that into a picture, a picture framed by your own personal wisdom, your glimpse of the American world" (29).

"*Any* point of view": this refusal to value one perspective over another is the cornerstone of a famous set piece in the Prefaces, the elaborate conceit of the "house of fiction." According to James, the house of fiction has "not one window, but a million – a number of possible windows not to be reckoned, rather; every one of which has been pierced, or is still pierceable, in its vast front, by the need of the individual vision and by the pressure of the individual will" *(Art, 46)*. As James takes pains to emphasize, all that distinguishes one viewer from another in the house of fiction is the "need" and the "pressure" of the "individual will." No viewing position is privileged; no window offers a more accurate or more preferable understanding of life than another:

> He and his neighbours are watching the same show, but one seeing more where the other sees less, one seeing black where the other sees white, one seeing big where the other sees small, one seeing coarse where the other sees fine. And so on, and so on; there is fortunately no saying on what, for the particular pair of eyes, the window may *not* open; "fortunately" by reason, precisely, of this incalculability of range. (*Art,* 46; James's emphasis)

The passage implies that the artist need not worry about justifying his vision; at the same time, however, the mere act of seeing through a window does not entirely take the place of more ordinary conceptions of value in this account. Although James declares that it is "fortunate" that there is "no saying what, for the particular pair of eyes, the window may *not* open," and thus makes it sound as if he values merely the incalculable particularity of individual perception, his preference for a view of "more" rather than "less" or of "fine" rather than "coarse" is unmistakable. Whatever his metaphor implies, James cannot bring himself absolutely to neutralize the differences in sensibility among viewers by treating those differences as nothing more than accidents of perspective. Yet his resistance in the Prefaces toward offering any more value-laden description of a superior artistic vision than that it sees "more" shows how James strives to preserve the relativity of perspective while also retaining a standard by which to judge artistic achievement.

This ambivalence in James's conception of the novelist helps explain a related doubleness in his account of a novelistic sincerity. On the one hand, James maintains that, to succeed in conveying a direct impression of life, a novelist must only be true to what he possesses in common with all other people: an identity defined by a unique point of view. In "The Art of Fiction" James asserts that the "first aid" to writing good fiction "is a capacity for receiving straight impressions" (21); "the only condition that I can think of attaching to the composition of the novel is . . . that it be sincere" (26). Yet a novelist must also be true to the view as well as to the point from which he sees it: he must experience life "directly," unmediated by any subjective partiality. Which, then, is the novel's proper subject: the viewer or the viewed? In the Prefaces, it seems, James outlines two competing ideals of novelistic authorship: on the one hand, the successful novelist is the one who most transparently expresses his unique "impression" of life; on the other hand, the successful novelist is the one who does not allow his own views to prevent life from making its "impression" on him. In the first case, the novelist is best when he projects his views; in the second, when he refuses to project them.

Once we appreciate this tension between projection and reception in James's account of novelistic point of view, we can better understand why James sometimes describes novel writing as a process of self-expression and other times as a process of recording. In his letter to the Deerfield students, for example, the great accomplishment of "doing something from one's own point of view" is inseparable from the project of considering "life directly and closely" (29). In "The Art of Fiction" James admonishes "novice" writers to "'Write from experience and experience only,'" yet the very next clause undercuts the leveling implications of this advice by upholding the standard of impression over that of expression: "I should feel that this was rather a tantalizing monition if I were not careful immediately to add, 'Try to be one of the people on whom nothing is lost!'" (13).

As a defining concept, "sincerity" proves insufficient to reconcile these conflicting demands that James places on the novelist; to mediate between the values of expression and impression, James must supplement his call for sincerity with the stipulation that the artist communicate his sense of "wonderment" too. On the one hand, James attributes the capacity for wonderment to people on whom nothing is lost:

> We care, our curiosity and our sympathy care, comparatively little for what happens to the stupid, the coarse and the blind; care for it, and for the effects of it, at the most as helping to precipitate what happens to the more deeply wondering, to the really sentient. Hamlet and Lear are surrounded, amid their own complications, by the stupid and the blind, who minister in all sorts of ways to their recorded fate. *(Art, 62)*

Hamlet and Lear are certainly not ordinary minds on ordinary days; their royal lineage suggests that, for James, the placement and trimmings of one's window might not, after all, be wholly irrelevant to an assessment of one's perspective, that sensibility may depend on the privileges of social position. But to underscore only the causal relation between status and vision implied by James's examples of "deep" sensibilities would be to miss the greater oddity in his invocation of these particular Shakespearean heroes: James's spectacular lack of concern for any specific attribute or action associated with these characters. Besides the related virtue of sincerity, wonder is the *only* character trait to which James wants to limit his novelist.

And wonder, as James describes it, necessarily diffuses an interest in the novelist's character by turning the act of novel-writing into a negotiation between viewer and viewed that relies as much on the worthiness of the view as on the viewer's capacity to "see." In James's formulation, "excited wonder must have a subject, must face in a direction, must be, increasingly, *about* something" (253). The view cannot be wonderful if the viewer thinks her sensibility makes it so; conversely, the viewer's sense that the view is so powerful as to transcend her comprehension of it always keeps her in "close connection" with the view. Such outward-directedness is, for James, the optimal condition for a novelistic creation because it can express the viewer's sensibility while at the same time maintaining the integrity of the view. It is the "subject" about which the artist wonders, James argues, that enables us to measure "his bias and his range":

> About what, good man, does he himself most wonder? – for upon that, whatever it may be, he will naturally most abound. Under that star will he gather in what he shall most seek to represent; so that if you follow thus his range of representation you will know how, you will see where, again, good man, he for himself most aptly vibrates. (*Art*, 253–4)

Paradoxically, the artist who most fully conveys this vibration of wonder to the reader is the least personal writer, insofar as he must remain true to his subject in order to vibrate "most aptly":

> the person capable of feeling in the given case more than another of what is to be felt for it, and so serving in the highest degree to *record* it dramatically and objectively, is the only sort of person on whom we can count not to betray, to cheapen or, as we say, give away, the value and beauty of the thing. By so much as the affair matters *for* some such individual, by so much do we get the best there is of it, and by so much as it falls within the scope of a denser and duller, a more vulgar and more shallow capacity, do we get a picture dim and meagre. (*Art*, 67; James's emphasis)

A superior sensibility is revealed precisely to the degree that it "records" "dramatically and objectively," without, that is, the self-interest that would interfere with the appreciation of the subject's virtues. By the same token, the more beautifully – which is to say, vividly and completely – the "thing" is represented, the more it bespeaks its indebtedness to the viewer/artist's sensibility.

Artistic wonder, as James thus describes it, establishes an economy of relation between viewer and viewed that is the basis for what I am calling the appreciation of alterity. The greater the artist's capacity for appreciation, the more capable he is of representation; to know the "thing" is irresistibly to reproduce it. In this economy, the greatest subjective investment results in a representation so objective (because so completely other) as to seem an actual object; the palpability of the artist's point of view – his interestedness – is imagined by James as a power to make palpable, not just to vivify but to instantiate the authentic identity of the thing that interests him:

> [the artist] lends and gives, only builds and piles high, lays together the blocks quarried in the deeps of his imagination and on his personal premises. He . . . can say to himself – what really more than anything else inflames and sustains him – that he alone has the *secret* of the particular case, he alone can measure the truth of the direction to be taken by his developed data. There can be for him, evidently, only one logic for these things; there can be for him only one truth and one direction – the quarter in which the subject most completely expresses itself. (*Art*, 122–3)

The desire to grasp the "secret" of what interests him leads James to plumb the "deeps" of his "personal premises," but this self-excavation results in no psychological or self-reflexive knowledge, no autobiographical association, nothing that might be considered a positive term of Jamesian identity. If the artist discovers himself in the process of representation, that is only because he has been guided by his subject to an objective assessment of the material within him – and this material, when "quarried," manifests the identity of the subject as an independent entity. Indeed, the workshop of the artist's imagination is nothing other than the "quarter in which the subject most completely expresses itself." Just as he hammers his imagination into the "blocks" that fit and fill in the "hard" outlines of his subject, so the artist will ultimately verify the autonomous substance of what interests him by transforming that interest into a material objet d'art.

Because the artistic subject is a key concept for James's aesthetic philosophy, its general definitional instability in James's critical writing becomes itself a significant component of the Jamesian version of the appreciation of alterity. In the Prefaces, James often uses the term "artistic subject" to refer to what he also calls the art work's "theme," "case" or "motive." But one of the most interesting aspects of the Prefaces is how little investment James has in saying what the theme of a particular novel is, what that work might, as we say, mean. The artistic subject thus is a concept that for James registers the art work's particular identity – this novel is "about" something different from that novel – while serving to define that identity less as something nameable and more as presence itself: what the work is finally "about" is the successful instantiation of the interesting object's coherent identity.

Finding the secret of the object of wonder, the "thing," transforms the nteresting object into a subject – almost a subjectivity – capable of self-expression. For James, the appreciation of alterity is, then, not only an economy of relation between representor and represented but a sequence of transmutation: the artist's identificatory understanding has the power to turn the object of interest into an artistic subject – and then to recast that subject as a self-expressive art work. In the Jamesian version of the appreciation of alterity, the artistic subject is ultimately defined by its hybrid nature: it is first of all both author and other, but it is also person and thing; the artistic subject is experienced by James as both a subjectivized object and an objectifiable subject. If the artist's appreciation discovers the object to be capable of humanlike self-expression, it is the objectiveness, derived from its objectness, of the artistic subject that allows James to believe that alterity can be instantiated through artistic form.

Given the complicated aesthetic philosophy that I have been describing, it is not surprising that James's followers needed to do some editing – and, in the name of editing, some out and out rewriting – if his work was going to lend itself to the systematic understanding of the novel they called theory. Yet even a quick look at the most influential work produced by a Jamesian, Percy Lubbock's *The Craft of Fiction,* can show us that the attempt to make the study of the novel more scientific results in the relocation, rather than the abandonment, of the appreciation of alterity. Lubbock believes that the first step in developing a theory of the novel is to limit the object of inquiry to the novel's form; he wants to tidy up James by extracting from his critical writing, and particularly from the Prefaces, the sections that pertain to technique. Lubbock declares at the outset of his study, "how [novels] are made is the only question I shall ask" (12). Although in this formulation Lubbock's question may seem identical to James's, the crucial distinction between master and disciple lies in the latter's narrower definition of "making." The Jamesian "questions of the intention of the novelist, his choice of a subject, the manner of his imagination, and so forth – these," Lubbock declares, "I shall follow no further than I can help" (12). Lubbock proposes instead what we might call an empiricist version of James's metaphorical materialism. Denying himself imaginative access to the quarry of the artist's imagination, Lubbock instead turns his inquiry to something that he thinks he can actually see: the techniques, or the "different substances, as distinct to the practised eye as stone and wood" (20), which constitute the novel's form. But to follow the issue of authorial agency "no further than can be helped" is, it turns out, to follow James more completely than Lubbock is able to theorize. By not asking about authorial intention, imagination, and subject choice, Lubbock does not in fact exclude these issues from his inquiry. If anything, not discussing these issues makes it easier for him to take for granted that his study of novel form can and should have ethical values inspired by James.

Ultimately, what it means for Lubbock to delimit his study of the novel is that authorial identity is itself delimited: authorial agency can seem more tangible if authorial identity can be thought of as objectively manifested, specifically if authorial identity can be defined as a feature of something that can be studied objectively – if it can be theorized as one of the stone- or woodlike substances of the novel. And it is James's own formalism that inspires Lubbock to make this move. Because Lubbock believes, as James does, that the art work holds "the silver clue to the whole labyrinth of [authorial] consciousness" (*Art,* 340), Lubbock concludes that one need only study the novel to know the essential truth of an author's identity. *The Craft of Fiction* explicitly reasserts James's definition of the novel's generic mission: to express its author's "vision of life." But whereas James had a large notion of how authorial identity might be embodied by the novel, Lubbock's empiricism encourages him to seek an objective correlative for authorial vision – and he finds it in the technical problem of point of view. For Lubbock, the relationship between a narrator and his character metonymically represents – and ultimately takes the place of – the Jamesian artist's relation to the interesting object in "life" to which the novel as a whole refers. Because narrative point of view stages a relationship between representor and represented, it becomes for Lubbock the novel's salient formal attribute: "The whole intricate question of method, in the craft of fiction, I take to be governed by the question of point of view – the question of the relation in which the narrator stands to the story" (251).

By equating authorial vision with novelistic point of view, Lubbock ascribes ethical value to technical effects even while he subtly departs from the values James assigns to the relationship between representor and represented. The best novelist, by Lubbock's lights, is not a wonderer but a dissembler: she expresses her own point of view by strategically pretending not to have a point of view of her own. Authors who can successfully pretend to disappear write better fiction, according to Lubbock, because they create the illusion of a social and material world:

> This is not *my* story, says the author; you know nothing of me; it is the story of this man or woman in whose words you have it, and he or she is a person whom you *can* know; and you may see for yourselves how the matter arose,

the man and woman being such as they are; it all hangs together, and it makes
a solid and significant piece of life.   (147, Lubbock's emphasis)

By appearing to disappear, the novelist creates "solid" subjects – characters
– whose very alterity, like that of the Jamesian artistic subject, gives the art
work its significant form. But, for James, the process of wonderful representation results in the construction and expression of an artistic subject,
which in turn produces an art work that gives meaning to life; for Lubbock,
the deliberate and strategic technical practice of authorial dissemblance results only in the novel's artful simulation of meaning, its illusion of a coherent and significant piece of life.

Lubbock's account of novelistic alterity thus seems more cynical than
James's: whereas James seeks to know and represent the intrinsic identity of
the object that interests him, the Lubbockian author seems to care for the
other only as a means for achieving a certain aesthetic effect. Yet for Lubbock the successful practice of dissemblance is itself a sign of a higher ethical good. The novelist's creation of seemingly self-expressive narrators and
characters evidences, according to Lubbock, her genuine capacity for alterity; an author who can successfully pretend to absent herself from her fiction
will crate an illusion not only of material reality but also of characterological autonomy. Her pretended ability to step outside her own point of view
becomes, in other words, evidence of her real respect for subjectivities other than her own, even if these subjectivities are fictional. Authors who create better novels – novels, that is to say, in which the characters seem real –
thus for Lubbock are also better people. If Flaubert is the positive example
of this Lubbockian version of the appreciation of alterity, Thackeray is the
negative example. For Lubbock, Thackeray's all-too-present and all-too-
Thackerian narrator represents the author at the expense of his characters:
"It is as though he never quite trusted his men and women when he had to
place things entirely in their care, standing aside to let them act; he wanted
to intervene continually" (103). The virtuous author, by contrast, treats her
characters so much as if they were both other and real that they seem to become so even to their own creator.

Lubbock's version of the appreciation of alterity simplifies and thus clari-
fies the ethical stakes in the theoretical tradition that I am tracing. The ethics
of James's paradigm are obscured in part because the value of authorial wonder is complicated by the hybrid nature – the extreme and simultaneous subjectivity and objectivity – of the artistic subject. By reducing the Jamesian
artistic subject to novelistic characters, Lubbock makes the double identity

of the represented other less confusing: the simultaneous "objectness" and subjectivity of a character are less in tension with each other because they are both novelistic illusions. The ethics of alterity that Lubbock relies upon thus seems more obviously recognizable as a kind of altruism: an author best represents himself by representing others; he represents his own vision of life by creating characters who themselves seem to possess their own visions of life. But if Lubbock's theory seems to allow a clearer – because more clearly human – ethical relation, this novelistic opportunity for virtue, is, importantly, predicated on a generic description of the novel as essentially rivalrous: for the author to do good, in Lubbock's theory, he must seem to step aside – and the only reason why he must make this sacrifice is because novelistic realism requires it. The novel's aesthetic success demands that the author choose between his own direct self-expression and the self-expression of an "other." Only for the virtuous author will this choice seem to require no self-sacrifice.

In her introduction to *Transparent Minds* (1978), the narratologist Dorrit Cohn adds a historical dimension – and a more sinister cast – to the economy of novelistic subjective relations that Lubbock describes. On her view, the development of the novel from the eighteenth century to the present is a story of the rivalry between an authorial narrator who "jealously guards his prerogative as the sole thinking agent within his novel" and a "fully developed figural consciousness" who seeks to "siphon away" the narrator's emotional and intellectual energy (Cohn, 25). The stakes of this rivalry have intensified in part due to Cohn's more specific and extreme account of how characterological autonomy should be defined – an account that is in turn predicated on her more specific sense of what distinguishes the novel as a genre. Because she believes that "fictional consciousness is the special preserve of narrative fiction" (Cohn, vi), in her theory the rivalry at the heart of narrative form finds its resolution in what she takes to be the evolutionary realization of the novel's technical potential: for Cohn, the novel fulfills its generic character by representing not an author's vision of life, but a character's vision of life, which she understands as the depiction of his or her consciousness. Now that we have looked at James and Lubbock, we can see how her account of novelistic form is informed by the ethical values she has in fact derived from the Jamesian theoretical tradition: the history of the novel for Cohn is the advance beyond selfish authors like Thackeray, who won't give their characters a chance to think for themselves, to more generous modern authors – James is one of her examples – who, in altruistically creating a consciousness that seems truly other, usher in the representation of "fictional minds with previously unparalleled depth and complexity" (26).

We can begin to understand Bakhtin's congeniality to the Jamesian tradition of novelistic alterity that I have been tracing if we turn to Wayne Booth's introduction to the first English edition of Bakhtin's *Problems of Dostoevsky's Poetics* (1984). Booth, who had published two decades before *The Rhetoric of Fiction* (1961) (a theory organized by headings and subtopics in the catalogue form so dear to the Anglo-American Jamesians), greeted Bakhtin's work with the enthusiasm of a convert. According to Booth, Bakhtin has taught him the limits of a strictly technical definition of the novel; Bakhtin's "challenge" to Booth's earlier way of thinking

> has little to do with whether or not the author claims privileges of omniscience or exercises inside views. Indeed it has nothing at all to do with the author's effort to produce a single unified effect. Its subject is not the ordering of technical means toward certain effects so much as the quality of the author's imaginative gift – the ability or willingness to allow voices into the work that are not fundamentally under the "monologic" control of the novelist's own ideology. (Booth, xix–xx)

What Bakhtin shows Booth, in other words, is how Anglo-American novel theory has over-valued technique in general and, since he singles out omniscience and inside views, "the whole intricate question" of point of view in particular. But whereas the new terms – like ideology and monologic – that Booth has derived from Bakhtin would imply that his rejection of formalism is based on an acceptance of a constructivist theory of social identity whose philosophical assumptions would radically reconceptualize the notion of authorial agency, the Bakhtinian step forward in the development of Anglo-American novel theory, at least as Booth construes it, leaves intact the Jamesian valorization of authorial point of view. Booth's account of Bakhtin reemphasizes, and helps make explicit, the ethical imperative – the altruistic relation between representor and represented – that has guided the Jamesian theoretical tradition from its beginnings. Booth understands Bakhtinian dialogism as nothing other than the appreciation of alterity; and he understands alterity as Lubbock and Cohn do, as the novelist's representation of realistic characters. According to Booth, the author's "imaginative gift" can achieve no greater end than to preserve "the autonomy of the novel's characters" (xxiii). If Booth's reading of Bakhtin marks a development in the Jamesian tradition, it is an advance in optimism about the novel's generic capacity for alterity: for Lubbock and Cohn the novel's generic form required that the successful representation of novelistic character be achieved through authorial self-sacrifice; Booth, by crediting Bakhtin with disconnecting technical effects from alterity, can now describe the novel as a veritable paradise of characterological autonomy where the author's imaginative gift, the gift for and of otherness, costs nothing to himself.

Although Booth's interpretation of Bakhtin thus does not radically change the Anglo-American understanding of the novel as the literary genre most dedicated to the appreciation of alterity, it does suggest Bakhtin's influence upon the conceptualization of characterological autonomy, a topic that, despite Booth's protestations to the contrary, brings us back to technique. Thanks to Bakhtin, Booth comes to believe that characterological identity is most authentically represented as self-expressive speech: the "freedom [of characters] to say what they will, in their own way" (xxii). The Jamesian emphasis on point of view, which culminates in Cohn's definition of characterological identity as most essentially a private and individual consciousness, is thus seemingly rejected in favor of a Bakhtinian understanding of people – and, by extension, characters – as pre-eminently linguistic subjects. Because Cohn believes that identity most essentially resides "inside" personal consciousness, she believes that only the novel, with its generic capacity for "inside views," can authentically represent character. Booth learns from Bakhtin that identity is not essentially private and ideal but social and linguistic; but because Booth's understanding of contructivism remains inseparable from his belief in the ethical importance of the novelist's imagination, he argues that the representation of social and linguistic alterity is achieved merely by the creation of fictional characters who speak with their own voices. For Booth, the author need only "allow [characters] to speak in ways other than his own" (xxii–xxiii) to represent them "dialogically" as autonomous social subjects. The author's imaginative gift is thus less one of invention – the creation of fictional characters who seem so real that even their maker regards them as autonomous – and more of reception: to represent authentic characters is to record and to respond to the social languages that even as fictional creations they somehow autonomously possess.

Despite the change in terminology – from individuals described as points of view to individuals described as specific social languages – Booth's understanding of Bakhtin reinscribes James's notion of authorial agency: the novel is again most essentially generated from the author's desire to understand an "other" who is experienced by the author as possessing an autonomous identity, distinct and different from his own. But in Booth's version of Bakhtin, the complexities of Jamesian interestedness – the notion that authorial point of view necessarily mediates its representation of the wonderful object – are exchanged for a conceptualization of alterity in which characterological language itself seems to solve the problem of representational mediation. The philosophically dense and difficult Jamesian "quarter in which the subject most completely expresses itself" is for Booth nothing more than the novelistic practice of quotation. No transmutation need take place, no evolution of interesting object to self-expressive subject, because the novelistic character is perceived as intrinsically capable of, and indeed defined by, her capacity for self-expression. If the move in Anglo-American theory from James to Bakhtin constitutes a progress, then, it is a journey toward, on the one hand, an increasingly utopian view of novelistic alterity (the representation of the other is achieved at no ethical cost to the self), and, on the other, an increasingly literalist understanding of how that alterity should be both defined and represented (from the Jamesian artistic subject to the Lubbockian and Cohnian character to Boothian/Bakhtinian quotation).

While Booth's interpretation begins to suggest what Anglo-American theorists have made of Bakhtin, a closer look at Bakhtin's work will show us that his compatibility with James is even more thoroughgoing than I have thus far suggested. By examining the philosophy of social language that grounds Bakhtin's theory of the novel, we will find that the basis of similarity between James and Bakhtin lies in what seems to be the definitive difference between them: their understanding of a novelistic form. When we analyze Bakhtin's account of novelistic representation, we discover that Bakhtin's philosophy of social language shares salient characteristics with what perhaps seemed the most complicated aspect of James's aesthetic philosophy: his description of the artistic subject.

We can begin to grasp what Bakhtin means by novelistic social language if we first understand what it is not. In "Discourse in the Novel," the essay in which his theory of novelistic language is most fully expressed, Bakhtin establishes an opposition between poetry and prose. Rather than distinguishing poetry from prose by any obvious formal differences – like short lines, rhythm, and rhyme – Bakhtin instead bases generic difference on the writer's *relation* to the language he employs:

> The language of the poet is *his* language, he is utterly immersed in it, inseparable from it, he makes use of each form, each word, each expression according to its unmediated power to assign meaning (as it were, "without quotation marks"), that is, as a pure and direct expression of his own intention.
>
> (285, Bakhtin's emphasis)

The poet's attempt to make language express only his own meaning denies what is for Bakhtin the true nature of language:

> Actual social life and historical becoming create within an abstractly unitary
> national language a multitude of concrete worlds, a multitude of bounded
> verbal-ideological and social belief systems; within these various systems (iden-
> tical in the abstract) are elements of language filled with various semantic and
> axiological content and each with its own different sound. (288)

The poet imagines – erroneously – that self-expression can be both private
and unmediated. By trying to make language express only his own intention, he seeks to strip the social multiplicity from language. He attempts,
in other words, to replace the socially and historically produced "verbal-
ideological and social belief systems" that, according to Bakhtin, inhere in
language with his own personal meaning.

By contrast, the Bakhtinian prose writer both recognizes and welcomes the
social diversity that constitutes language. He not only has a "sense of the
boundedness, the historicity, the social determination and specificity of one's
own language [that] is alien to poetic style" (285), but also is open to the alterity that inheres in language; he rejoices in expressing himself through languages not his own, is open to "alluding to alien language, to the possibility of another vocabulary, another semantics, other syntactic forms and so
forth, to the possibility of other linguistic points of view" (285).

The fact that Bakhtin begins with philosophical assumptions about life
and literature that seem so removed from James's makes it all the more powerful to discover that his definition of the novel also depends upon the appreciation of alterity – a version, moreover, that in its complicated definition
of the represented other is far more "Jamesian" than any of those we have
looked at so far. As I hope to show, by designating social *language* as the object of novelistic representation, Bakhtin conceptualizes alterity as more than
characterological vocal diversity. For Bakhtin, if the novelist represents language accurately, then the social subjects constituted by language will, as a
matter of course, be fully expressed. Language itself, in other words, enjoys
the respect that Lubbock, Cohn, and Booth accord to human subjects. Since
Bakhtin describes language as possessing both the qualities of radical subjectivity and radical objectivity – in his view language materializes and thus both
realizes and individuates the alterity of social subjects – Bakhtin's novelistic
language possesses a strong resemblance to the Jamesian artistic subject.

First of all, for both James and Bakhtin novelistic representation is grounded in what they take to be the essential feature of authorial identity: the felt
relation of the writer to the object of representation. The poet, for Bakhtin,
is the writer who has no sense of language's alterity, who uses language as a
means to an expressive end without realizing that it should also be a repre-

sentational end in itself. By contrast, the Bakhtinian novelist, like the Jamesian artist, represents the self in and through its relation to an other: the Jamesian artist strives to represent the essential nature of the "thing" that interests him; the Bakhtinian novelist also strives to represent the essential nature of the thing that interests him, social language. Of course Bakhtin and James do diverge in their understanding of the kind of identity that can be ascribed to the interesting object (James seems to be able to manage difference serially while Bakhtin embraces heterogeneity). But looked at another way, James's theory might be said to allow for more difference: for James the identity of the interesting object may be singular, but the potential sources of wonder are so various and unpredictable as to defy enumeration; for Bakhtin the object's identity may be multiplicitous, but the novelist's object of interest is always only one thing: social language. Whether singular or serial, the object's primary importance for both theorists is its latent subjectivity, called forth and made apparent only through the recognition of the artist/novelist. For both theorists, the artist/novelist's invested relation in the interesting object results in its objectivized representation of subjectivity: the Jamesian artist's wonder transforms the interesting object into a subject capable of self-expression; the Bakhtinian novelist's sensitivity to language as an end and not simply a means of representation unveils the social subjects that inhere in the linguistic body.

Bakhtin's theory seems even closer to James's when we discover why the Bakhtinian novelist is able to know and to practice the appreciation of alterity. The insight about language that distinguishes the Bakhtinian novelist from the poet is not garnered from any difference in social experience; Bakhtin instead invokes what we might call a generic essentialism: novelists are better able to know and represent the social nature of language, simply because they *are* novelists:

> all languages of heteroglossia, whatever the principle underlying them and making each unique, are specific points of view on the world, forms for conceptualizing the world in words, specific world views, each characterized by its own objects, meanings and values. As such they all may be juxtaposed to one another, mutually supplement one another, contradict one another and be interrelated dialogically. As such they encounter one another and co-exist in the consciousnesses of real people – first and foremost, in the creative consciousness of people who write novels. (291–2)

Bakhtin's "creative consciousness" thus seems indistinguishable from what James calls the artist's "responding imagination." In both cases, the quality that makes the appreciation of alterity possible is the sensibility of the artist.

And, like James, Bakhtin describes novelistic appreciation as essentially active and creative. The Bakhtinian novelist does not passively reflect the heterogeneous and dynamic social character of language; he imaginatively experiences what we might call a plethora of alterity: he identifies, occupies and interrelates the "specific points of view" that inhere in language. This imaginative engagement makes the Bakhtinian novelist an agent as well as a recognizer of alterity: his participation in the juxtaposition, supplementation, contradiction, and dialogical interrelation among points of view creates, as it were, *more* alterity by establishing new ways for points of view to interrelate. For Bakhtin, then, as for James, the appreciation of alterity is indistinguishable from the production of subjective relationality, which both theorists take to be definitive of the novel as an art form. For James the appreciation of the interesting object results in a work of art, an expression of the relation between author and object that creates a new identity, that of the artwork's artistic subject; while the "new" alterity, that produced by the relation between the author and the discourses he represents, is what, for Bakhtin, defines the novel as genre.

If so far we have seen that Bakhtin's social theory of the novel reinscribes an account of authorial agency that is compatible with James's, we have yet to examine the aspect of his thought that brings him closest to Jamesian formalism as I have been describing it. James's sense of the "objectness" of the artistic subject, we remember, helps him imagine that alterity inheres in form; the artist might express himself while retaining the integrity of the artistic subject thanks to the materializing power that he accords artistic form. Since Bakhtin does not define the novel as a form – much less a unified form – it would seem that his theory would be free from such mystification. But in Bakhtin's theory, the novelist could not represent social diversity at all if it were not for the materializing power that Bakhtin ascribes to language itself. The sociolinguistic appreciation of alterity that is staged in the novelist's creative consciousness depends upon the prior ability of language to instantiate social "points of view." When Bakhtin says that "elements of language" are "filled with various semantic and axiological content . . . each with its own different sound" (288), he means that language does not simply represent, but actually contains these different social identities. Linguistic form preserves the differences among points of view while allowing them to interrelate:

at any given moment of its historical existence, language is heteroglot from top to bottom: it represents the co-existence of socio-ideological contradictions between the present and the past, between differing epochs of the past, between different socio-ideological groups in the present, between tendencies, schools, circles and so forth, all given a bodily form.   (291)

Alterity can be manifested – points of view remain distinct, voices preserve their own "sound" – because linguistic form constitutes for Bakhtin an ideally self-expressive social "body": language becomes, in other words, the quarter that most completely expresses the multiple and multiply related social others who inhabit the novelist's creative consciousness. Like the Jamesian artist who is guided by his subject to an objective assessment of the material within him, the Bakhtinian novelist is led to discover the materiality of linguistic alterity that, when "quarried," manifests the identity of the social subject even as it expresses his own relation to it.

Thus, for Bakhtin, the language of the novelist never risks becoming merely poetic language because he is not only attuned to language itself as an other but also understands the expressive potential of linguistic *form*. Novelistic representation, for Bakhtin as for James, is ultimately as much about representing the other as an object as it is about representing it as a subject; indeed for Bakhtin the representation of the subjectivities that inhere in language can be accomplished only if social discourse is represented simultaneously as person and thing.

Having understood the specific kind of formalism that Bakhtin shares with James, we are also in a position to see why conceptualizing language in formalist terms leads Bakhtin to an ethics of alterity that differs from James's in crucial ways. For Bakhtin the novelist's representation of language ultimately allows him a subjective freedom that has no equivalent in James's aesthetic theory. James asserts that the connection between representor and represented is determined, we remember, by the essential and inescapable quality of the artist's interests; the artwork represents the artistic subject in and through representing this relation. By contrast, Bakhtin believes that, once the novelist learns to objectify language, to display it and not simply to speak through it, his relation to the object of representation becomes contingent: as a novelist, he by definition will necessarily choose to represent language, but he can, it turns out, remain only partially identified with, and thus expressed by, any particular languages he represents:

> The author does not speak in a given language (from which he distances himself to a greater or lesser degree), but he speaks, as it were, *through* language, a language that has somehow more or less materialized, become objectivized, that he merely ventriloquates.   (299; Bakhtin's emphasis)

Indeed, it is the process of instantiation and disinstantiation that, for Bakhtin, becomes the novelist's defining creative experience: "He can make use of language without wholly giving himself up to it, he may treat it as semi-alien or completely alien to himself, while compelling language ultimately to serve all his own intentions" (299).

The Bakhtinian novelist thus might seem to have a more contingent and more selfish, even "poetic," relation to his subject than novelistic discourse should allow; but the novelist's self-expression through language distinguishes itself from poetic language precisely because of its embodied expression of its own contingency: the poet treats language as if it were his own; the novelist as if it were other – even while it expresses his intentions. The contingency of the novelist's relation to any particular language results in the experience of his own identity as inexhaustible. Ventriloquization, made possible by the "objectness" of language, allows the Bakhtinian novelist to express himself constantly without ever fully expressing himself at all:

> such forms open up the possibility of never having to define oneself in language, the possibility of translating one's own intentions from one linguistic system to another, of fusing "the language of truth" with "the language of everyday," of saying "I am me" in someone else's language, and in my own language, "I am other."   (315)

A theoretical tradition that begins with the appreciation of the other thus culminates in the appreciation of the self as other. And the move to include authorial identity as the object of appreciation is predicated on what we might call a more cooperative version of the ethics of alterity, a difference from James that nonetheless is derived from the logic of ethical formalism. For James the artist wonders alone; the interesting object remains silent so he can speak for it; for Bakhtin the novelist who serves language is in turn served by language: language reciprocates by revealing to the artist the truth of his own alterity.

This Bakhtinian extension of the appreciation of alterity is made possible by a theoretical logic so enduring that I trust it now seems fully meaningful to call it novelistic: the hybrid quality James ascribes to the artistic subject, its ability to be author and other, person and thing, subjectivized object and objectifiable subject, becomes the definitive feature of both the Jamesian tradition of novel theory and the Bakhtinian alternative to it. James's emphasis on technique thus may be the impetus for the Anglo-American theory of the novel, but the ethical values that underwrite his understanding of form are what have resulted in the genre's subsequent valorization within Anglo-American novel theory. The contemporary Anglo-American enthusiasm for Bakhtin shows that novel theorists are no longer content with arguing that the novel is as good as other art forms; they no longer feel a need to assert, as James did, that the novel's aesthetic success depends upon what it has in common with painting, music, and poetry. Rather the appreciation of alterity has, through Bakhtin, become the generic feature that distinguishes the novel as a preeminent genre; to the degree that other genres incorporate this ethical quality, they become novelized or novelistic. But, as we have seen, the current valorization of the novel by theory is predicated on an enduring literary formalism that makes the appreciation of alterity a virtue only in theory.

NOTES

1 "The Writer and His Culture," and "Plots, Actions, Centers" are categories found in Miller; the rest may be found in Blackmur.
2 See my forthcoming *Social Formalism: The Novel in Theory from Henry James to the Present* (Stanford, Calif.: Stanford University Press).

WORKS CITED

Bakhtin, M. M. "Discourse in the Novel." 1934–35. *The Dialogic Imagination*, ed. Michael Holquist; trans. Caryl Emerson and Michael Holquist, pp. 259–422. Austin: University of Texas Press, 1981.

Beach, Joseph Warren. *The Method of Henry James.* 1918. Philadelphia: Albert Saifer, 1954.

Blackmur, R. P. Introduction to Henry James, *The Art of the Novel: Critical Prefaces*, ed. R. P. Blackmur. 1934. New York: Charles Scribner's Sons, 1962.

Booth, Wayne C. Introduction to M. M. Bakhtin, *Problems of Dostoevsky's Poetics*. 1929, ed. and trans. Caryl Emerson. Minneapolis: University of Minnesota Press, 1984.

Booth, Wayne C. *The Rhetoric of Fiction.* Rev. ed. Chicago: University of Chicago Press, 1983.

Brooks, Cleanth, and Robert Penn Warren. *Understanding Fiction.* 1943. 3rd ed., Englewood Cliffs, N.J.: Prentice Hall, 1979.

Cohn, Dorrit. *Transparent Minds: Narrative Modes for Presenting Consciousness in Fiction*. Princeton: Princeton University Press, 1978.

Hale, Dorothy J. *Social Formalism: The Novel in Theory from Henry James to the Present*. Stanford: Stanford University Press, forthcoming.

James, Henry. *The Art of the Novel: Critical Prefaces*, ed. R. P. Blackmur. 1934. New York: Charles Scribner's Sons, 1962.

James, Henry. "The Art of Fiction." 1888. In *The Future of the Novel,* ed. Leon Edel, pp. 3–27. New York: Vintage, 1956.

James, Henry. Henry James to the Deerfield Summer School. 1889. In *The Future of the Novel,* ed. Leon Edel, pp. 28–9. New York: Vintage, 1956.

Lubbock, Percy. *The Craft of Fiction.* 1921. New York: Peter Smith, 1931.

Miller, James E., Jr. Introduction to *Theory of Fiction: Henry James,* ed. James E. Miller, Jr. Lincoln: University of Nebraska Press, 1972.

5

ROBERT WEISBUCH

Henry James and the Idea of Evil

Henry James needed an imagination of Evil; it was a requirement of his artistic vocation as well as his personal identity. He had a huge ambition not only for his own fiction, but for the novel generally, which in his moment was still an adolescent inhabiting the outskirts of cultural respectability, where film (or "the movies") lived twenty years ago. James worked as a propagandist for the genre, playing a kind of shell game by worrying in his essays or prefaces over various aspects of fictional composition, as though one could simply assume for it the serious stature of lyric, epic, and dramatic poetry. But when in his own work he wanted to connect allusively to these established literary traditions, the problem of Evil became his chief conduit. I want here to examine this process in two of James's most famous short works, *Daisy Miller* and *The Turn of the Screw,* and one of the great novels, *The Portrait of a Lady,* to question why Evil so dominates his imagination when the very concept had, by his own estimation, become creaky, suspect, lame.

The greatness of the novel depended for James on subtlety and scope, the fineness of his work that everyone acknowledges, and the breadth, which James-haters miss. For fiction to be serious it had to be subtle, had to capture the essential tone of a moment or render the complexity of an attitude or situation in its subtlest shade. Characters in fiction seem never to have thought, really thought, until James; indeed, James invents interpersonal thinking, as his characters respond with the utmost consequence to each other's verbal and physical nuances to the point where a kind of mystical telepathy without the mysticism gets created. One such sentence in *Portrait of a Lady* reads "Not for an instant should he suspect her of detecting in his proposal of marrying her step-daughter an implication of increased nearness to herself, or of thinking it, on such a betrayal, ominous."[1] I promise – or threaten – to return to that sentence in its surrounding context, but here it exemplifies James's unrepentant stretching of the limits of language and syntax to render a complex situation exactly.

To make this project work, and to connect his finework of wrought intelligence with a human breadth, James required not so much the large social canvas of his Victorian contemporaries and predecessors but the great themes: and the greatest of all, from the earliest epics through Dante's *Inferno* and Milton's *Paradise Lost,* has been provided by the question of Evil. But James also knows not only that he requires this grand theme, but that it is an anachronism. When he brings his heroine in *Portrait* to the realization that her great friend and mentor has sold her like a mere thing into a loveless marriage, Isabel Archer does not simply ask herself whether Madame Merle is evil. Rather, James has her question "whether to this intimate friend of several years the great historical epithet of *wicked* were to be applied." And the epithet is introduced as strikingly second-hand, as if Evil is fustian, unreal: "She knew the idea only by the Bible and other literary works." This belatedness of Evil, this understanding of it as a matter of texts and letters, ultimately became James's great contribution to the imagination of Evil. It leads James to the strategy of reasserting its importance by questioning it, challenging it actively, not asserting flatly its existence but making it a competitor in a world acknowledged to be skeptical of it.

James's strikingly original strategy, then, is – paradoxically – one of restoration: he renews the consequence of Evil by problematizing its reality – this is the very plot, in fact, of *The Turn of the Screw.* And he gained the freedom to do so because he had recourse not only to the Bible or to "literary works," but to another imaginary of Evil: a New World of Evil. If James freely "picks and chooses" in his allusions to Evil, he does so in a strikingly American context. Those diminishings of Evil we might locate in the British eighteenth and nineteenth centuries – where the grand supernatural Evil that Milton made the subject of his epic became gothicized, parodied, attenuated, or psychologized in fiction and poetry alike – do not happen in the literature of the United States of the same period. In fact, the snobbish disdain that Britain, as a former imperial power, has toward its lost colony adds a postcolonial piquancy to the notion of Evil. When the British argue that Americans have no literature because America lacks a history, writers like Charles Brockden Brown and Hawthorne respond by invoking an American Puritan past with all its emphasis on negativity and evil. The didactic theological ideas of the Puritans will not be accepted by American writers two centuries later, but they will continue to excite their imaginations, and never quite get disowned even when they are transformed into more secular and psychological versions of themselves. And again, in response to an associated British taunt that America lacked a sufficiently complex society to be worthy of literary treatment or even human interest, Americans could argue that the very lack of a historically rich social configuration freed them to think largely about the permanent aspects of the human estate. Emerson proclaimed that every individual "can live all history in his own person," that "all facts of history preexist the mind as laws, and Thoreau saw whole past cultures recapitulated in our momentary moods – "the history which we read is only a fainter memory of events which have happened in our own experience."[2] Freed of the clutter of history and an intricately corrupt social arrangement of classes and experience, these Americans argued, we can contemplate Self, Other, and God in an open field.

Admittedly, Henry James is not about to chase Melville's white whale – aside from his temperamental limits – it is a few very packed American decades too late. Yet, in accepting whole cloth the great theme of British fiction, courtship, and marriage, and its famous arena of domestic interpersonal language, conversation, James never forgoes his own dictum, "it's a complex fate, being an American," and one of its responsibilities is fighting a mystified valuation of Europe. At age 21, with an American's pride in epistemological enterprise, he writes, "Mr. Dickens is a great observer and a great humorist, but nothing of a philosopher," and much later he will relegate George Eliot to the occupation of a historian and Anthony Trollope to that of an undisciplined windbag.[3] It is by reinvoking mystery and metaphysics that James stakes out his postcolonial claim as an American writer: the great issue of Evil, the one that fixed the gaze of Dante and Milton, would provide the American tone in the British fictional territory James occupies.

One more problem faces this project, however: the new American tradition in literature also provides James with his opposition, a great mind that did not contain the notion of Evil. "Our young people are diseased with the theological problems of original sin, origin of evil, predestination and the like," wrote Ralph Waldo Emerson. "They never presented a practical difficulty to any man, – never darkened across any man's road who did not go out of his way to seek them. They are the soul's mumps and measles, and whooping coughs."[4] Sometimes Emerson can sound the more orthodox note of Evil as "merely privative, not absolute; . . . like cold which is the privation of heat."[5] Elsewhere, more rebelliously proclaiming, "I unsettle all things," "no evil is pure, nor hell itself without its extreme satisfactions,"[6] James puts on a face of astonishment in relation to these notions in his essays and letters, where he famously speaks of Emerson's "ripe unconsciousness of evil."[7] In his fiction, he creates a whittled, more naive version of that figure, where he serves as a model for the innocent Americans who visit Europe. In the passage I cited above, he attributes Emerson's naiveté to the "plain, God-fearing, practical society which surrounded him," and wonders at the fact that Emerson thrice journeyed to Europe, "a more complicated world," without changing his "spirit, his moral taste, as it were [, which] abode always within the undecorated walls of his youth. There he could dwell with that ripe unconsciousness." Characters like Isabel Archer and Daisy Miller were versions of Emerson on the move, making the same journey from the same beginning place of ideas that does not include Evil; and each of them is tested by whether they can grow beyond their youths as Emerson cannot. But, to complete the dilemma, Emerson must also be retained, or at least part of him: staying Emerson may lead to disaster, but losing him, as expatriates who seek to shed their American identities lose him, means losing one's soul and perpetrating "the dark, the foul, the base" that James's Emerson did not even acknowledge to exist (Gard, p. 227).

Now for the fun of seeing what James can do with his clunky Satanic subject. We know that James needs to doubt the wicked even as he insists on its plausibility, that he must establish some allusive networks that relate spiritual absolutes to social living while not allowing them to encourage a reductive escape from thinking of people in their complexities and not as mere representations of a single idea. We know that he is going to make his characters travel for that expansion of intelligence that eluded Emerson and that they must grow beyond but not out of who they have been. But we do not know yet, until we enter the fabric of the fiction, how terrible it can be.

When we go looking for evil in *Daisy Miller,* what we first find is a simple, then awful, joke: that while the expatriate idler Winterbourne worries over the morality of the young American woman, it is his own behavior that constitutes immorality. He is a new Ethan Brand, committing an unpardonable sin in his overly intellectualized searching out of the moral fault of another. The same awful joke informs *The Turn of the Screw.* At one moment the Governess, thinking she sees one of the ghosts haunting the children outside the window of a dining room, runs outdoors to investigate: "I applied my face to the pane and looked, as he had done, into the room" where the servant, Mrs. Grose, had come; at the sight, Mrs. Grose "pulled up short as I had done; I gave her something of the shock that I had received."[8] Is the Governess the protectress of the children or the only real ghoul at Bly? In her attempts to save them from the phantoms that may be of her own making, she too may cause the very evil that she means to prevent.

The early tale of an international tragedy and the later tale of official evil bear much in common, and what most connects them is the evil they depict.

It is borne of a self-denying libido that somehow encourages a refusal to entertain possibility without irritably and simplistically demanding an answer. Winterborne must know if Daisy is an innocent or corrupt; for the Governess, Miles and Flora are either the most innocent children or they are terribly, demonically corrupted. And in each case as well, this need to know in absolutes and allegories is linked to a stunning self-ignorance in regard to desires and resentments both social and psychological.

The trick of *Daisy* is that the narration places itself close by Winterborne's mind, making his confusions seem like complications ascribable to Daisy's character. To cite one particularly important example, as Winterbourne follows Daisy to the physically dangerous, literally miasmic and brokenly enclosing Colosseum, an unwanted chaperone or even a voyeur at what he takes to be a clandestine meeting with a near-gigolo, he hides "not from the fear that he was doing her an injustice, but from a sense of danger of appearing unbecomingly exhilarated by this sudden revulsion from cautious criticism. He turned away," hiding his perverse relief in solving, all wrongly, his ambivalent and ambiguous view of Daisy, happier to have achieved his deadly peace of mind than upset to find his beloved is corrupt.[9] Daisy sees him nonetheless and calls out to him, prompting Winterbourne to scold Giovanelli for exposing the girl to the ruins in which Roman fever is potent. This warning is made less gallant by half, given that Winterbourne had meant to retreat before issuing it, thereby leaving the girl to a possible death which he will go on to cause. For he kills her spirit by his dismissal. When she asks if he wants to know whether she is engaged to Giovanelli, he responds, sneeringly, "it makes very little difference whether you are engaged or not" (47). Daisy, echoing his phrase, soon replies, "I don't care whether I have Roman fever or not" (48). In the tale's sentimental causality, Winterbourne's renunciation of interest in Daisy creates her renunciation of interest in life.

Just so, in *Turn,* James shifts our interest from what the protagonist's mind perceived to the nature of her perception and its disastrous effects in the world she perceives. As such, the governess – who becomes the first-person narrator of this fiction – bears a startling resemblance to Winterbourne. If Winterbourne is an American who opted out of the capitalist nation just at that moment when the definition of manhood is shifting from the inherited aristocracy to a rude economic competitiveness, the Governess suffers from both social and economic unimportance. And, like Winterbourne, she invests herself overmuch – in all senses of that word – in the situation she observes. And, like Winterbourne again, leaking libido and a need to possess work themselves out in a drama of perception that has malignant, even horrific consequences in the lives of those perceived. "They had nothing but me; and I – well, I had *them*," she says at one point: precisely this complex of desires borne of inner impoverishment unites these two protagonists, and defines their capacities for evil (28).

In both texts, these points are made clearest in the thematics of vision, and I want to compare two distinct moments of such perception to get at the nature of the evil to which each character falls prey: the Governess's final sighting of a specter and Winterbourne's first view of Daisy. In each case, a kind of intense but awkwardly sublimated sexual desire may initiate the evil but the evil will go far, far beyond any single aspect of the self.

Commentators have so often cited the various sexual shadings of the Governess's visions that it seems almost shameful to rehearse them, but every sighting of the ghosts includes a potentially sexual implication: Quint's phallic appearance takes place just as the Governess wonders if she is to see her desirable employer; the Governess sees Miss Jessel in communion with Flora as Flora makes a toy boat by sticking a mast like stick into a flat piece of wood. This is truest in the final scene, where the Governess's forcing Miles to view the apparition of Quint – "the devil," "the hideous author of our woe" (88) – is rendered in a language suffused with double entendres ("with a moan of joy, I enfolded, I drew him close" [85]) and energized by orgiastic, superhot syntax. What is interestingly anomalous to these exclusively sexual readings is the presence of an equally inappropriate language: that of a cold yet egomaniacal scientist. In the final, fatal confrontation with Miles, she is "so determined to have all my proof": contradicting utterly her earlier attempt to keep the specter from Miles's sight, she requires him to view Quint "for the demonstration of my work." Both qualities – the eroticism, the unnatural intellectual removal – are functions of egotism, as the Governess is by now far more concerned with her own dramas than with protecting her charges. Flora goes mad and Miles dies in her arms; she imagines the latter as a creature hurtling over an abyss: "I caught him, yes, I held him – it may be imagined with what a passion" and yet "his little heart, dispossessed, had stopped" (88).

The tale will not tell us whose evil is responsible for this death – perhaps his corruption has been so utter that salvation required it, perhaps her possessive clutching of him is suffocating, both figuratively and literally. Whatever one feels, the language of blindness supplants that of vision to measure the Governess's self-incriminating complicity with evil: "My equilibrium depended on my rigid will, the will to shut my eyes as tightly as possible to the truth that what I had to deal was revoltingly against nature" (80); Quint's return outside the window "reduced me to the mere blind movement of getting ahold of [Miles], drawing him close"; and finally, "I was infatuated, I was blind with victory," where again lover and logician combine in egotism at a mothering seduction turned suffocatingly murderous (88). One finally asks whether the striking absence of a final framing device is James's way of leaving meaning utterly open – as many critics have hypothesized – or whether the Governess's tale swallows the frame text narcissistically, as her subjectivity has suffocated all else.

James dares to warp the very form of his tale, then, to dramatize even in its structure the evil he is defining there. This damnation begins with a worrisome but not terrifying desire to be loved, which leads to what we might consider a prurient perception, to a final, self-confirming, self-advertising narrative told to sustain a self's sense of worth. Much of this is what one might want to call fault, or even error: what raises itself to the level of Evil is not merely egotism but egotism's disregard of the Otherness of other people, even and especially helpless children. Authentic hauntings or no, the evil is the forcing of children to confront what their psyches, tender or corrupted or tainted, cannot bear; whether or not Quint or Jessel began the ruin of their childhood, the Governess ends it, and ends it for reasons all her own.

If the Governess's sightings end in blindness – a blindness correlated with a treacherous perception that traduces the otherness of others – Winterbourne's radical insecurities leads to a treacherous perception, and this in turn to something like the Evil that is our concern. Indeed, Winterbourne is not so much a moral toad (although he becomes that) as an epistemological disaster-site; his very manner of perceiving reveals layers of emotional distress. Here is how James describes his first set of observations upon Daisy:

> They were wonderfully pretty eyes; and, indeed, Winterbourne had not seen for a long time anything prettier than his fair countrywoman's various features – her complexion, her nose, her ears, her teeth. He had a great relish for feminine beauty; he was addicted to observing and analysing it; and as regards this young lady's face he made several observations. It was not at all insipid, but it was not exactly expressive; and though it was eminently delicate, Winterbourne mentally accused it – very forgivingly, of a want of finish. (7)

Winterbourne's acquisitive perception itemizes Daisy's features in such a way as to make her an object and himself a horse trader. His "relish" for "female" beauty is awful too, suggesting an emotional distancing that is inappropriately aesthetic and thus both prurient and affected. Indeed, as he wonders if the face lacks a finish, we wonder about *his* – about who is setting the standards for this snob, and about how a man can fall in love when he is so distracted by social acceptance. But even though these perceptual habits problematize the perceiver, they also suggest his undoing: the sins of the spectatorial characterize a man who does not quite so much live as watches the motion picture of his own living. Winterbourne Studios is consistently flattering to its star, to be sure, but this narcissism is also self-negating, since one cannot lead a life by observing it.

The effect of this – and other – perceptions of Daisy is to launch a crime against otherness: for whether he itemizes, categorizes, or fictionalizes Daisy, he refuses her the reality and integrating wholeness that makes women – and men – people. Is Winterbourne, then, evil? Like the Governess, he *commits* evil by rendering his own self-doubts upon the viewed body of another, requiring certitude to fight off the openness required to view each individual person and encounter as exactly that, individual. Like the Governess, he misapprehends and ultimately refuses Otherness, in this case an even more stringently gendered Otherness, as the terrible result of a misapprehension of the self. And yet, like the Governess, Winterbourne is not evil by intent; he is, even, and like her, meaning to be very, very good. They do not commit evil in the usual sense; it happens to them, from the deaths they do not understand and thus cannot shape within them. Both are haunted by themselves.

But this is not to say that there is no room in these tales for Evil in the grand, old, theological, sense of the word: on the contrary. In both tales, in very different ways, James makes direct contact with the mythic materials of Judeo-Christian culture equally to gloss his sense of evil and measure its fate in the modern world. In *Daisy*, this is performed by ironic contrast: indeed, the entire narrative of the tale can be understood as a commentary on a culture in which gossip has replaced the gospel. The demands of the social conformity forwarded by the culture of American expatriate women to which Winterbourne clings have usurped the place of the Church: in a remarkable scene set in St. Peter's, "a dozen of the American colonists in Rome came to talk with Mrs. Costello, who sat on a little portable stool at the base of one of the great pilasters. The service was going forward in splendid chants and organ tones in the adjacent choir, and meanwhile, between Mrs. Costello and her friends there was a great deal said about poor little Miss Miller's going really 'too far'" (42). In this truly grotesque scene, as scandalizing chatter ignores and disturbs the lovely music of Spirit, the women have taken to themselves the heavenly judgment that is St. Peter's office. And it is just then that Winterbourne hears from a friend that Daisy and Giovanelli have been sighted viewing the portrait by Velazquez of Pope Innocent X, a rendering that reveals the ill-named Pope as a worldly cynic. By this juxtaposition of the women gossiping in a church and the representation of a corrupt pope, James extends the evil beyond Winterbourne to the Europe-aping Americans of the expatriate society and then beyond them to the history of Europe and its religions.

We are given, in other words, an audacious sense of the origins of Winterbourne's weakness, as James provides us an encapsualted history of Western religion by the tale's oscillation between Geneva, "the little metropolis of Calvinism" (4), and "the cynical streets of Rome" (42). With its accusatory religion of the doctrine of innate depravity and Winterbourne's apparent attempt to live down to that doctrine in his misprising of Daisy's innocence, Geneva begins the process of destroying Daisy that Rome, city of ordained convention and a too-worldly Church, completes. It is thus appropriate that Winterbourne ends the tale back in Geneva, "whence there continue to come the most contradictory accounts of his motives of sojourn: a report that he is 'studying' hard – an intimation that he is much interested in a very clever foreign lady" (50). A larger, more courageous return, back across the ocean with a hard-won knowledge, is forfeited for this cowardly small one: going back to Geneva is going nowhere, and Winterbourne's life becomes an empty circle. And at the final moment of the tale, James reaches back beyond even the ecclesiastical history he is invoking to a mythmaking tradition where sin is equated with fixity and names rich with allegorical meaning betoken both crime and punishment. I am thinking here, of course, of Dante's *Inferno*. Not only do Winterbourne's fate – utter stasis – and name link him to the wintry Satan of Dante; they become allegorically appropriate to his status, and emblematic of his punishment: the endless repetition, icily fixed in loneliness, of his self-love, which is encompassed – "bourne" – as it originates in – is "born" by – winter. The only motion available to Winterbourne, as to Dante's Satan, is the futile beating of wings that immures him all the more fixedly in an ice that represents his fear and hatred of others. This is not to say that Satan is Winterbourne's real identity, but something less crude and worse, that this is what Winterbourne, by his failure of thinking of Daisy outside of old categories and by his success at thinking himself out of love, has become.

The Governess is likewise given moments of near-escape from the Evil that is herself, and, when she fails so to evade them, is invested with a language yet more frankly theological. Thus, she asks herself what she is if the children are innocent, and again when she confronts "the appalling alarm of [Miles] being perhaps innocent." (87). But these fears are quickly dismissed in the rush of the Governess's self-justifying certitude; and with these certainties comes a language that not only describes her theology but also judges her theologically. She renders that last scene as a Christian narrative, in which Quint's thrice-named "white face of damnation" (5, 88) has gone beyond the gothically ghostly to become Satanic. The Governess even terms him, paraphrasing Milton's famous phrase, "the hideous author of our woe" (88) and describes her struggle as like "fighting with a demon for a human soul" (85). But when she dispossesses Miles of this demon and possesses him for herself, it is the boy who has become the archangel: "With the stroke of the loss I was so proud of, he uttered the cry of a creature hurtling over an abyss, and the grasp with which I recovered him might have been that of catching him in his fall" (88). In this frantic theologizing, not only is Miles one moment Adam, the other Satan hurled out of the heaven; the Governess's initial phrase – "with the stroke of the loss I was so proud of" (88) – names herself either a prideful God preening himself on creating a fortunate fall or, more likely, a Satan celebrating the wrecking of Eden out of a monomaniacal attempt to give his own meaning to the brave new world. At moments like this, as in Miles's ambiguous address to either the ghost or the woman who compels him to witness that apparition ("Peter Quint – you devil" [88]) we note another candidate for Satanic majesty in the scene, our "hideous author" herself.

And with that last Jamesian turn of the screw, in which the narrator's very narrative is inculpated in the very Evil that she seeks to delineate and order, we come to our final understanding of the role of Evil in these tales: the grounding of Evil in the self, in the narcissism of these two characters, is less about the evils of narcissism (although it is clearly about *that*), and more about the terms for living in a modern world where all comforting authority has been lost – even, in *Turn,* the authority of the author herself – and where the utter freedom of the subjective self obtains. This freedom, in these tales, is a terror rather than a liberation for the characters who confront it, and leads them to attempts to impose meaning on a recalcitrant world that leads in turn to the violation of others. Because the Governess will not live with uncertainty, one child loses sanity and another life. Because Winterbourne will not live with this openness, will not accept the extraordinary challenge of self-awareness and truly devoted perception required of a world where we are alone, Daisy goes to her death and he learns nothing. These tragic works may measure themselves against the theological language of evil and its Miltonic or Dantean mythopoesis, but they define an evil fit for the century of Henry James and for our own, informed by what James termed "the imagination of disaster."

Daisy Miller's late-night conversings with men scandalize Rome, or at least the false Rome of the American expatriates. When Isabel Archer considers remaining in conversation with a man after other members of the household have retired, her aunt warns her against "taking what seems to me too much liberty." Isabel, thanking her, insists that she always wants to know the conventions of "things one shouldn't do." Mrs. Touchett responds, "So as to do them?" and Isabel, shooting ahead of Daisy, replies, "So as to choose" (67). Like Daisy Miller and like Christopher Newman in *The American*, Isabel Archer is an Emerson on the road, a young woman who reads German Idealist philosophy in the locked office at Albany that occludes a view of the street; an overly theoretic, though wonderfully fresh and earnest self-realizer. She is not merely a typical American – in this novel Henrietta Stackpole, a flattened version of Margaret Fuller in her role as a correspondent for the *New York Herald,* full of prefabricated attitudes toward Europe and immune to growth, exists to be that. But the novel's title, *The Portrait of a Lady,* implies by the word "Lady" an achieved maturity, the goal that James held for an America in need of cultural growing-up, just as a "portrait" suggests a cultural maturity in acknowledging the world of art. Unlike Daisy Miller Isabel Archer is booked to grow up, and on that development James stakes his epic attempt to write a novel that will be a great work of art.

It is probably just a coincidence that the initials of the main words in the title of James's novel are those of Milton's epic *Paradise Lost,* but one is tempted to call it an accident made in Heaven, for Milton's epic is very much the basis for James's attempt. Eventually we will examine the multitude of allusions and their meanings, but here it is enough to say that this is a novel of *felix culpa,* the fortunate fall, much like the Genesis story and even more like Milton's rewriting of it. But just as in Milton's poem, everything is pointed toward a defining of freedom. The novel certainly concerns the unexpectedly far-reaching consequences of a character's inadequacies of perception, and in that it is wholly reminiscent of *Daisy* and *Turn.* But here alone we have a full development of necessity and freedom, circumstance and free will, in which each, bewilderingly, may take on the appearance of the other. And here alone, perhaps, until James's very last works will this freedom be achieved, precisely because a character will learn the deep comprehension of necessity.

That necessity is insisted upon in the first three words of the novel – "Under certain circumstances" – which acknowledge the reality of a world not created by the self but independent and sometimes governing. And we are introduced to the Edenic Gardencourt before we are introduced to Isabel for the plain reason that England and Europe exist, individually and culturally, before the American girl does; it is the world that by its priority of time – the world into which she and America are born – becomes her circumstance, hard lesson as it is to an Emersonian young woman. But this part of the pre-ordained is indeed lovely, as the very name Gardencourt implies the best merging of ordered nature and noble civilization; and, as two of the three figures in this "peculiarly English picture I have attempted to sketch" (17) are American – though Americans who retain their national identities while acclimating wonderfully to their British surroundings – Gardencourt suggests the best merging of England and America. But it is a declining, drowsy Eden. It is a lovely dusk, but night will fall. Mr. Touchett is dying, his son Ralph is deathly ill as well and living under a sure sentence of premature death, and their visitor the handsome Lord Warburton is a member of a British aristocracy that no longer knows what to do with itself. (Later Warburton will be posed in Rome standing on a cracked pavement by the portrait of "The Dying Gladiator.") The moment Isabel enters, the dog barks, she scoops it up, and the place begins to move. That is why the two younger men will fall in love with her and the older one will dower her: she renews the vitality of this fatigued Eden. But for Isabel herself, once she struggles to an understanding of Gardencourt's high values, she will have to transform the lost place into an aspect of her spirit and have it inform her actions in a world where even civilized Edens are always being lost. For James, the new American frontier is eastward, reintegrating the Old World; but what happens to Gardencourt is what happens to the frontier of writers like Twain. It remains available at all only if it is internalized, for it is going, going, gone.

As for Isabel, within moments her rejoinder to learning the identity of Lord Warburton – "Oh, I hoped there would be a lord; it's just like a novel!" (27) – puts her in a league with Jane Austen's Catherine Morland and the entire tradition of heroines in the British realistic novel, all of them remarkable but self-deluded, in need of an encounter with the real. The carefully delineated linear time scheme – broken only, if brilliantly, by a gap of several years in the middle of the book, during which all is changed utterly for Isabel – and the tone of the patience-demanding narrator create a link to the British tradition as well. But Elizabeth Bennett and Dorothea Brooke never had to deal with anyone like Gilbert Osmond or Madame Merle. They never, that is, had to deal with that wickedness we defined earlier as personified Evil that is the special realm of American romance. But it is most Osmond who moves the novel's self-definition away from England into the mid-Atlantic.

To say that Osmond is James's personification of aspects of Evil is to put it with too much cold logic; Osmond is the name for what James hates. Some commentators have associated Osmond and Isabel's wonderful cousin Ralph as art-substituting-for-life ghouls, but, in fact, it is the distinction between them that makes Osmond a ghoul indeed and Ralph an avatar for James himself. At one point Isabel compares the two. For both, "life was a matter of connoisseurship," but she makes the distinction that "in Ralph it was an anomaly, a kind of humorous excrescence, whereas in Mr. Osmond it was the keynote and everything was in harmony with it" (220). This is almost true – not everything in Osmond's life will turn out to be in harmony with a principle of beauty – and yet it is awful, because Isabel thinks the distinction is to Osmond's advantage. Ralph compares Isabel's arrival to receiving "a Titian by post, to hang on my wall," but he quickly notes that the young woman's "passionate force" is "finer than the finest work of art – than a Greek bas-relief, than a great Titian, than a Gothic cathedral" (63). Art is to serve life, which surpasses it. Osmond's desire, "to make one's life a work of art," is an aestheticism to make the skin crawl. If Osmond's duplicitous life – he has had an affair while married, has advertised the child as his dead wife's, marries Isabel for her money and because she turns down the proposal of an English lord, and so on – fulfills his aim, that is only because (and this is James's great laugh) his taste in art is itself poor. In the words of the young man in love with Osmond's daughter, Ned Rosier – another, rosier, aesthete, physically healthier than Ralph and morally healthier than Osmond – his taste is atrocious.

And Isabel falls in love with him. And then, even after she learns all about his evil, she returns to him. This is how the novel is structured. In both cases, Isabel will make a decision that will surprise and disappoint any reader of spirit. This is James's daring, to have Isabel choose in a way that might appear wholly at odds with our sense of her, but which in each case, on closer examination, is completely, even lavishly, prepared for by what James has told us of her. And that is the point, the demand for closer examination. It is what is required of Isabel within the novel and of us without, as the narrator abjures us not to judge too quickly and then almost punishes us by our surprise at Isabel's two major decisions. James makes us aware of the barbarisms of perceptions to which we as well as Isabel are prone – the same doubling of character and reader's predicament we found in the tales, an epistemological problem made as warm as life's heartbeat.

For when we look back to comprehend Isabel's choice, we learn her character as if for the first time. The motives are shockingly multiple. "Isabel had in the depths of her nature an . . . unquenchable desire to please" (40); Osmond, with his judgmental reserve, encourages this desire in Isabel as her other suitors, falling over themselves, have not. Osmond appears wonderfully unconditioned – as Merle describes him, "No career, no name, no position, no fortune, no past, no future, no anything" (169), a string of negatives that reminds one of Emerson's definition of evil as "merely privative." But Madame Merle, pimping toward the marriage she desires, desiring it after all for the good of her daughter and her lover, counts rightly upon Isabel's fear of constriction. And she is also playing upon another of Isabel's facets, her "certain nobleness of imagination which rendered her a good many services and played her a great many tricks" (53), in Osmond and in Europe on her tour, "seeing often in the things she looked at a great deal more than was there, and yet not seeing many of the items enumerated in her Murray." Thus, when she hears Osmond exulting over an art find, "her imagination supplied the human element which she was sure had not been wanting" (223). Yet, even without her mixture of imaginative generosity, careless perception, and cultural insecurity, Isabel would find Osmond's "studies, my willful resignation" attractive, as confirming her own decisions against marriage to Goodwood or Warburton. She can give herself completely, yet safely, to this paragon of the Nothing.

Isabel's final choice, to return to her marriage, is her triumph, as this choice to marry in the first place is her utter defeat; and that intelligent readers wish to deny this simply underscores the difficult logic of any fortunate fall. If, then, Isabel had been led by that "deepest thing" of giving herself completely, now "Deep in her soul – deeper than any appetite for renunciation – was the sense that life would be her business for a long time to come" (458). The new formulation of the deep thing is a huge advance, no longer self-referential, but acknowledging a world in which the self participates. Many American novels end with a new quest just defined, and Isabel's notion of life "business" to transact suggests that this is another such one. Her decision, then, has nothing to do with resignation nor with duty. She returns not at all to save Osmond; indeed, she could ruin him, given her knowledge. Though she never will do that and he may never even know that she could, the power in this marriage has shifted. Nor does she return simply to save her stepdaughter, though Pansy does have something to do with it. Isabel instead follows the words of Osmond, redeeming them from his emptiness, giving them meaning for the first and only time: "I think we should accept the consequences of our actions, that what I value most in life is the honour of a thing," says the most dishonorable of men (438).

James is daring here in giving his villain something of the truth to state. It is not a matter of honor but of acknowledging the self, albeit a self understood, with Hawthorne and against Emerson, as a result of accumulated experience. Isabel must return to Osmond, as Hawthorne's Hester finally must return to the Boston that victimized her, to affirm her identity. This is where her life has taken place, and anywhere else would mark not a fresh start but a dissolution. If she is to see her earlier decision to marry Osmond as solely the result of the deceptions of others – and she has reason to do so – then she defines herself as Osmond's creature indeed. If she instead affirms that she was complicit in this terrible decision, that confession allows her to retain a sense of her earlier choice as free. By returning to Osmond, Isabel thus literally defeats his freedom-killing powers and affirms herself, then and now.

And with this return come a cluster of Miltonic allusions, turned on themselves. "The world lay before her – she could do whatever she chose" and she lost her way, "almost on purpose, in order to get more sensations" (257). Now, after Goodwood's white-lightning kiss (which does not, as the "frigid" theory argues, frighten her back to Osmond – rather this "act of possession" reminds her that she is right to desire a self-determining life), Isabel discovers "a very straight path" (482), home to her struggle, her "business," her life. Earlier, a dismal Isabel had envied Ralph his dying and wished "to cease utterly," seeing death as "sweet as the vision of a cool bath in a marble tank, in a darkened chamber, in a hot land" (457), while Goodwood's passion had made her see a train of images akin to "those wrecked and under water . . . before they sink," dying in the sense of giving control of her life to her American suitor. Such a return to her initial state, to the America of her emigration, would be a return to a false Eden now, a regressive doubling, a death. Instead Isabel chooses to make her world.

This choice thereby *rewrites* the Miltonic epic it invokes, and it gains expanding resonance by James's dealings with this equally allusive progenitor. The echoes occur on almost every page. Gardencourt is a civilized Eden and Isabel's "nature had, in her conceit, a certain garden-like quality" (53). But Isabel is a prideful Eve, "very liable," the narrator playfully admits, "to the sin of self-esteem" (53); and like Eve, she bears a "general disposition to elude any obligation to take a restricted view" (99). She wishes to look upon "the cup of experience" without touching it (132). Mr. Touchett, with his "unlimited means," is something of a god with whom Ralph as a sort of Christ intervenes on behalf of Isabel, who in this sense plays the role of humanity. In her confusion, Isabel mistakes this god and his free gift of money (which is tantamount to free will) for Satan, naming him "the beneficent author of infinite woe" (351), like Quint to the Governess. And Ralph, like Christ, heals Isabel by his dying.

Osmond, of course, takes the money Mr. Touchett and Ralph had provided for Isabel – just as Satan takes the free will provided for humankind by God and Christ. Goodwood says Osmond possesses "a kind of demonic imagination" (415). Like Satan, he corrupts the Church, not only by his fantasy of becoming pope (surely he would take the name Innocent), but more by sending Pansy to a convent, converting it to a prison. "His egotism lay hidden like a serpent in a bank of flowers" (353) and, like Satan, he is a disappointed, envious revenger. He has, as his faithful assistant Merle says, enacted his revenge on Isabel, who mistook the devil for an instrument for expanding freedom: "Instead of leading to the high places of happiness, . . . it led rather downward and earthward, into realms of restriction and depression where the sound of other lives, easier and freer, was heard from above, and where it served to deepen the feeling of failure" (349). Life with Osmond is Hell.

Ashamed and with "infinite dismay," Isabel cannot confess her unhappiness to Ralph, much as "he made her feel the good of the world." She hides her reality from him as Adam and Eve, fallen, hide from the Angel, but then "women find their religion sometimes in strange exercises" (357). But this antireligion gives way: In "a tone of far-reaching, infinite sadness" (the counter to her "infinite dismay" earlier), Isabel must visit the dying Ralph. He "spoke at last – on the evening of the third day" (469), recalling the Resurrection. And Ralph, who earlier, in recognizing Isabel's hidden misery, "feels as if I had fallen myself," releases Isabel's sorrow in a theologically tinged emotion: "'Oh my brother!' she cried with a movement of still deeper prostration" as Ralph tells her that "if you've been hated, you've also been loved. Ah but, Isabel – *adored!*" (471). Her confession that she has suffered wins her, the next morning, a witnessing of the ghost of Gardencourt, a holy rather than a gothic ghost as Ralph's spirit and the suffering-achieved higher innocence of a ruined but persisting Gardencourt become hers.

Yet, in that final interview, which is one of the greatest scenes in literature, Ralph tells Isabel never to wish for death. "Dear Isabel, life is better; for in life there's love. Death is good – but there's no love" (470). This is not a particularly Miltonic view; and, in fact, James employs all of the Miltonic allusions so tellingly yet without urging us to obey their spirit entirely. Indeed, in the passage I noted in the first part of this essay, where Isabel considers whether Madame Merle is evil, "wicked," James pins Isabel's salvation on refusing that mode of understanding. Of course, Merle requires that epithet if that is to be our mode of understanding: Merle, who cannot shed tears, who is beyond redemption, who is in Ralph's description "the great round world itself," constitutes with Osmond the world in their false appearings, the flesh in their illicit relations, the devil in their forfeiture of the free will of others. But that is not where Isabel's thought takes her, even as she is recognizing Merle's calumny for the first time. The long paragraph that begins with Isabel questioning whether the great historical epithet fits, ends with Isabel imagining how Osmond must be punishing Merle for procuring him a marriage so little to his liking: "What must be his feelings to-day in regard to his too-zealous benefactress, and what expression must they have found on the part of such a master of irony?" Even this vision recalls Milton's Satan, in his hateful encounter with his antifamily of Sin and Death; and yet Isabel's thoughts proceed to a far more lovely secular vale. James writes, "It is a singular, but a characteristic, fact that before Isabel returned from her silent drive she had broken its silence by the soft exclamation: 'Poor, poor Madame Merle'" (425).

The biblical and Miltonic lexicon is insufficiently flexible, too impoverishing of a full and empathizing consciousness, a complete recognition of self and other, which is Jamesian salvation. And even earlier, once Isabel is alerted to how deep in Hell she lives by Osmond's plea to her to marry off Pansy to Warburton, we see in action that same imagination that will save Isabel. You will recall that nearly impossible sentence that I mentioned toward the beginning of this essay. It occurs when Isabel is speaking with Warburton, and she is hoping to warn him that his desire for Pansy is neither really healthy nor legitimate, that it is, in fact, a substitute for his feelings for Isabel and thus not very kind in regard to Pansy. But what we read is, "Not for an instant should he suspect her of detecting in his proposal of marrying her step-daughter an implication of increased nearness to herself, or of thinking it, on such a betrayal, ominous." That is, she discovers a way to say to him by an undertone, a glance, an air, "I trust you, so do look to your motives and I give you perfect freedom to do as you will knowing you will do rightly." Meanwhile she spares him all the pain of a direct confrontation. Asked by Osmond to manipulate crudely, as do he and Merle, Isabel employs a tender half-manipulation, not to enslave Warburton as Osmond would do, nor to brand or moralize upon him as Milton might, but to free him into his best self, his generously thinking self. And Isabel accomplishes this by her own act of generous and intensely subtle thinking, thinking that is beautiful and self-expelling. This is Jamesian Good.

Isabel is no goody. She never really accepts the Countess Gemini's suggestion to be a little wicked and take revenge, but she does exult in noting to Osmond, "How much you must want to make sure of him!" (388) in regard to Warburton; a "horrible delight" precedes for a moment her exclamation of pity for Merle, and Isabel does say enough to banish Merle back to her native, and hated, Brooklyn. Yet Isabel really does not take the real revenge that a moral condemnation would bring. She chooses, with her eyes painfully open, not to live in a world of moral absolutes or to act upon others as if moral epithets could sum them. It is not so much that such a revenge would make her like her enemies, always the paradox in revenge, but that it would be based on a reduction of experience that would rob the self. She accepts the challenge of excruciatingly careful and self-aware perception that is James's answer in this undoctrinaire time for ridding our new freedom of the horror it holds for those who, like Winterbourne or the Governess, cannot substitute this rigor of the heart's intelligence for imposed dogma. The world is now truly all before Isabel and all before us, we who have been shorn of the comforting simplifications, and who must live now by our wits and by our love.

NOTES

1   *The Portrait of a Lady*, Riverside reprint of the New York edition, ed. Leon Edel (Boston: Houghton Mifflin, 1963), p. 366. Subsequent quotations refer to this edition.

2   Ralph Waldo Emerson, *Collected Works,* Centenary Edition, ed. Edward Waldo Emerson (Boston and New York: Houghton Mifflin, 1903–4), Vol. 2, pp. 6, 3; Thoreau, *A Week on the Concord and Merrimack Rivers* (Boston: Houghton Mifflin, 1961), p. 323.

3   Quoted in Cornelia P. Kelley, *The Early Development of Henry James* (Urbana: University of Illinois Press, 1930), p. 53.

4   "Spiritual Laws," in *The Portable Emerson,* revised ed., ed. Carl Bode in collaboration with Malcolm Bradbury (New York: Viking Penguin, 1981), p. 199.

5   "The Divinity School Address," in *The Portable Emerson,* p. 75.

6   "Circles," in *The Portable Emerson,* p. 238.

7   Review of *A Memoir of Ralph Waldo Emerson,* in *The Critical Muse: Selected Literary Criticism,* ed. Roger Gard (London: Penguin, 1987), p. 213.

8   *The Turn of the Screw* (New York: Norton, 1966), p. 21. Subsequent references in the text are to this edition.

9   Henry James, "Daisy Miller: A Study," in *Tales of Henry James,* ed. Christof Wegelin (New York: Norton, 1984), p. 46. The text follows the first English edition published by Macmillan and Co. in February 1879. This remains the preferred version of the tale for me and many other readers who consider James's revision of this particular work for the New York Edition to be particularly unfortunate. Subsequent references in the text are to this edition.

6

HUGH STEVENS

Queer Henry *In the Cage*

Who is queer Henry, and how might he be described? The story of Henry James's sexuality has certainly held us sufficiently breathless round the fire, yet it remains as elusive and difficult (and as compelling and disturbing) as James's own *Turn of the Screw.* This tale's first (fictional) auditors aired what were to become unresolvable critical dilemmas even before they had heard the tale:

> Mrs Griffin . . . expressed the need for a little more light. "Who was it she was in love with?"
> "The story will tell," I took upon myself to reply.

Like Mrs. Griffin, we might at this point feel, "Oh, I can't wait for the story!" Yet, of course, as Douglas insists, "The story *won't* tell . . . not in any literal, vulgar way."[1] Need this be the only way we ever understand?

It seems appropriate to begin an essay on "queer Henry" with a theoretical quandary embedded in *The Turn of the Screw,* if only to point out that the critical assumptions of a certain mode of twentieth-century life-writing, assumptions that the story of a subject's romantic and sexual life can be told in a literal way, are explored and questioned in James's own fiction. Within the framework of *The Turn of the Screw,* the governess's tale has the status of a nonfictional autobiographical memoir, one which, notoriously, refuses even to give its subject's name. The prevalent mode of anonymous first-person life narration in the late nineteenth century is, of course, the sexological case study, a mode of narration that might be seen to tell in literal, vulgar ways.[2] The influence of the sexual sciences on twentieth-century biography and criticism can be strongly felt in writing on James. Leon Edel's monumental biography exhibits a Freudian confidence in the interpretation of signs to uncover hidden sexual and familial truths. In Edel's portrayal, James the writer creates remarkable fictions to compensate for repressed transgressive passions; James is exemplary of sublimation as a psychoanalytic theory of creativity. Another biographical writer on James, Richard

120

Hall, states that "Edel wants to find the hidden truth, the face behind the mask. His is the approach of an artist and a Freudian psychologist, ferreting out unconscious motives, as long as the hypotheses offered can be based on data, to some extent" (Hall 83).[3] Such an uncovering of the eroticized secret, such a fixing of its terms, can only reduce its fascination ("so it is only *that*").

This discursive procedure contains its subject and turns its subject into an exhibition piece, with peculiarities safely understood and labeled.[4] Whereas the narrator of James's "The Figure in the Carpet" fails utterly to uncover Hugh Vereker's secret,[5] psychoanalytic critic Melissa Knox believes that a certain secret is legible in everything James wrote, including the commas:

> With a prose that suggests narcissism and femininity, James avoids directly stating his homosexual wishes, but nevertheless exhibits them. This is a typical resolution of conflict in which the defense against a particular thought or activity – the decorated circumlocutionary prose – itself gratifies the forbidden desire. In other words, seeking to conceal his homosexuality, James cultivates a style that expresses it; it "governs every line, it chooses every word, it dots every i, it places every comma," as Hugh Vereker – Henry James? – says in "The Figure in the Carpet."
>
> (Knox 221)

Here James is formulated, sprawling on a pin. We see what Eve Kosofsky Sedgwick calls "the insulting presumption of the [twentieth-century] reader's epistemological privilege" ("Queer Performativity," 27), a privilege that was denied the nineteenth-century writer. James is constructed as a writer, but not a reader; at least, he cannot read himself as well as we can (thus he fails to realize an Emersonian self-knowledge). It is simply not countenanced that James might consciously be exploring erotic possibilities, taking prose as his medium; nor is it considered that James might be a subtle manipulator of the dynamics of secrecy and knowledge, rather than their mere victim. Yet who has explored such dynamics more perceptively than James? There is another problem in such an interpretation. Are we to understand that a writer whose work simply overflows with double entendres – whose prose is an extraordinary erotically charged vehicle – was simply unaware of this fact? Whether we say that James creates such erotic meanings "consciously" or "unconsciously," we are equally involved in constructing or creating a "James" who is prior to the act of writing, confusing cause (the biographical James who writes) with effect (the James who is an effect of our reading). And such interpretive acts are repeatedly allegorized in James's fiction.

In countless fictions ("The Figure in the Carpet," *The Aspern Papers,* and

In the Cage are notable examples), James is fascinated with the epistemology of the secret that will not reveal itself. Jamesian criticism has often been content to read such reticence as an ambiguity that enhances aesthetic pleasure through endlessly prolonging the work of interpretation.[6] In this article I will be exploring some of the ways in which Jamesian secrecy and ambiguity intersect with a discursive regime of power, knowledge and public representations. In *In the Cage,* such mechanisms operate in a quite specific historical context: not just that of "modern sexuality" (as identified by writers like Michel Foucault and Jeffrey Weeks), but also the fraught and lurid atmosphere of publicity and secrecy ushered in by the Wilde trials and other scandals such as the Cleveland Street scandal of 1889–90.[7]

In a review of a new Shelley biography published in 1927, Virginia Woolf wrote that "There are some stories which have to be retold by each generation, . . . because of some queer quality which makes them not Shelley's story but our own" ("Not One of Us," 465). James is certainly one such figure, a figure whose life and works will bear any number of re-tellings. New versions might be seen not as displacing earlier versions, but as existing alongside them. As queer activism is gaining a firmer foothold in the academy, it is not surprising that critics in the 1990s should be engaged in the creation of "queer Henry." Such a project derives its energy from several sources, including queer theory, queer activism, feminism, and, from within the academy, an ever-growing body of historiographical writing charting the development of sexual subjectivities.

Despite some groundbreaking work, in particular by Sedgwick,[8] there is still much to be said about how James's fiction interrogates the construction of homosexual identities across the turn of the century. Since Weeks and Foucault published their influential historical studies of sexuality in the 1970s, the belief that there are ahistorical, essential sexual "identities" that can be traced in literary writing has progressively weakened. Recent scholars view literary writing as participating in the *construction* of identities within a certain historical context.[9] This entails a shift in the ontological status of the writing. Rather than expressing the prior identity of its creator, it might be seen as a site where, within given historical constraints, identity itself is constituted; hence identity might be performed rather than expressed in a literary text.[10]

James's writing has played an important role in this reconceptualization of the relation between literary writing and identity. Sedgwick sees James's prefaces to the New York Edition of his works "as a kind of prototype of – not 'homosexuality' – but *queerness,* or queer performativity." Sedgwick is using the term "queer performativity" to name "a strategy for the production of meaning and being, in relation to the affect shame and to the later and related fact of stigma" ("Queer Performativity," 11). This strategy locates agency within the text itself rather than within the biographical writer: meaning, being and identity might be constituted in a particular way in a given text, but no one text will express the writer's "essential" being. The very concept of an essential being is called into question by such a concept of performativity, in which "being" could be conceived of as perpetually subject to re-making, re-forming, within a series of performative acts.[11]

Sedgwick's formulation links "queer performativity" to a broader spectrum of transgression rather than to homosexuality per se. Its particular attachment to homosexuality derives from the strength of the taboo against homosexuality; hence, the "queer performative" is not necessarily dependent on modern conceptions of homosexuality as a particular sexual identity. The queer performative could attach to any shameful sexual transgression: one might then expect a puritanical culture to spawn queer performativity. It is difficult to think of a more memorable literary example of queer performativity than "the spectacle of guilt and shame" constituted by Hester Prynne on the scaffold, "under the heavy weight of a thousand unrelenting eyes, all fastened upon her, and concentrated at her bosom" (*The Scarlet Letter*, 56–7). James's queer performativity, instead of distancing him from the New England Puritanical culture he frequently disparages in his critical writing, might be thought of as showing his own intimate connections with this culture.[12]

Queer performativity, then, does not oppose an already constituted individual subject to the social world, but locates ontologically charged moments when subjectivity is formed through negotiation with social stigmas, with the taboo. If we consider that "identity" might be up for grabs, might be worked out (rather than expressed) within a text, then James's writing itself can be thought of as the scene of erotic exploration: it is not necessary to conceive of a Jamesian body prior to the scene of writing. Freed from the burden of biographical priority, James's fictions emerge as dynamic in their erotic adventurousness.

Sensitivity to the historical conditions of James's writing, and to the social setting this writing addresses, can only enhance our sense of how very daring this fiction is. Of great interest here is the efflorescence of literary and historiographical scholarship on Oscar Wilde, which asks both how Wilde himself constructs and manipulates understandings of sexuality and eroticism, and how "Wilde" has been constructed as exemplary of the modern "queer" or "camp" sensibility.[13] This genealogical inquiry points to the enormous importance of the Wilde trials in shaping modern notions of queerness. How does James's fiction respond to these developments? How might we locate the specters of Wilde in James's writing?

In my reading, James's writing is always "queer,"[14] from the early fiction onward. This queerness might be measured in the fiction's persistent eroticization of the transgressive, of the forbidden. An early novel like *Roderick Hudson* (1875) explores the effect of a transgressive homoerotic passion in a cultural context preceding the formation of modern queer identities: here "queerness" might be thought of as a highly private, heroic mode of suffering. In the 1890s, however, James's fiction increasingly registers the public circulation of queer identities: queerness is present as a condition to be denied, to be attributed to others, as a possible threatening identification made about oneself.[15] The stakes have changed. At issue, in James's fiction from the fin de siècle onward, is the understanding of a queer identity in a queer culture.

To "out" Henry James, then, could only ever be a bathetic gesture, as James can only ever be queerer than any portrayal that would lend him a stable, identifiable sexual identity. Rather than asking whether James is or is not "homosexual," criticism might examine how his writing examines the workings of sexual identity within culture, without the assumption that James's own identity might be so simply uncovered.[16] Caution on the issue of James's "own" identity might accompany a certain boldness in reading his fiction. Such an inquiry will, I believe, eventually show James to be as important a figure as Wilde in the formation of modern queerness: whereas Wilde represents the public face of queerness, James might be seen as one of the great explorers of queer interiority, as (to paraphrase Conrad) an early "historian of queer consciences."[17] Whereas a certain construction of Wilde as loud, dramatic, flaunting, might be seen as the very type of modern queerness, to the extent that this type circulates publicly as an identifiable figure,[18] James might be seen as exploring private psychic difficulties associated with queerness in its social context. One might aim to recover not James's "identity," but his agency as a thinker, or theorist in his own right, which might emerge through situating his writing in its historical context. For his writing explores what would become some of the most important dilemmas and tensions in modern queerness: such questions as the ability to mourn in a homophobic culture, or the difficulty of an identity which will admit homoerotic affection. The rest of this essay describes how James examines issues of public naming, of knowledge, denial, and of the circulation of knowledge in *In the*

Cage, written and published in 1898.[19] This tale's self-consciousness and hypersensitivity around the very issue of sexual representation foreground issues that have become central in our understanding and experience of modern homosexuality.

In a number of tales published after 1895, the year of the Wilde trials, James explores issues of secrecy and publicity, blackmail, scandal, fear of exposure, and suicide, and these explorations may be related to the simultaneous repression and promotion of sexuality engendered by the trials.[20] Often, within the tales themselves, these issues are explored within an ostensibly heterosexual context. Some tales establish a queer thematics more boldly – "The Altar of the Dead," for instance, issues from the very tension between a "straight" and a "gay" reading, asking whether George Stransom can light a candle for his dead friend Acton Hague.[21]

In this reading of *In the Cage* (1898), I want to propose that there is no vulgar division between "straight" and "queer" tales, but that these tales interrogate (and participate in) the production of sexual identities, and register the ethical complexities such a production produces. First, some comments about the notion of a "queer" fiction might be helpful. In a discussion of the contemporary reception of *The Picture of Dorian Gray,* Regenia Gagnier argues that the novel "conceded to two distinct audiences": "members of the homosexual community could read *Dorian Gray* sympathetically," whereas "the story's obliqueness regarding Dorian's sins and . . . its entirely moralistic conclusions" could free Wilde from any public airing of hostile suspicions (61). Indeed, if *Dorian Gray,* as this reading suggests, contains a coded, flirtatious discourse, some of the hostile comments it attracted were also encoded, most famously when a review in the *Scots Observer* claims that Wilde "can write for none but outlawed noblemen and perverted telegraph boys" (Beckson 75).

Describing the increasingly hostile reception accorded the English decadents in the early 1890s, which associated Decadence with "'merely limited thinking' at best and unhealthy effeminacy at worst," Gagnier regards James as one of the "subtlest authors" who "could employ the decadent themes of the time and remain above suspicion" (154–5). In Gagnier's view, even when James publishes in a little magazine notoriously associated with Decadence, such as the *Yellow Book,* he is "responsible for no more than upholding the dignity of art and poking fun" (155).

Yet if James resists the clarion call of decadence, and toes no particular party line in his public persona as a writer, the subtlety with which he supposedly remains "above suspicion" is impressive indeed. Certainly the very rarefied nature of his fiction, and his relatively small readership, meant that the fiction escaped the kind of attention received by *Dorian Gray*. Moreover, the late fiction is fascinated with barely visible queer scenarios, which might create suspicion but which give no firm diagnostic evidence to any scrutinizing gaze.[22] The way in which the fiction repeatedly flirts with queer possibilities, without substantiating them, becomes the occasion for fine Jamesian humor; but one might also say that such "subtle" flirtation is the very stuff of queerness in a homophobic culture.

These tensions are evident in *In the Cage,* which takes the relation between hints and the narratives that might be construed from them as its very subject. In this tale a nameless young woman, employed as a telegraph clerk, worries away at the jigsaw puzzle made up by the private lives of the Mayfair aristocrats whose messages she conveys. Here, the trackings, the dissemination and the concealment of sexual knowledge are very much at stake, and James implicates the reader by giving her no more knowledge – indeed less knowledge – than he gives the telegraphist. Here, the reader's epistemological privilege, the staple ingredient of dramatic irony – and, as Sedgwick points out, of a prominent mode of twentieth-century psychoanalytic life writing – is stripped away; and although at times we might be encouraged to smile at the young woman's naiveté, the story comes to allegorize our own curiosity, our own voyeuristic impulses, as we endeavor to follow her mind's deft movements. Thus we fit together the pieces of her life: the petty class tensions that characterize her dealings with the other telegraphic employees and the decoratively named Mr. Cocker's "young men" (*Complete Tales* 10:140), the anxieties concerning her mother, "too often, alas! smelling of whisky" (141), the progress of her engagement with yet another decoratively named grocer, Mr. Mudge.

Our fascination with the materiality of the young woman's life[23] is surpassed only by our involvement in her imagination. The girl's growing obsession with the liaison between two of her customers, the married Lady Bradeen and the bachelor Captain Everard, is such that she postpones the promised pleasures of domesticity with Mudge in Chalk Farm for a prolonged existence "in the cage." She eventually learns from Mrs. Jordan, who has learned from her newly affianced Mr. Drake, who has recently been "engaged" by Lady Bradeen to become her butler (although the story follows Mrs. Jordan and the young woman in refraining from so violently naming this profession), that Lady Bradeen is to marry Everard, Lord Bradeen having most considerately ceased to live. This information, despite its typically circuitous provenance, is decisive in making the young lady take those steps that will at last give us a name for her: at the close of the tale we learn she is to become Mrs. Mudge not "next month" but "next week" (242).

This is the apparently clear scenario of the tale. But when it is thus tidily resolved into one plot much is left out. Interpretational possibilities abound as freely as the names the girl's customers affix to their telegraphic communications. Lady Bradeen, for instance, can be Cissy, or Mary, or Doctor Buzzard at Brickwood, whereas Everard is, on varying occasions, "Philip with his surname," "Philip without it," "merely Phil" or "merely Captain," "the Count," "William," "the Pink 'Un," or, "coinciding comically, quite miraculously, . . . 'Mudge'" (152). It will be noted that his soubriquets are as sexually suggestive as his (im)proper name, although the telegraphist assumes early in the tale that this is "doubtless not *his* true name either" (147). Only imagine the effect of so many such names in Cocker's! Small wonder that our heroine's regard for the Captain would appear to exceed that of strict professional propriety, and even to exceed her regard for her own "oleaginous" and "comparatively primitive" Mudge (166–7). She takes to imagining Everard's hourly movements, loitering outside his London residence; she shares a possibly compromising walk with him in Hyde Park one evening; she regards his face as "the most beautiful [object] in the world" (214).

James figures her involvement as "the queer extension of her experience, the double life that, in the cage, she grew at last to lead" (152). Later, he writes that Everard is "the alternative self who might be waiting outside" (214). Here, the story anticipates aspects of "The Jolly Corner," whose hero Spencer Brydon divides his life between his "dim secondary social" existence and "the real, the waiting life; the life that . . . began for him, on the jolly corner" (208): in the late nineteenth century "doubleness" comes increasingly to invoke the contrast between a socially acceptable exterior and an erotic, transgressive, hidden self.[24] If the telegraphist's experience then comes to seem paradigmatic of late-nineteenth-century queerness, with the cage echoing the spatial dynamics of the closet, our position as readers is analogous to hers. Our own imaginations go to work on the telegraphic messages we are given, and the queer extension of our experience might consist in noticing the proliferation of (fragmentary) queer scenarios in the cage. Like the telegraphist, we must negotiate a coded discourse, as the tale's narrator refuses to break the code for us.

Our ability is unlikely to match that of the betrothed of Mr. Mudge, who comes to alarm her aristocratic customers by becoming more capable than they of writing their own telegrams, and acquiring an extraordinary command over the details of their correspondence. Lady Bradeen is "confused and bewildered" (182) when the telegraphist suggests that the telegram to Miss Dolman, ending

> Make it seven nine four nine six one. Wire me alternative Burfield's   (181)

should in fact end "alternative Cooper's." (The telegraphist glibly explains: "for Miss Dolman it was always to be 'Cooper's'" [183].)[25] A couple of months later the young woman is able to recall for Everard the exact date and code of this telegram: having feared that the telegram might compromise him in some way, Everard is relieved that the code was "wrong." A conversation between Mrs. Jordan and the telegraphist at the close of the tale enables us to connect this fear with the hostile Lord Bradeen, who was going to act, presumably, to put an end to the liaison or file for divorce.

> The telegraphist feels deeply implicated in these events: She felt . . . as if she might soon be pounced upon for some lurid connection with a scandal. It was the queerest of all sensations, for she had heard, she had read, of these things . . . Scandal? – it had never been but a silly word. Now it was a great palpable surface, and the surface was, somehow, Captain Everard's wonderful face. Deep down in his eyes was a picture, the vision of a great place like a chamber of justice, where, before a watching crowd, a poor girl, exposed but heroic, swore with a quavering voice to a document, proved an *alibi,* supplied a link.
>
> (224–5)

The spectacle of a young telegraphist possessing too much knowledge of the aristocracy, knowledge to be aired in the courts and to be given the publicity of scandal, suggests not only aristocratic divorce cases that were reported in detail in the press of the 1890s (and dramatized in *What Maisie Knew*), but also the Cleveland Street Scandal of 1889–90, involving liaisons between members of the aristocracy and a number of telegraph boys (the intended audience of *Dorian Gray,* according to the review cited earlier) in a brothel run by Charles Hammond at 19 Cleveland Street, in the West End of London.[26] Only Henry James, one would think, could have imagined such names for the boys in the Cleveland Street Scandal as Charles Thomas Swinscow, George Alma Wright, Henry Horace Newlove, and Charles Ernest Thickbroom. Another figure associated with the scandal whose freedom with notions of identity might be regarded as Jamesian was "Reverend" George Daniel Veck, who lived with Hammond at the Cleveland Street house as a clergyman, decked out in clerical robes despite having never been in holy orders. The principal aristocrat in the affair was Lord Arthur Somerset, who left England for good to escape arrest: the idea that justice was being delayed in order to allow such evasions became central to the scandal, which was reported in detail by Earnest Parke in the *North London Press*. The nickname of Somerset, a major in the Royal House Guards, was "Podge," and his father was known as "The Old Blue 'Un." One might wonder whether Everard's aliases "Mudge" and the "Pink 'Un"[27] are mere uncanny echoes of the scandal. Certainly James could have been well informed of the scandal's finer details: his close friend Howard Sturgis, who was regarded as lucky not to have been publicly connected with the affair, is a likely source of information.[28]

Whether these echoes are unconscious or not, *In the Cage* and the Cleveland Street Scandal have shared concerns: prominently, the fact of scandal itself, and an aristocracy compromised by having its private life made public. These concerns coalesce in the sordid act of blackmail, with which James's tale is preoccupied. Our heroine, sullied by being the vehicle through which so many potentially indecent details are transmitted, considers the idea of becoming an avenging angel. As she tells Mrs. Jordan, "*my* place" – the post office – "is filled with all the smart people, all the fast people, those whose names are in the papers" – and she knows all "their affairs, their appointments and arrangements, their little games and secrets and vices" (163). The line between novelistic imaginings and more sinister forms of observation is fragile as she develops "an instinct of observation and detection" (153), and takes note of her customers'

> squanderings and graspings, . . . struggles and secrets and love-affairs and lies, [which are] tracked and stored up against them, till she had at moments, in private, a triumphant, vicious feeling of mastery and power, a sense of having their silly, guilty secrets in her pocket. . . . There were those she would have liked to betray, to trip up, to bring down with words altered and final. (154)

In *In the Cage* the Jamesian technique of encouraging the reader to imagine monstrosities but refusing to divulge particulars is carried to humorous extremes: the telegraphist "read into the immensity of [her customers'] intercourse stories and meanings without end" (155). Here the tale's discretion passes ironic commentary on its own public status: if the details are compromising, the tale will not be responsible for passing them on, just as the telegraphist ultimately refrains from any violent exercise of her "mastery and power." The reader's active curiosity is thus gently mocked by not being satisfied. We mimic the telegraphist by reading *into*. We know that her ladies are "*almost* always in communication with her gentlemen, and her gentlemen with her ladies," but also bear in mind "that it was much more the women . . . who were after the men than the men who were after the women" (155, my emphasis). It is interesting to hear from Mrs. Jordan that the "bachelors" are "the most particular" about their flower arrangements, given that the late 1890s saw homosexuality increasingly associated with a public iconography of flowers.[29] We might wonder whether there is indeed "something auspicious in the mixture of bachelors and flowers," a mixture which does not result in a "positive proposal" for Mrs. Jordan from Lord Rye, who makes for his floral arrangements "the most adorable little drawings and plans" (162, 165). (The positive proposal, of course, issues from Lord Rye's "awfully handsome" butler and "loved friend," Drake,[30] who has to leave Lord Rye's service on the occasion of his marriage to Mrs. Jordan, as Lord Rye cannot agree that Mr. Drake should "sleep out" [231, 237].) Yet we may wonder in vain for any proof we might obtain, even if, like the telegraphist, we find it a "torment" that we cannot "touch . . . on some individual fact" (173). Thus the tale diagnoses our own modes of reading, so that the hierarchical relationship of critic and fiction is reversed.

The telegraphist might consider herself a benign observer, but Everard and Lady Bradeen are not always so sure. When she corrects the details of Lady Bradeen's telegram, we are told, "It was as if she had bodily leaped – cleared the top of the cage and alighted on her interlocutress" (182). The tale may not be suggesting we can refrain from curiosity, but, like *The Aspern Papers*, it certainly foregrounds the damaging forms curiosity can take. Here the language of beastliness associated with the cage recalls the blackmailing beasts made prominent in the Wilde trials. On 28 April 1895 James had written to Edmund Gosse "that the wretched O.W. seems to have a gleam of light before him . . . in the fearful exposure of his . . . little beasts of witnesses[.] What a nest of almost infant blackmailers!" (*Letters* 4:12). Since the Labouchere Amendment to the Criminal Law Amendment Act of 1885 – known familiarly as the "Blackmailer's Charter" – had criminalized all sexual acts between men, blackmail had become rich in queer associations. The telegraphist of *In the Cage* "quite thrilled herself" with the prospect of becoming a little beast of a witness, of saying to Everard:

> I know too much about a certain person now not to put it to you – excuse my being so lurid – that it's quite worth your while to buy me off. Come, therefore, buy me! (176)

She interprets Everard's smile as saying to her, "you have me by this time so completely at your mercy" (173), and soon she finds him "putting down redundant money – sovereigns not concerned with the little payment he was perpetually making" (215). The story's discretion may once more be seen in its refusal to characterize this act as blackmail; it is noted that "she might well have marvelled [Everard's giving her the money] didn't seem to her more horrid," and she finds an "amount of excuse, with some incoherence . . . for him" by reasoning that "he wanted to pay her because there was nothing to pay her for" (215).

More ghostly echoes of Wilde can be found in the coded discourse of the telegrams, and the multiplicity of names adopted by their authors. Of Everard's first communication, we are told that "*His* words were mere numbers," and we have already considered the opacity of Lady Everard's (erroneous) "seven nine four nine six one" (181). Similar humor may be found in a letter Alfred Douglas sends to George Ives on 22 October 1897 after Wilde's release from prison, mocking Ives' excessive caution:

> O showed me your letter. We are here at N or rather P which is close to N. We met a charming fellow here yesterday. I wonder if you know him; his name is X and he lives at Z. He was obliged to leave R on account of a painful scandal connected with H and T. The weather here is D today but we hope it may soon be L again.
>
> Yours in strictest privacy.
A. B. D.
(quoted in Gagnier, 158)

Similarly, the correspondents' false names recall how Wilde, in 1897, had been traveling under the name of "Sebastian Melmoth"; in 1889, Lord Arthur Somerset, fleeing from "justice," had briefly traveled under the names "Arthur Short."[31] Name-changing shenanigans are again portrayed by James in "Fordham Castle" (1904), in which Abel Taker becomes Mr. C. P. Addard (again that syllable "ard"!), and Mrs. Magaw becomes Mrs. Vanderplank; both these characters adopt their new identities in a Swiss hotel, safely removed, respectively, from wife and daughter to whom they constitute embarrassments.[32]

Such associations, of course, can proliferate indefinitely without adding up to anything conclusive. Yet to ignore them would be to ignore how the spectacle of queerness, as constituted in prominent trials and scandals, the question of homosexuality and the criminalization of homosexual acts, and the ugly proliferation of blackmail attending this criminalization, all mark British culture of the 1890s and are registered in *In the Cage*. This tale's refusal to specify, all the while casting out lurid innuendoes, may be seen as passing ironic comment on a culture obsessed with naming, while making public naming a matter of great risk. If we ask that *In the Cage* should divulge, in a "literal, vulgar way," the "silly, guilty secrets" of the aristocratic patrons of the telegraph office, we risk deluding ourselves, taking on that same "triumphant, vicious feeling of mastery and power" felt by the telegraphist; we risk becoming detective, judge, and executioner. On the other hand, a refusal to ask after the details literally strewn in our investigative paths might entail a refusal to trace a queer history. Might it be that such a history is constituted precisely in such hints and such evasions? in such problematic meetings of public and private? Further, might the tale's (and much of James's fiction's) "queerness" consist in this very crossing of sexual scenarios, the radical way in which his sexual scenes endlessly suggest other scenes, so that *In the Cage,* a tale of a heterosexual adulterous liaison, can pass commentary on the fraught secrecy and knowledge characterizing the meeting of Victorian queer subcultures with the public sphere?[33] Asking the tale to yield a consistent interpretation would be to ask it to provide the notion of a coherent (sexual) identity, yet James's late fiction is fascinated by the incoherence, the polymorphousness, of identity; any reductive interpretation of *In the Cage* will do injustice to such multiplicity. Hence, rather than choosing between an originary "gay" reading (James was fascinated by the spectacle of homosexual blackmail, but as a tale explicitly about such a spectacle could not be published, we see it transmuted into a heterosexual scenario in his fiction), and a literal "straight" reading (the tale is about adulterous heterosexual passion and the risks of such a passion), we might queerly read the tale as refusing to let one scenario displace the other, and as dramatizing the anxieties and the thrills and the play of desire in a culture both sexually censorious and addicted to sexual sensationalism. The coexistence of secrecy and publicity can be felt in the "appointments and allusions, all swimming in a sea of other allusions still, tangled in a complexity of questions" observed by the telegraphist in the cage. Henry James himself is the absent creator who will not unpack the allusions, untangle the questions. Yet if they can bestow such pleasures on his bewildered readers, might such pleasures not also have been his at the time of writing?

To return to the question with which I opened this essay: who is queer Henry? The "epistemological privilege" assumed by James's critics would seem to be somewhat compromised by the James I have portrayed in this essay: the playful erotic punner, the teaser, taking pleasure in weaving a polyvalent erotic web which flickers between revelation and concealment. Eric Savoy connects the tale to James's "panicked response" to the Wilde trials, and hypothesizes that "James negotiated and perhaps contained his anxiety by displacing it into a heterosexual register in *In the Cage*" (294, 296). Certainly the tale represents panic about sexual revelations, yet my reading of the playful allusions and punning games, and of the jocular control over the movement of knowledge and secrecy, suggests that the "heterosexual register" is ironic rather than defensive. Leon Edel suggests that "laughter" rather than panic lies behind James's refusal to portray the adulterous liaison of *In the Cage* more directly: André Raffalovich, the Russian "author of a book of homosexuality . . . said to have wooed John Gray away from Wilde" had asked James to explain the wrongdoings of the tale, at which James "swore he did not know, he would rather not know" (*Life* 2: 695–6).

If the claims we make about James involve us in truth games, James explores the dynamics of such discursive maneuvers and relentlessly interrogates the relations between identity and speech. The exploration of such relations in *In the Cage*, a tale fascinated with the spectacle of blackmail and with blackmail's abuses of power and knowledge, passes commentary on the emergent queer culture of 1890s Britain. The tale's ethical dimension might consist in its search for modes of sexual curiosity and speculation not directed to fixing and compromising the subject under consideration; its ethical question might be, when does a telegraph clerk become a pouncing beast? Such questions should surely be raised when considering our own positions as writers on James. We should not assume that our "superior" knowledge will enable us to discern how James is implicated in anxieties concerning sexual identity: rather we might ask how James's fiction examines the anxieties produced by a culture that is also our culture. In asking after "queer Henry," it seems worthwhile to take account of how James, in fictions like *In the Cage*, is already investigating the processes and ethics of queer reading.

NOTES

1   *The Turn of the Screw*, in Vol. 10 of *The Complete Tales of Henry James*, p. 18. This edition of the tales consistently gives the text of the tales' original publication in book form.

2   See Weeks, *Coming Out* and *Sex, Politics and Society,* and Christopher Craft, *Another Kind of Love,* for accounts of sexological narrative.

3   See also Edel's essay, "The Figure Under the Carpet."

4   Such "truth games" are of course discussed and critiqued by Michel Foucault in *The History of Sexuality: An Introduction* and in *Discipline and Punish.*

5   See Hillis Miller (1980): "James uses all the realistic detail of his procedure as a novelist to name in figure, by a violent, forced, and abusive transfer, something

else for which there is no literal name and therefore, within the convention of referentiality which the story as a realistic novel accepts, no existence. This something else is figure, design, the embroidered flower itself."

6 See Mark Seltzer, *Henry James and the Art of Power,* pp. 12–18. and passim, for a discussion of the tendency of James's critics to avoid political readings of James.

7 My essay here affirms the claims made by Eric Savoy's recent article, "'In the Cage' and the Queer Effects of Gay History." Savoy objects that the tradition of formalist readings of the tale – in which the telegraphist is read "as an unreliable 'artist figure'" – elides "the important question of the tale's historical register, the spectacular scandals of the 1890s" such as the Cleveland Street Scandals and the Oscar Wilde trials (286–7). Savoy convincingly shows how the blackmail plot, deriving from the "palpable, provable knowledge" the telegraphist obtains about her customers (303), responds to "the sexual panic and class panic" (287) generated by these scandals. The associations between tale and these scandals are extraordinarily rich, and the present essay discusses many connections not explored by Savoy.

8 See Sedgwick, "The Beast in the Closet: Henry James and the Writing of Homosexual Panic," in *Epistemology of the Closet,* pp. 182–212. "Queer Performativity: Henry James's *The Art of the Novel,"* and "Is the Rectum Straight? Identification and Identity in *The Wings of the Dove,"* in *Tendencies,* pp. 73–103. Other important readings include Robert K. Martin, "The 'High Felicity' of Comradeship: A New Reading of *Roderick Hudson"* (1978), Richard Hall, "Henry James: Interpreting an Obsessive Memory" (1983), Michael Moon, "A Small Boy and Others: Sexual Disorientation in Henry James, Kenneth Anger, and David Lynch" (1991), and Wendy Graham, "Henry James's Subterranean Blues: A Rereading of *The Princess Casamassima"* (1994). See also my "Homoeroticism, Identity and Agency in James's Late Tales," in Gert Buelens, ed., *Enacting History in Henry James* (Cambridge University Press, forthcoming).

9 Two of the most influential works stating the case for constructionist work on sexual identity are Diana Fuss's *Essentially Speaking* and Judith Butler's *Gender Trouble.* For examples of recent queer scholarship see Fuss, ed., *Inside/Out* and the periodical *GLQ.*

10 See especially Judith Butler's *Bodies that Matter,* which combines theoretical inquiry into the materiality and ontological status of the body with exemplary readings of literary texts by Willa Cather and Nella Larsen.

11 See Butler, *Gender Trouble,* p. 145. Note that Butler's argument should not be interpreted as implying that identity, or gendered identity, can take any form: her work in *Bodies that Matter* is particularly attentive to the *constraints* that surround any performative act, to the limits as well as to the possibilities of agency.

12 Notably in *Hawthorne, Literary Criticism* 315–457. In *Caught in the Act* Joseph Litvak compares the private theatricals that make up Jamesian identity (in particular, the "act" of "making a *scene"*) with the workings of the public trial.

13 Especially worthy of attention are Regenia Gagnier, *Idylls of the Marketplace:*

Oscar Wilde and the Victorian Public (1986); Neil Bartlett, *Who Was That Man? A Present For Mr Oscar Wilde* (1988); Christopher Craft, "Alias Bunbury: Desire and Termination in *The Importance of Being Earnest*" (1990); Eve Kosofsky Sedgwick, *Epistemology of the Closet* (1991); Jonathan Dollimore, *Sexual Dissidence: Augustine to Wilde, Freud to Foucault* (1991); Ed Cohen, *Talk on the Wilde Side: Toward a Geneaology of Male Sexualities* (1993); Alan Sinfield, *The Wilde Century: Effeminacy, Oscar Wilde and the Queer Movement* (1994); Joseph Bristow, *Effeminate England: Homoerotic Writing after 1885* (1995).

14   For the record, the first recorded use in the OED of "queer" to mean "homosexual" is 1922. However, this usage must have enjoyed considerable oral circulation before this date. Interestingly, E. M. Forster uses "queer" with homosexual connotations three times in *Maurice,* which he wrote in 1913 and 1914: see *Maurice,* pp. 85, 141, 152. Bristow, in *Effeminate England,* writes that "there were groups of men – such as Henry James and E. M. Forster – who, in the 1890s and early 1900s, discreetly gave this epithet a homophile inflection" (p. 3). I want to retain some of the uncertainty in the precise meaning of "queer" in this essay, as this uncertainty lends the word a radical charge.

15   See Sedgwick, "The Beast in the Closet," in *Epistemology of the Closet.*

16   Some of James's most erotic writing is of course contained in a number of letters addressed to younger men, especially in the years after 1895. The biographical construction of a sexually timid James should bear in mind that in the wake of the Wilde trials, such erotic *writing* is more daring and more risky than illegal sexual activity conducted in secrecy.

17   Conrad calls James a "historian of fine consciences" (21).

18   This argument is made especially well in Ed Cohen's *Talk on the Wilde Side* and Alan Sinfield's *The Wilde Century.*

19   James wrote the tale soon after moving into Lamb House in June 1898 (Edel 2:263).

20   The notion that a "repression" of alterior sexual experiences and identities might in fact constitute a promotion of subversive sexuality is central to Anna Marie Smith's *New Right Discourse on Race and Sexuality.* Her insights, although derived from a study of Thatcherite Britain, can productively be brought to consideration of the 1890s. The staged suicide of Sir A. B. C. Beadel-Muffet in "The Papers" (1903), and the actual suicide of Newton Winch in "A Round of Visits" (1910), can both be related to a queer context, but there is not space to discuss the issue of suicide here.

21   See my "Homoeroticism, Identity and Agency in James's Late Tales" for a detailed reading of queer mourning in "The Altar of the Dead."

22   I am thinking of such tales as "The Altar of the Dead," "The Papers," "Mona Montravers," and "A Round of Visits," to name only a few. Although there is not space to advance readings of all these narratives here, I hope that my reading of *In the Cage* might suggest how queer readings of other tales might be developed through attention to James's narrative obliqueness and fascination with secrets.

23 The care with which James describes her working conditions, and also those of her friend Mrs. Jordan, who has "invented a new career for women – that of being in and out of people's homes to look after the flowers" (142), makes the story an interesting portrayal of women's labor.

24 See Karl Miller, *Doubles,* Elaine Showalter, *Sexual Anarchy,* Gagnier, *Idylls of the Marketplace.*

25 Thirty years later, another fictional queer couple, Orlando and Marmaduke Bonthrop Shelmerdine, Esquire, employ "a cypher language which they had invented between them so that a whole spiritual state of the utmost complexity might be conveyed in a word or two without the telegraph clerk being any wiser" (*Orlando,* p. 269). The fact that Orlando and Shelmerdine are themselves "cypher" characters, fictional representations of the married (lesbian) Vita Sackville-West and (homosexual) Harold Nicolson, can only intensify Virginia Woolf's ironic commentary on the use of coded discourse and the discrepancies between public form and public lives.

26 For a full account of the scandal see Hyde, *The Cleveland Street Scandal,* which has formed the basis of my account here.

27 In 1912 James could joke in a letter to Sturgis that A. C. Benson is writing Symonds's biography "in the Key of Pink" (*Selected Letters,* p. 397) – here "pink" replaces the blue of Symonds's book of essays *In the Key of Blue* (1892). Here effeminate pink is associated with homosexuality; the ambiguity of "pink 'un," then, suggesting both "penis" and homosexuality, is a typically rich Jamesian pun.

28 Hyde quotes a letter from a stockbroker named Hugh Weguelin to Somerset's friend Reginald Brett, which reads: "I think it very unfair that other people whose names are mentioned in this business should not bear some of the heat of the day. I think Eric Barrington, Howard Sturgis and one or two others should be called upon to assist" (41).

29 See especially Bartlett, *Who Was That Man?,* and Gagnier, *Idylls of the Marketplace,* pp. 163–4. These works describe Wilde's ironic use of the motif of the green carnation, associated with Wilde in Robert Hichens's novel *The Green Carnation* (1894).

30 Another pun: given that *In the Cage* is about the process of decoding, and is largely set in a grocer's named Cocker's, it seems hardly too free to connect the name Drake with the word used to designate another male domestic fowl. I am constantly surprised by the number of people who resist my claim that James's puns are a quite self-conscious erotic register.

31 See Hyde, *The Cleveland Street Scandal,* pp. 95, 103.

32 James even pays attention to the luggage (shades of *The Importance of Being Earnest?*). Whereas Somerset rejected the name "Winter" as clashing with his initialed luggage (Hyde, 62), Reggie Turner gives Wilde traveling bags named S. M. (Ellmann, 491). Abel Taker has not been so thoughtful: his luggage still reads "A.F.T.," thus compromising his claim to be Mr. Addard.

33 See Weeks, *Sex, Politics and Society,* pp. 99–121, and Bartlett for good descriptions of sexual subcultures at the turn of the century.

WORKS CITED

Bartlett, Neil. *Who Was That Man? A Present for Mr. Oscar Wilde.* London: Serpent's Tail, 1988.

Beckson, Karl. *Aesthetes and Decades of the 1890s: An Anthology of British Poetry and Prose.* New York: Vintage, 1996.

Bristow, Joseph. *Effeminate England: Homoerotic Writing After 1885.* New York: Columbia University Press, 1995.

Butler, Judith. *Bodies that Matter: On the Discursive Limits of "Sex."* New York: Routledge, 1993.

Butler, Judith. *Gender Trouble: Feminism and the Subversion of Identity.* New York: Routledge, 1990.

Cohen, Ed. *Talk on the Wilde Side: Toward a Genealogy of a Discourse on Male Sexuality.* New York: Routledge, 1993.

Conrad, Joseph. *Notes on Life and Letters.* London and Toronto: J.M. Dent and Sons, 1921.

Craft, Christopher. "Alias Bunbury: Desire and Termination in *The Importance of Being Earnest.*" *Representations* 31 (1990), 19–46.

Craft, Christopher. *Another Kind of Love: Male Homosexual Desire in English Discourse, 1850–1920.* Berkeley: University of California Press, 1995.

Dollimore, Jonathan. *Sexual Dissidence: Augustine to Wilde, Freud to Foucault.* Oxford: Oxford University Press, 1991.

Edel, Leon. "The Figure Under the Carpet." In *Telling Lives: The Biographer's Art,* ed. Marc Patcher. Washington, DC: New Republic Books, 1979, pp. 17–34.

Foucault, Michel. *Discipline and Punish: The Birth of the Prison.* New York: Pantheon, 1977.

Foucault, Michel. *The History of Sexuality: An Introduction.* New York: Pantheon, 1978.

Forster, E. M. *Maurice: A Novel.* New York: Norton, 1971.

Fuss, Diana. *Essentially Speaking: Feminism, Nature, Difference.* New York: Routledge, 1989.

Fuss, Diana. *Inside/Out: Lesbian Theories, Gay Theories.* New York: Routledge, 1991.

Gagnier, Regenia. *Idylls of the Marketplace: Oscar Wilde and the Victorian Public.* Stanford, Calif.: Stanford University Press, 1986.

Graham, Wendy. "Henry James's Subterranean Blues: A Rereading of *The Princess Casamassima.*" *Modern Fiction Studies* 40 (1994), 51–84.

Hall, Richard. "Henry James: Interpreting an Obsessive Memory." In *Literary Visions of Homosexuality,* ed. Stuart Kellogg. New York: Haworth, 1983.

Hawthorne, Nathaniel. *The Scarlett Letter,* in *Novels,* Vol. 2. New York: Library of America, 1983.

Hyde, H. Montgomery. *The Cleveland Street Scandals.* London: W. H. Allen, 1976.

James, Henry. *Literary Criticism: English and American Writing.* New York: Library of America, 1984.

James, Henry. *Letters,* ed. Leon Edel, Vol. 2. Cambridge: Harvard University Press, 1975.

James, Henry. *Complete Tales of Henry James,* Vol. 10, ed. Leon Edel. Philadelphia: Lipincott, 1962.

Knox, Melissa. "Beltraffio: Henry James's Secrecy." *American Imago* 43 (1986): 211–27.

Litvak, Joseph. *Caught in the Act: Theatricality in the Nineteenth-Century English Novel.* Berkeley: University of California Press, 1992.

Martin, Robert. "The High Felicity of Comeradeship: A New Reading of *Roderick Hudson.*" *American Literary Realism* 11 (1978), 100–8.

Miller, J. Hillis. "The Figure in the Carpet." *Poetics Today* 1 (1980), 107–18.

Miller, Karl. *Doubles: Studies in Literary History.* Oxford: Oxford University Press, 1985.

Moon, Michael. "A Small Boy and Others: Sexual Disorientation in Henry James, Kenneth Anger, and David Lynch." In *Comparative American Identities: Race, Sex and Nation in the Modern Text,* ed. Hortense Spillers. New York: Routledge, 1991.

Savoy, Eric. "In the Cage and the Queer Effects of Gay History." *Novel* 28 (1995), 284–307.

Sedgwick, Eve. *Epistemology of the Closet.* Berkeley: University of California Press, 1990.

Sedgwick, Eve. *Tendencies.* Durham, N.C.: Duke University Press, 1993.

Seltzer, Mark. *Henry James and the Art of Power.* Ithaca: Cornell University Press, 1984.

Showalter, Elaine. *Sexual Anarchy: Gender and Culture at the Fin de Siècle.* New York: Viking, 1990.

Sinfield, Alan. *The Wilde Century: Effeminacy, Oscar Wilde and the Queer Movement.* London: Cassell, 1994.

Smith, Anna Marie. *New Right Discourse on Race and Sexuality.* Cambridge University Press, 1994.

Symonds, John Addington. *In the Key of the Blue and Other Prose Essays.* London: E. Matthews and J. Lane, 1893.

Weeks, Jeffrey. *Coming Out.* London: Quartet, 1977.

Yeazell, Ruth, ed. *Sex, Politics and Society: The Regulation of Sexuality since 1800.* London: Longman, 1989.

7

MILLICENT BELL

The Unmentionable Subject
in "The Pupil"

James's great short story, "The Pupil," is, among other things, about something considered nearly unmentionable by the genteel – money. By an extinct code of manners and taste that James examines and turns inside out, refined persons were still, in the last decades of the nineteenth century, not supposed to talk much about money, even though their liberty to avoid its mention depended on its sufficient supply. The monetary sufficiency that silenced mention varied – a moderate amount would do if it enabled the possessor to appear to have no worries about his material basis. But the decorum of reticence about money implied, clearly, upper class security. A genteel appearance of indifference to such crude facts as income and expenditure probably implied also that one had never needed to "make" money, had never been forced into a daily preoccupation with it. Ideally, a gentleman's money arrived of itself in the form of quiet, automatic increments to his bank account, which was never overdrawn.

James's gentlemanly young tutor, Pemberton, has clearly been bred to the polite concealment of anxiety about dollars or pounds. But it is precisely this anxiety that is really uppermost in his mind when he applies to the Moreens for the position of tutor to their son. He has no private income, having exhausted a year of travel after coming down from Oxford (where he had studied after four years at Yale). His "university honours had, pecuniarily speaking, remained barren," and he cannot afford to be indifferent to what these prospective employers will pay him (513). In this situation he is not quite typical of the English university men among whom he has recently lived. His is an upper-class membership less long established, perhaps, than theirs, and less secure. Perhaps the fact that he is an American is meant to suggest a more advanced stage of the economy of wealth than of the hereditary upper class – wealth that is not only more recent in its notions but more liquid and more subject to rapid fluctuation – and necessarily discussable.

Nevertheless, he observed the traditional proprieties of the upper-class gentleman unquestioningly. Though "he would have liked to hear the figure of his salary," he has no difficulty in asking about it; he hesitates and pro-crastinates (511). He is further inhibited by the apparent character of the lady with whom he is negotiating. As the opening sentence of the story tells us, "It cost him such an effort to broach the subject of terms, to speak of money to a person who spoke only of feelings, and, as it were, of the aris-tocracy" (511). He feels compelled to stay not only within his own bounds for gentility but within the restraints that her appearance, her manner, and her speech seem to demand.

But Mrs. Moreen's reluctance to discuss the amount of Pemberton's salary is not the expression of her refined distaste for a gross topic. It is a calculat-ed evasion. James's narrator, who will enter into Pemberton's feelings throughout the story, sees the falsity of the Moreen claim to gentility. He re-veals it to us in a striking visual image when he says that Mrs. Moreen "sat there drawing a pair of soiled *gants de Suede* through a fat jewelled hand and, at once pressing and gliding, repeated over everything but the thing [Pemberton] would have liked to hear" (511). Those suede gloves, the more elegant because described as such in the French phrase, are soiled – a give-away of the insufficiency of Mrs. Moreen's claims to the aristocratic chic. The nervous motion by which with one hand she pulls them back and forth through the other is also curiously suggestive in other ways. It corresponds to the way she is trying to manipulate the other person by the repetition of her blind assurances. It also seems obscurely sexual – and perhaps it intro-duces into the story on a still more covert level a subject even more forbid-den than the subject of money: that of sexual pleasure. This conjunction of suggestions sets in motion the faint suggestion that Mrs. Moreen has a pro-curess's instinct for the way love may be made to have an exchange value, may be made equivalent to money.

Mrs. Moreen seems to guess, accurately enough, that Pemberton will feel young Morgan's appeal. She sends the boy out of the room to fetch her fan in order to "say some things about her son that it was better a boy of eleven shouldn't catch" (512). Though Pemberton is disappointed to realize that she does not intend to "approach the delicate subject of his remuneration" (512) – a matter that is not for delicate ears – there remains an implication that what she is actually doing is also, somehow, a "delicate" subject; like a brothel keeper, she is advertising her young man's charm and promise in or-der to excite the young man's interest. "He's a genius . . . you'll love him," she says at the end of this first of their conversations (516). That this is ac-tually a sexual invitation is doubtful, but it is the first of a continuous series of remarks of this sort made by Mrs. Moreen throughout the story; she will never cease to remind Pemberton of the reward he gains by knowing her son. She will encourage the tutor's discovery of the precocious youngster's charm in order to arouse and to strengthen his delighted affection – and so to justify her claim that the teacher's pleasure in his student's rare qualities is itself ample payment. And further – even more shocking, probably – she will convert the boy's own return of devotion to Pemberton into a substitute for money owed by his parents. The child himself assists her game as he calls after Pemberton at the close of this interview, "We shall have great larks!" (516).

Pemberton's first impression of Morgan Moreen is "not quite the soft solicitation the visitor had taken for granted." Morgan seems "sickly without being 'delicate,' and that he looked intelligent – it is true Pemberton wouldn't have enjoyed his being stupid – only added to the suggestion that, as with his big mouth and big ears he really couldn't be called pretty, he might too utterly fail to please" (512). The applicant is not yet so attracted to the job he is asking for that he forgets altogether that it is a job, and he manages at last to squeeze out "a phrase about the rate of payment." But Mrs. Moreen, overlooking this vulgarity, "became still more gracious to reply: 'Oh, I can assure you that all will be quite regular'" (513). Meeting her husband for further discussions he again stammers out his modest ideas about salary, and Mr. Moreen meets them with enthusiasm, but makes plain that they are wanting in "style." The prospective pupil has uttered a warning with his "Oh la-la!" and the remark "The less you expect the better" (513–14). But Pemberton glimpses in his face a "far-off appeal" (515).

If refined indifference to money is deliberately urged upon Pemberton by his new employers, their own existence is a grotesque literalization of the snobbish pretense of living on air. They really do live on "nothing a year," like Thackeray's Becky and Rawdon Crawley, and they are, like Thackeray's characters, social types, though types on the margin of social classification. It has been customary for critics to see the Moreens as expressions of James's realist observation of the deracinated expatriates whom he had observed in their wanderings along the edges of European society. *Their* Americanism has helped them to be free of the constraints imposed by stable tradition; having abandoned their native land with its greater freedom from prescription, they literally belong nowhere. Unlike Pemberton, they are Americans who have lost all sense of their own moral traditions and failed to replace them by any European set of values.

All they know are manners and appearances, their art of impersonation endlessly attempted in a succession of settings to which they bear no essential relation. They know how to appear "polite" in addition to being equipped with cosmopolite graces, knowing a dozen languages and being familiar with art and music, informed about stylish resorts and the right circles in European capitals and the habits of the titled and the fashionable. They move continually from one place to another in search of landing in some elite social set. They sometimes seem to live well and sometimes very meagerly, dining on "macaroni and coffee" (520) although they know the recipes for a hundred dishes. But, above all, whatever the hidden facts of their situation, they have mastered the art of never appearing to be anxious about the money that is their chief object.

One may be tempted to see these impostors as more like Thackeray's pretenders than is the case. James's vision is, actually, a surreal version of the social-satiric mode. The short-story form permits a more cartoonlike characterization, reduced to the scale of an epigram. We see once and forever Mr. Moreen with his imposing white moustache and the ribbon of an unidentified "foreign order" in his buttonhole bestowed for undeterminable "services," and his weakly imitative son, Ulick, with "a buttonhole but feebly floral and a moustache with no pretensions as to type," and Mrs. Moreen, whose elegance is "intermittent and her parts didn't always match." We need to know nothing about the two Moreen daughters beyond the fact that they "had hair and figures and manners and small, fat feet" (517), and are the bait by which the Moreens hope to achieve alliance with families of wealth and prestige.

Their marginality to the "normal" social world is, in fact, so extreme that we feel them to be more exaggeratedly marginal than any real persons James could have found on the social scene. They seem to Pemberton like a band of gypsies, a tribe unaffiliated with any fixed place or nation. It is not surprising that they speak a special argot of their own, the family language which Morgan calls "Ultramoreen." In their travel from one location of possible – and generally disappointed – social opportunity to another, they resemble even more a gang of pickpockets or a company of strolling players. And perhaps they really do not exist as realities credible even among such groups.

Hardly human, unpossessed of heart or soul, they are elfin creatures of fantasy, exaggerated and darkly comic representations of the strangeness in ordinary life when human beings seem no more than circus animals dressed like men and women and dancing to a devil's pipe. In an epiphanic moment, Pemberton sees that "their whole view of life, dim and confused and instinctive, like that of colour-blind animals, was speculative and rapacious and mean" (534). We share Pemberton's feeling – at some undesignated, remotely later hour – that his association with the Moreens had something dreamlike about it. Today, after a considerable interval, there is something phantasmagoric, like a prismatic reflection or a serial novel, in Pemberton's memory of the queerness of the Moreens. If it were not for a few tangible tokens – a lock of Morgan's hair cut by his own hand, and the half-dozen letters received from him when they were disjointed – the whole episode and the figures peopling it would seem too inconsequent for anything but dreamland (518–19).

One can, however, see the Moreens neither as literal social phenomena nor as irreal dreams. They can be understood as symbolic forecasts of a future only beginning in James's day. Their reality is the momentary validity of appearance in a postmodern world where all is appearance, the values of the stock market governed by the latest rumors jockeyed by brokers and tipsheets. Or, we can even say, it is the reality of a culture completely ruled by publicity and advertising, and news that is "true" only if it is published, of a society in which whole classes of persons simply cease to exist because they are not the subject of media mention – or exist only when they are. They are frauds, but they bring into question the very foundation of truth. They are as elegant, as witty, as plausible, as any of the persons they sponge on or swindle, and we are never quite sure of how they do what they do. Even Morgan, who is their closest observer, is unable to solve their appearance of living so well that money is hardly mentionable. He will cry out to Pemberton

I don't know what they live on, or how they live, or *why* they live! What have they got and how did they get it? Are they rich, are they poor, or have they a *modeste aisance?* Why are they always chiveying me about – living one year like ambassadors and the next like paupers? Who are they, anyway, and what are they? I've thought of all that – I've thought of a lot of things. They're so beastly worldly. That's what I hate most – oh I've *seen* it! All they care about is to make an appearance and to pass for something or other. What the dickens do they want to pass for? What *do* they, Mr. Pemberton? (549)

The question is one Pemberton cannot answer, the money mystery behind the Moreens' appearance of carefreeness remains impenetrable.

It is in contrast with such alien creatures that Morgan's humanity seems so remarkable when he undertakes to warn his tutor about his parents. It is the beginning of Pemberton's education in the surrender of false delicacies; eventually he will have to admit to the boy that he doesn't really respect Mr. and Mrs. Moreen and that they don't pay him properly. The boy's appeal is, however, both compensation and trap. He turns out to be as remarkable as promised: "supernaturally clever," with "a kind of homebred sensibility which might have been bad for himself but was charming for others," and, deprived of school, still "unconscious and irresponsible and amusing" (523), and yet something of a small stoic, a creature of touching honorableness. But these very superiorities, and especially the moral ones, promote that seduction of Pemberton on which the Moreens count. They promote his entrapment. Morgan responds in turn to the tutor so that the Moreens

> were delighted when they saw Morgan take so to his kind playfellow, and could think of no higher praise for the young man. It was strange how they contrived to reconcile the appearance, and indeed the essential fact, of adoring the child with their eagerness to wash their hands of him. (522)

Like a pair of neglected children, like the brother outcasts they really are, the young man so youthfully naïve and the preternaturally mature boy become closer. The Moreens' luck breaks down, and the family passes four pinched months in Paris. Tutor and pupil wander about together in their tattered clothes, figuring themselves "as part of the vast hand-to-mouth multitude of the enormous city" (530). After a year with the family, Pemberton has received only a hundred and forty francs by the way of salary, and he cannot go on without something more.

To this appeal Mr. Moreen tolerantly "listened . . . as he listened to every one and every thing like a man of the world, and seemed to appeal to him – though not of course too grossly – to try to be a little more of one himself" (531–2). Here is the first sounding of one of the story's key phrases, to be repeated with a gathering ironic meaning until it is the very last thing heard at the close. The injunction to be a man of the world instructs the young man to think nothing of the small monetary matter he has had the bad taste to bring up. Poor Pemberton "recognized in fact the importance of the character – from the advantage if gave Mr. Moreen" (532).

To Mrs. Moreen he makes his appeal more bluntly nonetheless; he will have to leave unless something is paid on account on the spot. And she replies, with her confidence, not at all misplaced, that he is caught first:

> "You won't, you *know* you won't – you're too interested. . . . You *are* interested, you know you are, you dear, kind man!" She laughed with almost condemnatory archness, as if it were a reproach – though she wouldn't insist; and flirted a soiled pocket handkerchief at him (533)

– the flirted soiled handkerchief, like the soiled suede gloves she held earlier, somehow again suggesting her spurious gentility along with sexual innuendo. He stays on. Mrs. Moreen was right. "He couldn't bear at the pitch to leave the child . . . he had seen fully for the first time where he was." He knows this just as surely as he knows the Moreens for what they are: "a band of adventurers" to whom he has "given himself away" (533), as one might give oneself away to hobgoblins by some demonic contract or as one might lose all one's goods to supreme con artists.

Months later, Mr. Moreen counts out another three hundred francs, "with the sacrifice to 'form' of a marked man of the world" (533), and Pemberton refurbishes his wardrobe, prompting this false gentleman to make another sacrifice of the same sort. "If Mr. Moreen hadn't been such a man of the world he would perhaps have spoken of the freedom of such neckties on the part of a subordinate. But Mr. Moreen was always enough of a man of the world to let these things pass" (535). Morgan, grown older, knows the situation has no promise. "You ought to *filer*," he tells Pemberton, "You can't go on like this. . . . You know they don't pay up." And Pemberton makes his last feeble attempt to suppress the unmentionable topic, to feign that there's no problem of money, protesting, "They pay be beautifully" – an untenable "whopper" (536). "What do I want of money." (537), he also says, and *that* misrepresentation, given his feelings for Morgan, is almost the truth; his love makes him imagine he has no other wants, though that morning ends with Morgan breaking down in tears.

So again, he tells the Moreens to pay what they owe on the spot. But, "counting on the superstition of delicacy" (538) they are secure in the knowledge that he has not told Morgan the truth. His threat to do so produces another appeal from Mr. Moreen "on every precedent, as a man of the world" and causes his hostess to cry out "touchingly," "You do, you *do*, put the knife to one's throat" (539). The next morning, however, she comes to Pemberton's room very early with fifty francs in her hand, in a scene in which her sexual provocation plays a role as "she squeezed forward in her dressing gown and he received her in his own, between his bath-tub and his bed" (539–40). Again, she tries to convince him that "he was really too absurd to be *paid*. Wasn't he paid enough without perpetual money" by his life with this family, "above all by the sweet relation he had established with Morgan – quite ideal as from master to pupil – and by the simple privilege of knowing and living with so amazingly gifted a child, than whom really (and she meant literally what she said) there was no better company in Europe?" (540). And she is right. He is too charmed to do anything but accept the situation, for a while longer, of not being paid in any other way. "Your calculation's just – I *do* hate intensely to give him up; I'm fond of him and he thoroughly interests me, in spite of the inconvenience I suffer" (542). He refuses her fifty pounds on the condition that he can at last be frank with his pupil – but since he has rejected the money he does not need, of course, to talk to a son about the "turpitude of the parents" (535). Money is no longer due, and he has accepted the idea that the relation with his pupil pays for itself.

But Morgan knows without being told. He tells Pemberton the story of his nurse, Zenobie, who stayed as long as she could, though she never received her wages. Morgan guesses, after all, that his parents don't pay his tutor, though they would pretend, if asked, that they do. "I know all about everything," says this child, who has nearly lost what remains to him of childish innocence. He is poised on that turn from childhood into adult knowledge that James would study even more elaborately in *What Maisie Knew* a few years later.

The next act of the common life of Pemberton and the Moreens is played out against the backdrop of the most beautiful of meretricious old cities, Venice. "The sunsets were beautiful and the Dorringtons had arrived" (555), and then they departed, having proposed for neither of the daughters. Late autumn brings cold rain and wind, like a warning of judgment.

> One sad November day, while the wind roared around the old palace and rain lashed the lagoon, Pemberton, for exercise and somewhat for warmth – the Moreens were horribly frugal about fires; it was a cause of suffering to their inmate – walked up and down the big bare *sala* with his pupil. The scagliola floor was cold, the high battered casements shook in the storm, and the stately decay of the place was unrelieved by a particle of furniture. Pemberton's spirits were low, and it came over him that the fortune of the Moreens was now even lower. A blast of desolation, a portent of disgrace and disaster, seemed to draw through the comfortless hall. (556)

But James's satiric humor resumes, even as he offers this Dies Irae description. "Mr. Moreen and Ulick were in the Piazza, looking out for something, strolling drearily, in mackintoshes, under the arcades; but still, in spite of mackintoshes, unmistakeable men of the world" (556). A crisis had been reached. Mrs. Moreen plunges into the *sala,* sends Morgan off – even now he musn't hear anything about the improper subject of money. But with Pemberton there is no longer any pretense of ladylike indifference to such matters; she asks the poor tutor (who hasn't "three louis"!) for the loan of sixty francs.

Morgan is now fifteen; he looks forward to going to Oxford, with Pemberton's help, but the money basis is hardly clear. "He, Pemberton, might live on Morgan, but how could Morgan live on *him?*" (557). There is nothing for it but for Pemberton to go off for a while and earn something – and he gets the chance when a relative in London finds him a job tutoring an "opulent youth." Mrs. Moreen, with her new abandonment of all reserve, now accuses him of bolting for fear they might "get something out of him" (with reference to the loan he refused to supply). But Mr. Moreen and Ulick, when "*they* heard the cruel news, they took it like perfect men of the world" (563).

After months at his new post, Pemberton – moved by a reluctant compunction – sends Mrs. Moreen some money from his earnings, and gets in response a frantic appeal for his return; Morgan is very ill. The Moreens are in a hotel in Paris in the elegant Champs Elysées quarter. "They couldn't be vulgarly honest, but they could live at hotels, in velvety *entresols,* amid a smell of burnt pastilles, surrounded by the most expensive city in Europe" (565). They have bounced up again, evidently; it will appear that they have now pitched their hope for one of the girls on a rich American. Morgan doesn't seem quite so ill, either, or at least is better now.

But Mrs. Moreen is triumphant that her ruse had worked. "She was enchanted that she had got him over . . . it was useless of him to pretend that he didn't know in all his bones that his place at such a time was with Morgan. He had taken the boy away from them and now had no right to abandon him" (566). Her statement is patently false and yet it has a certain truth. Morgan's attachment to Pemberton *has* become stronger than his attachment to his dreadful family. Pemberton *has* created an affiliation. Perhaps it is possible to call this tender friendship an erotic affiliation, though how clearly James understood the bond between his characters as a homosexual one is not determinable, and may be doubted. But Morgan has now arrived at an age when, at any moment, his own masculinity will reach a new level of sexual awareness, and – to speak in up-to-date terms quite alien to James's way of thinking – he can become a "consenting adult."

Precisely now, when Morgan begs to be taken away from his family, Pemberton is nonplussed, for more evident reasons. He is, more than ever, really too poor for generosity. Earlier he had carelessly said to Morgan, "We ought to go off and live somewhere together" (545). When he had resolved to take another job, he had said, "I'll make a tremendous charge: I'll earn a lot of money in a short time, and we'll live on it" (560). But he has just thrown over his only immediate prospect of earning anything. For this, if for no other reason, their dream of their joining life together must be given over. He groans, "Where shall I take you, and how – oh *how,* my boy?" (567).

This is not yet what Mrs. Moreen has in mind. The tutor is simply to come back on the old basis. Mr. Moreen and Ulick "accepted the return like perfect men of the world" (570) and again Pemberton and Morgan are companions in Paris while the Moreens' fortunes teeter before another fall. Pemberton knows that Morgan expects that when this happens they really will go off together for good: "He talked of their escape – recurring to it often afterwards – as if they were making up a 'boy's book' together" (570). But "for the first time in this complicated connection, our friend felt his collar gall him. . . . He could neither really throw off his blighting burden nor find in it the benefit of pacified conscience or of a rewarded affection" (572). "Blighting burden" – the relation with Morgan? He ruefully "sees his youth going and that he is getting nothing back for it. The return that is not material, the "rewarded affection," no longer is enough, after all. It is only Morgan – whose highmindedness is both exaltedly romantic and childishly naïve – who still believes in the exchange of love for love.

> It was all very well of Morgan to count it for reparation that he should now settle on him permanently – there was an irritating flaw in such a view. He saw what the boy had in mind; the conception that as his friend had had the generosity to come back he must show his gratitude by giving him his life. But the poor friend didn't desire the gift – what could he do with Morgan's dreadful little life? (572)

When the storm overwhelming the Moreen fortunes comes, finally, James figures it by means of another passage of powerful description to match the moment of autumnal change in Venice:

> One winter afternoon – it was Sunday – he and the boy walked far together in the Bois de Boulogne. The evening was so splendid, the cold lemon-colored sunset so clear, the stream of carriages and pedestrians so amusing and the fascination of Paris so great, that they stayed out later than usual and became aware that they should have to hurry home in time to arrive for dinner. They hurried, accordingly, arm-in-arm, good-humoured and hungry, agreeing that there was nothing like Paris after all and that after everything too that had come and gone they were not yet sated with innocent pleasure. When they reached the hotel they found that, though scandalously late, they were in time for all the dinner they were likely to sit down to. Confusion reigned in the apartments of the Moreens – very shabby ones this time, but the best ones in the house – and before the interrupted service of the table, with objects displaced almost as if there had been a scuffle and a great wine-stain from an overturned bottle, Pemberton couldn't blink the fact that there had been a scene of the last proprietary firmness. The storm had come – they were all seeking refuge. (574)

It is too late for the "innocent pleasures" of which they are still not weary. It is the final exposure, so long delayed, of the real condition of the Moreen economy. Mrs. Moreen no longer minces words; Pemberton must simply take over Morgan altogether.

> Cruel as it was for them to part with their darling she must look to him to car-
> ry a little further the influence he had so fortunately acquired with the boy –
> to induce his young charge to follow him into some modest retreat. They de-
> pended on him – that was the fact – to take their delightful child temporarily
> under his protection: it would leave Mr. Moreen and herself so much more free
> to give the proper attention (too little, alas! had been given) to the readjust-
> ment of their affairs. (575–6)

The Moreens, who have so long maintained the appearance of gentility along with its hypocritical pose of living on nothing – by whatever dodges and de-vices – are at last persons with no money to be silent about. Mrs. Moreen's game is what it has always been. Now that she feels she must unburden her-self of Morgan altogether she continues to exploit the way he will pay his way by his beautiful nature, the interest of helping him, his grateful love. She needs to offer nothing more to his caretaker.

Morgan responds with rapture. "Do you mean he may take me to live with him for ever and ever?" He stammers to Pemberton, "My dear fellow, what do you say to *that?*" (576). And then we are hurtled to the end of the story, a conclusion much discussed and debated. James says (it is not the most transparent of sentences) that the boy "had a moment of boyish joy, scarce-ly mitigated by the reflexion that with this unexpected consecration of his hope – too sudden and too violent; the turn taken was away from a *good* boy's book – the 'escape' was left on their hands." The ending of the "*good* boy's book," the boy's adventure tale with a happy ending that they had played at writing together, won't close the story. Real escape – in the adult world he has suddenly entered – is hardly possible. "How could one not say something enthusiastic" (576) is Pemberton's distressed thought. But he does not have to say anything. Morgan may have already understood something; and this understanding may have stopped his heart.

With their dead child in their arms the Moreens debate the cause of Mor-gan's heart failure. "I thought he *wanted* to go to you" wails Mrs. Moreen, while Mr. Moreen insists, "I told you he didn't, my dear" (577). Mr. Moreen, of course, to whom appearances remain all, "took his bereavement like a man of the world." As in the similar ending of *The Turn of the Screw,* James permits the stricken boy to die without answering any questions, including the reader's. It seems clear enough, though, that the story has prepared us to realize that poor – that is, penniless – Pemberton would have had to disappoint Morgan.

NOTE

All citations in this essay refer to the *New York Edition,* Volume 11.

8

SARA BLAIR

Realism, Culture, and the Place of the Literary: Henry James and *The Bostonians*

In his 1907 preface to *The American,* on the subject of editing his own voluminous oeuvre for the New York Edition of his work, a meditative Henry
James wrote that "it is as difficult . . . to trace the dividing-line between the
real and the romantic as to plant a milestone between north and south."[1]
The question of James's commitment to literary realism dogged him throughout his career, and it would continue to be linked (as his image suggests) with
the problem of his commitment to national traditions and cultures. Some
readers have argued that the whole body of James's work is marked by traces
of the realist project; others argue that only specific texts stake their claims
under the sign of realism, understood as an interest in contemporaneity and
its psychic and social effects. The only point of consensus on this issue, it
seems, concerns James's fiction of the mid-1880s, particularly *The Princess
Casamassima* and *The Bostonians.* Taken together, these novels are said to
instance the power and limits of James's experiments with realism, marking
an "episode" in his evolving authorial practice.[2]

   In this essay I look more closely at one of these texts, *The Bostonians,*
which has occasioned powerful disagreement among James's readers about
the nature and value of his strategies for representing social reality. From the
outset, we need to concede the mixed affect of the novel in generic terms.
Even James's record of his intentions for the novel in his writing notebooks
suggests this fact: on the one hand, he is determined to explore, with "pic-
torial" accuracy, the new social types of modern America; on the other, he
is fascinated by the sphere of women's relations and desires – "the situation
of women" – in which the institutions and narratives of love, marriage, and
desire figure so prominently.[3] Thus straddling that notoriously wavering
dividing-line between those notoriously intransigent provinces, realism and
romance, *The Bostonians* brings the machinery of the latter to bear on its
protagonists – particularly on the question of women's destiny and freedom
in an emerging social order – in startlingly uneven ways. Nonetheless *The
Bostonians,* like James's writings of the 1880s at large, intently engages

American literary realism. And the most productive way of understanding that engagement may be to suggest that James's interests in the sociology of feminist struggle are knottily entangled with, and perhaps even a kind of red herring for, a far broader set of concerns: ultimately nothing less, in the realist moment, than the project of building a national culture itself.[4]

How does this project intersect with literary realism? To address that question, we can consider the pronouncements made by the novel's studiously disinterested narrator. Of Miss Birdseye he remarks that, "in a career in which she was constantly exposing herself to offence and laceration, her most poignant suffering came from the injury of her taste."[5] He notes with aspersion of Mrs. Tarrant's morality that "Her husband's tastes rubbed off on her soft, moist moral surface . . . she found herself completely enrolled in the great irregular army of nostrum-mongers, domiciled in humanitary Bohemia" – not surprisingly, since "a woman who had had the bad taste to marry Selah Tarrant would not have been very likely" to practice "a very straight judgement" (865–6). By contrast, the nervous rectitude of Olive Chancellor is "a sign of" the "culture and quiet tastes" that prevail in her quintessentially Bostonian salon (909) – tastes she "sacrifice[s]," according to Basil Ransom, in submitting Verena's special gifts to the "puffery" of the new techniques of advertising (1200). With similar *dis*taste, Dr. Prance pronounces professionally that she would be surprised if the "anaemi[c]" Verena "didn't eat too much candy" (841). This symptomatology implicates not only the heroine's questionable aesthetic preferences, but the threatened fitness of the "consummate" modern woman, "the American girl" (913–14), on which the future of the American social body turns.

In other words, I am suggesting, the central concern of *The Bostonians* is the production, experience, and social vitality of "culture" in its myriad and changing forms. Indeed, the defining contest between Olive and Basil – admittedly inflected by the gap between the "habits and tastes" of bourgeois Boston and "the old ideas in the South" – can be read as a contest not only for Verena but over the import of culture at the moment of realism (814, 818). Here as throughout James's writings of the 1880s, "the great modern question" is not female suffrage per se, but complex changes in the Anglo-American public sphere – particularly in middle-class habits of taste, consumption, and culture-making – wrought partly by the increasing activity of women as readers, writers, and targeted consumers of new forms of culture and entertainment (934). Central to James's "very *American* tale" of reform is a vested interest in the "spell," the "romance," of these (mostly popular) cultural forms, and in the lineaments of the "general culture" (1009) – aesthetic, social, national – they register and aid in shaping.[6]

This concern, it must be noted, is hardly unique to James. The notion of culture, understood as a set of institutions and exchanges in which citizens are made, definitive communal and national ideals are forged, urged itself with extreme pressure throughout American public life during the late 1870s and 1880s. With the withdrawal of Federal troops from the American South in 1877, the project of Reconstruction came to an end and a rapid reorganization of American public life ensued. Among the many changes unleashed during the following decades was the meteoric rise of an industrial urban life-world and of new technologies and organs for representing it: photography, film, popular music, and other modes of training and entertaining its citizens. When Basil Ransom is "conscious . . . of a bigger stomach than all the culture of Charles Street" – that is, of the "oldest and best" of Yankee "*bourgeoisie*" – "could fill," he is hardly an unreconstructed southerner (816, 832). In fact, he heralds a historic shift in symbolic and material power from Boston to New York, from the old "stock" of New England Brahmin gentry to the vigorously entrepreneurial classes represented here by Matthias Pardon, figure and transcriber of the new "public life": the emerging culture of "publicity" and "of the metropolis" (867, 1038).

Zealously baiting his acquaintances for interviews, feeding the mill of the "personals" and gossip columns of a new national press, adopting an aggressively instrumental stance toward human beings – "'There's money for some one in that girl,'" he declares; "'you see if she don't have quite a run!'" (859) – Pardon emblematizes the rise of commodified selfhood, and of mass cultural institutions for exploiting it, as a norm of American public life.[7] Its hallmark creation is the New Woman, both the subject and the intended object of advertising, popular fiction, and a new journalism of celebrity and sensation. If the death of Miss Birdseye marks the end of a feminist and political era – the complete extinction of "the heroic age of New England life" (1167) – it also marks the advent of a femininity constructed via the consumption of leisure articles (Verena's candy and celebrity photographs) and emerging forms of "home-culture" (lectures, séances, musicales) that would evolve into more aggressively commercial spectacles, like the planned triumph of Verena as speaker in the Boston Music Hall. "Naturally theatrical," with "queer, bad lecture-blood in her veins" (848, 1030), the Verena who is eager to "raise my voice in the biggest city" figures not only the more circumscribed "question" of female suffrage and civil liberties, but the problem of identity in a collective life increasingly dominated by the logic of mass media and entertainment (886).

James's interest in this cultural transformation is not only that of the realist historian he styles himself, as narrator of his tale, to be. His novels and criticism throughout the 1880s and early 1890s pointedly but unevenly consider the role literature will play as a cultural force in this "age of new revelations" (850). In this particular respect James is at odds with – exceeds – the American realist project. Such conspicuous apologists of literary realism as William Dean Howells (whose own New Woman novel of 1883, *A Woman's Reason*, provides the title for Verena's undelivered lecture) and Richard Watson Gilder (editor of the *Century*, the genteel journal in which *The Bostonians* originally appeared in serial form) argued for the special power of realist literature to promote a more progressive, enlightened "new Americanism."[8] Howells would influentially define literary realism as an organic outgrowth of Americans' distinctive nature: sympathetic, liberty-loving, and determined to resist "the paralysis of tradition."[9] *The Bostonians* itself stands in uneasy relation to these notions, and to the high-mindedness with which Gilder and other exponents of realism pursue them. Although James too presses claims about the role of literature in the formation of the "general culture" of "the great Democracy," he takes a quite different view of its limits and effects (1009, 903). Far from naturalizing its generic conduct as the product of a national or broadly racial character, James understands literature as a contestant in the volatile, highly theatrical, public sphere of modern America – a contestant for the power to create, shape, and redirect fictions of country, community, and self.

Accordingly, when Basil Ransom lambastes Selah Tarrant, the "mesmeric healer," as "the cheapest kind of human product" (830, 853); when James's narrator dismisses the culture of reform as the work of "lady-doctors, lady-mediums, lady-editors, lady-preachers, lady-healers" (878); when the novel inhabits the cultural spaces of the drawing-room, the hotel, the salon, and the Music Hall, with their distinctive leisure activities; then, James actively pits literature as a form of experience and an institution against competing (especially mass) cultural forms. Within the pages of James's novel, vastly different and emerging forms of narrative jostle against one another, vying for cultural power: the seductive, cliff-hanging "serial fiction" (itself the genre of *The Bostonians*) Pardon disingenuously recommends to Olive Chancellor; the gossip columns he produces for that bible of the new, *The Vesper;* the work of such high culture heroes as Comte and Carlyle (who are Ransom's favorite authors) and George Eliot (who is Olive's); drawing-room lectures on ever-more-novel subjects, like "the Talmud," for "the fashion-able world" (1032, 1033); the dime novels with lurid paper covers to be found in cheap bookstalls and hotels (1197); the "personals" of the new cheap daily newspapers, in which Selah Tarrant longs to read his name and so confirm his power to pulse on the "national nerve-centres" (897). To-gether, these different genres of culture, "distinction," and "taste" constitute a booming trade in narratives of "the American people," in and through which American sociality is constituted as powerfully as in "the domain of practical politics" (917, 1087).

Given James's long-time reputation as the very embodiment of high gen-teel culture, we might expect that distinctly literary texts would be granted a special status in this trade, as more valuable discourse protecting the body politic against the "contagion" of popular narrative (860). But literature rep-resents itself here with great ambivalence and unevenness; and the narrative fails to resolve itself in favor of high culture, or the self-consciously literary, in quite the ways we anticipate. By turns, both Olive Chancellor and Basil Ransom serve as surrogates for the high cultural author, whether realist or romantic: Olive is said to be "a spinster as Shelley was a lyric poet," will-fully determined to create Verena in the image of her own conceptions of en-lightened womanhood (816); Ransom mounts his dissent against reform cul-ture in "terms of opprobrium extracted from the older English literature," styling himself a latter-day Carlyle with "a vision of distinction" to be ful-filled in a burgeoning career as a man of letters (853, 1150). For James, both these styles of authorship turn out to amount to forms of possession, the de-sire to "get hold" of Verena and transform her into an icon of the feminini-ty each desires differently to install (1150). Both are more than a little akin to the project their authors so vigorously detest in connection with the "lit-erary enterprise" of Matthias Pardon (915). Furthermore, the distinctly elite tendencies of the two cousins smack of a certain atavism. Just as the "Ger-man" tomes and "big books from the Athanaeum" with which Olive schools Verena in "the fields of literature" seem to constitute a bulwark against real and social experience (1132, 960), Basil's perusal of conservative, distinctly Anglo-Saxon cultural texts – "volumes of rusty aspect, picked up at New York bookstalls" (1159) – suggests a willed failure of engagement with the conditions of contemporary America.

Nor is the genteel culture, the purview of America's aspiring bourgeois and moneyed classes, a more promising site of cultural activity or training. Al-though the "chatty . . . style of literature that seemed to take most to-day" – the work of "'lady-writers'" producing for a popular "gynecaeum" (917)

– comes under indictment, the novel finds the kind of thoroughgoing aestheticism often associated with James himself conspicuously wanting as an alternative. The languid self-indulgence of Henry Burrage, a wealthy suitor of Verena's who "collected beautiful things . . . that he sent for to Europe" (938), remains unthreatening to Olive precisely because his "exquisite taste" in music, "*bibelots,*" and atmosphere creates a kind of "harmony" – a hermetic "Civilization" – from which the rough and tumble of contemporary social life, its contests over the forms of culture, are shut out; in the Burrages' elegant New York salon, every effect is calculated to produce a seductively decadent atmosphere of "fragrance" and "perfumes" and "precious object[s]," the whole scene lit by "covered lamps" (943). In no other Jamesian text of this decade (not even *The Portrait of a Lady,* featuring the baneful aesthete Gilbert Osmond) does the "*dilettante*" cut such an obviously insufficient figure, performing the rites of taste with the effect of narrowing, rather than enlarging, the boundaries of culture (940).

Such observations can help us make sense of *The Bostonians'* palpable and surprising discomfort with literariness, with the cultural authority of the high style. This discomfort is most obvious in the novel's emphatic insistence that its narrator is a mere reporter or transcriber of "occult information," "incompeten[t]," "forbidden" or "denied" the "opportunity" to speculate more closely on motive and circumstance (809, 1181, 954, 972). In "The Art of Fiction" (1884), James would famously declare under the lofty banner of realism that the novelist must first and foremost "speak . . . with the tone of the historian" so as not to give the representational powers of the novel away.[10] Here, however, the withdrawal of the narrator from the authority of omniscience does quite different work. It reveals James's intention to forestall a merely reactionary investment in high culture in favor of more flexible and strenuous thinking about the role of literary texts, values, and institutions in the general culture of American modernity. Such a description of James's project explains the novel's instability more productively than charges of misogyny or a failed interest in reform on his part. In particular, it helps us address the novel's increasingly insecure rendering of Ransom's violent opposition to women in the public sphere.

Nowhere is that opposition more complexly recorded than in the novel's most intensely public scene, the spontaneous outing of Ransom and Verena in New York's Central Park. Desperate to "detach" her "a little from your ties, your belongings" (1099), Ransom doesn't succeed in "pressing" Verena to have lunch with him in the city, as he fantasizes doing; but "an irrepressible desire urge[s] him on to taste, for once, deeply," the pleasure of her undivided attention (1098). In the Park, they visit "the little zoological garden," observe "the swans in the ornamental water," "threa[d] the devious ways of the Ramble," "los[e] themselves in the Maze," and "admir[e] all the statues and busts of great men with which the grounds are decorated" before "resting on a sequestered bench" for an interval of intimate conversation about liberty, writing for the public, and the dangers of the feminization of American culture (1103). It is here, in the Park's pastoral precincts and far from the maddening crowds, that Verena is converted to Ransom's vision of her own destiny; and it is here that the novel gives expression to his infamous outburst:

> "The whole generation is womanized; the masculine tone is passing out of the world; it's a feminine, a nervous, hysterical, chattering, canting age, an age of hollow phrases and false delicacy and exaggerated solicitudes and coddled sensibilities, which, if we don't soon look out, will usher in the reign of mediocrity, of the feeblest and flattest and the most pretentious that has ever been. The masculine character, the ability to dare and endure, to know and yet not fear reality, to look the world in the face and take it for what it is – a very queer and partly very base mixture – that is what I want to preserve, or rather, as I may say, to recover; and I must tell you that I don't in the least care what becomes of you ladies while I make the attempt!" (1121)

To what extent does James invite us to identify the novel's observations on the condition of American culture with Ransom's harangue? Many scholarly readers have made this very link.[11] But a more complex set of intentions becomes evident when we consider the setting of this scene in Central Park, and the role of the park itself as a U.S. cultural institution during the late 1870s and early 1880s. For Central Park – America's first landscaped, public, natural preserve – functioned as a literal and symbolic arena for the staging of vexed questions about the state of American general culture, the character of its urban users, and – perhaps most salient – the status of women in the public sphere. Opened in stages between 1858 and 1860, the Park was explicitly designed by chief architects Frederick Law Olmsted and Calvert Vaux to serve as "the big art work" of a modern Republic in which citizens would create their own civic institutions.[12] Its chief goal was "to empower each individual with the confidence of personal aesthetic judgment," promoting "civic order achieved through the refinement of taste."[13] Their design strategies – the revolutionary greensward plan, which interspersed broad expanses of lawn with groves of trees and bodies of water; the "separation of ways" that sank transverse roads below ground and kept pedestrians from crossing paths with carriage-riders – were intended to immerse the park-goer in a pastoral oasis, psychically removed from the conflicts and demands of the city. Through this kind of experience, a "thoroughly American" revision of European aesthetic models, Olmsted believed that the new populations of New York could be "trained" in civic feeling.[14] In particular, immigrants and laborers could be "educat[ed] to refinement and taste," endowed with "the mental and moral capital of gentlemen."[15]

However suspect Olmsted's investment in gentlemanliness, Central Park was indeed an important site for testing claims about the character of the American mass public. During the postwar decades, users became increasingly mixed in terms of class and ethnic affiliation and "taste." Newspaper reports celebrated the Park's accommodation of "the ragged urchin" and "the millionaire," "hard-handed labor" and "soft-palmed wealth," nicknaming it "The People's Pleasure Ground."[16] Engaging in the varied activities catalogued by Verena and Ransom – strolling through the "pseudo-tropical" Ramble, boat riding, promenading on the Mall, feeding swans on the Lake – the Park's users shaped an emerging culture of leisure, spectacle, and display even as they enjoyed controlled contact with urban life, mores, institutions, and one another. At free concerts in the Ramble, these mixed audiences heard music "of the higher and more instructive kind . . . intermingled with what is commonly known as 'popular music'"; programs were self-consciously arranged "so as to give each class a fair share of its favorite music" while remaining "a little in advance of the average taste."[17] These kinds of public cultural events not only constituted new forms of mass entertainment; they promoted – if unevenly – contact between racial communities, ethnic groups, and classes as well as a certain level of tolerance for cultural difference. Central Park simultaneously symbolized and provided a new kind of space for the formation of a more genuinely democratic "general culture," a public sphere of open exchange.

The salience of Central Park as a cultural project to James's designs is even more pronounced when we consider the explicit claims made by and about women with respect to their freedom of movement and association in this new kind of public space. If the Park allowed a certain controlled contact between class and ethnic groups, it also provided an enormously liberating opportunity for middle-class women – those, as Ransom puts it, "only thought safe when . . . between four walls" (1101) – to break out of the confines of home and hearth, the symbolic spaces of true (that is, genteel, white, and Protestant) womanhood. As early as 1861, a popular magazine notes that "many ladies walk daily" in the Park "without attendance"; in the ensuing decades, bourgeois women – especially the young and unmarried – increasingly availed themselves of opportunities provided by the Park for unchaperoned display, informal socializing, courting, and vigorous physical exercise. Widely popular sports like skating and cycling afforded a liberating physicality and a sanctioned release from rigid middle-class conventions of femininity; in fact, skating in the Park was one of the few activities in which "ladies" might "properly" exercise with men, or display their ankles![18] The effects of such freedom of movement on Verena Tarrant, we might note, are immediate and striking: walking in the Park, "enjoy[ing] the sense of wandering in the great city," her experience is "more intense, more full of amusing incident and opportunity"; free to "stop and look at everything" and "indulge all her curiosities," she can recapture the less regulated experience of girlhood, when she "strayed far from home . . . playing she was a gipsy" (1102).

Not surprisingly, as Verena's image of herself as "gipsy" suggests, the increasing freedom of middle-class women in public occasioned deep anxiety about attacks on that most prized of bourgeois commodities, female purity.[19] In 1888 Joseph Pulitzer's *World* would send its sensationalist woman reporter Elizabeth Cochrane (better known as Nellie Bly) undercover to pose as an innocent "country girl" to be approached by men – presumably working men and foreigners – with erotic designs. Such prurient expectations were hardly borne out by the facts of contact; between 1879 and 1886, fewer than 6 percent of arrests in all New York parks were accounted for by crimes against women and only one arrest was for rape.[20] But these anxieties suggest what is at issue in popular narratives about the Park, as in the fate of Verena Tarrant. What is the character of the masses assembled for spectacular entertainment: are they a united body of "picturesque beauty," as one Park-goer noted in his diary, or "*essentially a mob, lawless and uncontrollable*," as Olmsted would complain? And what is the place, both physical and symbolic, of "ladies" and femininity in this rapidly changing social order?

Set within the arena of these contestations, Basil Ransom's apostrophe to Verena reverberates with varied overtones. When he declares that there is "No place in public" for such a beautiful woman, that his "'plan is to keep you at home and have a better time with you there than ever'" (1112), it is precisely the unprecedented "public" opportunity for contact and exchange afforded by their outing in the Park that makes possible his declaration. Insisting on a natural distinction between the "public, civic" world and "the realm of family life and domestic affections," Ransom belies the powerful possibilities for cultural redefinition opened up within the complexly public yet intimate space in which his exchange with Verena occurs. On her side, Verena too is fatally short-sighted; succumbing to "a spell . . . as she listen[s]" (1105), she conflates the moment's rare freedom of movement and conversation with the achievement of a "real self" that can be transported to, and sustained within, the traditional female sphere of love, "outside and above all vulgarizing" – and energetically social – "influences" (1115, 1114).

The novel itself, it must be said, entertains notions of femininity and publicity that partially link James with Ransom's cultural politics. It reads Verena's about-face on the role of women as predictable, but in such a way as to beg the question of an essential, biologized female "nature" ("it was *her* nature to be easily submissive, to like being overborne" [1105; emphasis mine]). And it gives Ransom's "narrow notions" – "the rejection of which by leading periodicals was certainly not a matter for surprise" (1111) – a kind of legitimacy through their affective power over the "brilliant, successful" heroine (1117). But Ransom's anxiety about the cultural fate of "the masculine character" in the era of "hysteri[a]" and "magazines" is finally revealed as insufficient by the context of democratic publicity in which he gives it voice. As he and Verena trade talk about women in civic life, they "emerg[e] into the species of *plaza* formed by the numbered street which constitutes the southern extremity of the Park" (1116). Passing over the threshold of the Park – beyond its "bowers and boskages," its "artificial lakes and cockneyfied landscapes" – the couple is confronted with the spectacle of the new, mass-mediated, bourgeois city:

> The chocolate-coloured houses, in tall, new rows, surveyed the expanse; the street-cars rattled in the foreground, changing horses while the horses steamed, and absorbing and emitting passengers; and the beer-saloons, with exposed shoulders and sides, which in New York do a good deal towards representing the picturesque, the "bit" appreciated by painters, announced themselves in signs of large lettering to the sky. Groups of the unemployed, the children of disappointment from beyond the seas, propped themselves against the low, sunny wall of the Park; and on the other side the commercial vista of the Sixth Avenue stretched away with remarkable absence of aerial perspective.
>
> (1116)

In this variegated scene, the heterogeneous elements of urban modernity – the new street-cars and Elevated lines and the traditional horse-drawn conveyances; the excrescences of uptown development and the "signs" of an urban "picturesque"; the culture of leisure and that of commercial activity; the perspective of the bourgeoisie "survey[ing] the expanse" from on high and the vantage-point of the "unemployed," the immigrant, "the low" – "expos[e]" themselves, rub "shoulders" with one another, to remarkably energetic effect. Commenting on the aesthetics of this raw mixture, which prominently features "a remarkable absence of aerial perspective," James's narrative can also be said to comment on its own intended commitments, to locate its interest and curiosity precisely here: in the urban street, where the signs of American identity and sociality are being vigorously, variously produced.

To this process, Ransom's terms are deeply inadequate. What he cannot do, under the brief of a radical cultural conservatism, is "look the world" of urban heterogeneity "in the face and take it for what it is." With respect to the contentious "mixture" – the perhaps "queer and partly very base mixture" – of cultural styles, identities, and affiliations that comprises modern America, Ransom's gospel of "masculine character" turns out to mean an embrace of forms of regulation and control that violently oppose the cultural demands and opportunities of a more expansive democracy. In his narrow but historically conditioned vision – Ransom has, after all, survived "various engagements" and "forgotten Southern battles" in the recent war; he desires nothing so much as to "leave [the South] alone with her wounds and her memories, not prating in the market-place either of her troubles or her hopes" (1024, 846) – the urban spectating classes of the Union can figure only as an ungovernable "rabble" (1214). Increasingly, as the novel unfolds, James tests the limits of this view, and thus measures his own disaffection from the emergent culture of the gilded age *and* from merely genteel forms of reaction to it. Rather than simply concede Ransom's radical "suspicio[ns] of the encroachments of modern democracy" (975), the novel hazards various notions of literature as a cultural activity and of the literary as a profession – a profession of cultural engagement – that departs from Ransom's project of containment and possession.

Here we must consider not only the famous, famously unsatisfying ending of the novel (a reviewer in the *Atlantic,* for example, scoffed at "its almost indecent exposure" of Olive Chancellor[21]) but also the energy of its movement toward that closing. After Verena and Ransom's outing in Central Park, we see Ransom become increasingly reckless and without "scruple"; he graduates from illegal entry in Olive's summer home in Marmion to contemplated assault and battery backstage at the Music Hall to the virtual abduction of Verena. What precipitates this conduct – or, perhaps better, this protocol for privatizing Verena's natural resources – is hardly an avowal of love on the heroine's part. Rather, the "sense of elation and success" that

"throb[s] in his heart" and emboldens Ransom to make his stand is occasioned by the acceptance of one of his "articles": one he rates "the best,"
"the most important thing I have done in the way of a literary attempt"
(1139, 1140–1). Having this article published confirms not only his cultural prospects but his "manhood"; it "makes an era in [his] life" and gives permission to his waging of a "war to the knife" for possession of the "consummate[ly] innocen[t] . . . American girl" (1141, 1155, 913–14).

It is certainly open to us to read Ransom's pivotal declaration as a representative statement of the double bind of the writer, the figure of culture, in
late nineteenth-century America. James himself – the very icon of the artist
who derides even as he woos an indifferent public – would wistfully write
brother William of *The Bostonians* that, "having got no money for it, I hoped
for a little glory," and more theatrically bemoan to Howells the "inexplica-
ble injury wrought . . . upon my situation" by *The Bostonians* and *The
Princess*, which "have reduced the desire, and the demand, for my productions to zero."[22] Howells himself would advance the project of literary realism in part so as to secure for the realist writer in America a public, distinctly masculinized, cultural function, famously equating the man of
business with the man of letters as the active shapers and strivers of the new
republic. Certainly Ransom's anticipated publication in the pages of the *Ra-
tional Review* gives expression to a broadly cultural desire for the possibility of sustaining a vital public sphere ungoverned by the logic of con-
sumerism, novelty, and sensation.

But James is ultimately too canny about such desires, even as motive forces
in his own fiction, to let them stand uninterrogated. For the drift of *The
Bostonians* is toward an ever more acute recognition of the continuity of apparently opposing cultural forces – not only of realism and romance as generic expressions of cultural desires and possibilities, or of Verena and Ransom,
but of Ransom and the forms of culture-building he strives to transcend.
Ironically, even as his notice of publication makes James's protagonist an author of genuine "articles" – and thus himself a genuine article, rather than
merely an instance of retrogression and failure – it allows him to become a
contestant for the disposition of Verena, that "article for which there was
more and more demand" (1097).

Styling himself a figure of opposition to, and indeed of *ransom* from, the
"unhealthy," "extravagant," "false" character of American modernity (975),
Ransom arrives at the Boston Music Hall on the eve of Verena's performance
charged with the certitude that he is "apart, unique," "not one of the audience" (1198). Shockingly, however, he experiences this form of distinction

as an intermittent identification with "a young man . . . who, waiting in a public place, has made up his mind, for reasons of his own, to discharge a pistol at the king or the president" (1198). This resonantly historical image, recalling the theatrical setting of Abraham Lincoln's assassination some twenty years earlier, suggests just how much is at stake in the imagination of an oppositional public culture. It also suggests that Ransom's will to power must end up being indistinguishable from the very forms of "hysteri[a]," ill cultural health, and sensationalism he so actively derides (975). In fact, as he inspects the Music Hall's facilities and architecture, Ransom becomes precisely the kind of spectator from whom he ostensibly desires to "save" Verena; he buys "one of the photographs" of the heroine and "also the sketch of her life" in preparation for his own unfolding "exhibition of enterprise" (1200).

Even more tellingly, Ransom will become something of a figure for the very lawlessness and unregulated desire he identifies as the definitive characteristic of the modern public sphere. In the breathless atmosphere of the Music Hall, he waits outside Verena's locked door with a frantic Matthias Pardon, a pompous Mr. Filer, managing "agent" for "prima donnas" and "natural curiosities" (1206), and a hired "guardian of order" who refuses his request to speak to Verena "in private" by replying sardonically, "'Yes – it's always intensely private'" (1201–2). The ensuing scene stages not only the immediate issue of Verena's recantation – her "submiss[ion]" to Ransom's erotic "spell" (1210) – but the problem of how the general culture of an "enlightened democracy" is being forged (1097). In this heated moment Ransom presses his claim to Verena by insisting on the vulgarity and uncontrollability of the audience, the "city of Boston" assembled "under this roof": "'What do they care for you but to gape and grin and babble?'" he demands. "You are mine, you are not theirs" (1211). But it is Ransom who presses the rights of ownership and consumption, declaring, "She's mine or she isn't, and if she's mine, she's all mine!" (1212). It is Ransom who takes possession by laying hands on Verena, getting her bodily out of the place, much as Selah Tarrant does in the "grotesque manipulations" that mark her earliest and most vulgar performances (855). And it is Ransom who resorts to "muscular force" to break free of the "house" and its restless "raving rabble" (1218, 1214).

Even though Ransom has his way with Verena, triumphing over the "new system of advertising" and its self-serving "agents" (1202), the public against which he acts is powerfully transformed. Or rather, Ransom's language for describing and constituting that public is found conspicuously wanting. Numerous readers have commented on the shifting balance of sympathy in the novel's closing pages, as Olive, "[d]ry, desperate," her "pale glittering eyes straining forward, as if they were looking for death," braves the wrath of the crowd, virtually "offering herself to be trampled to death and torn to pieces" (1216, 1217). Here, perhaps, for the first time – as Ransom predicts that the people, "senseless brutes!", will "howl and thump according to their nature" (1216); as Olive herself predicts she will "be hissed and hooted and insulted!" (1218) – Olive Chancellor becomes an authentic heroine, a figure of "revolutions" and "sacrific[e]" to "the furious mob" (1217).

Importantly, Olive's heroism is made manifest precisely in the failure of the multitude to insist on the appearance of the real heroine, that attractive commodity they have paid so dearly to see. Even as Ransom spirits the material girl away from her mother and from Olive's "tremendous entreaty" to "mingl[e] in the issuing crowd" of the Hall, Olive mounts the stage her ambition has erected, in front of which "the great public waited" (1212, 1218). At just this moment, the narrative eerily occupies Ransom's point of view: it is the "Mississippian," so powerfully "palpitating with his victory" that he can afford to feel "a little sorry" for his foe, who "perceive[s] the quick, complete, tremendous silence which, in the hall, . . . greeted Olive Chancellor's rush to the front" (1217–18). In that echoing silence – an *absence* of hooting, hysteria, and derision, in which "[e]very sound instantly dropped" – a "respectful" quality of attention reigns: whatever Olive "should say to them . . . it was not apparent that they were likely to hurl the benches at her" (1218). The violence of desire and self-indulgence is finally on Ransom's side; the "ferocity" that ostensibly "lurks in a disappointed mob" is displaced by intelligent, or at least "not ungenerous," curiosity (1201, 1218).

Ransom, then, not only underestimates the capacity of the urban crowd for civil forms of contact and exchange, but himself enacts the very vulgarity his intervention is intended to overturn. It is this highly unsympathetic Ransom who enables the novel's transfer of sympathy to Olive, as well as its pointed interest in the public performance she undertakes. Struggling to wrench Verena away from her entourage, Ransom fails to observe Olive's rush to the platform; oddly, the narrative remarks that, "had" he done so, "She might have suggested to him some feminine firebrand of Paris revolutions, erect on a barricade, or even the sacrificial figure of Hypatia, whirled through the furious mob of Alexandria" (1217). Why, we might ask, does the climactic scene of the novel comport itself this way, inhabiting a perspective that is in effect vacant, invoking a mythic iconography that likens this scene in the hidden rooms of the Music Hall to decisive moments in the founding of Western civilization?

The answer resides in James's ultimate commitment not to realist representational modes, but to rethinking the act of culture-building. With the pointedly conditional imagery of Olive as revolutionary martyr – "*If* [Ransom] had observed her"; "She *might* have suggested to *him*" (italics added) – James simultaneously brings into view Ransom's insufficient imagination of the contemporary public sphere and the role that literary narratives play in the formation of collective values. The reference to Hypatia recalls the female philosopher of fifth-century Alexandria; but it also recalls the popular historical novel *Hypatia, or New Foes in Old Clothes*, written by the conservative English curate Charles Kingsley and enjoying a thirteenth printing in 1881. In Kingsley's novel, the philosopher-virgin attacks "the hateful and degrading" status of women as "the property, the puppet, of m[en]," and she dies at the hands of a venomous mob.[23] But what makes Kingsley's Hypatia relevant to James's Olive is the larger contest she embodies, between "paganism" and the Christian Church, "two great rival powers, in deadly struggle for possession of the human race" (Kingsley, viii). *Hypatia* is a barely concealed allegory for the state of contemporary Anglo-Christian culture, an "age" whose "manners, and its literature," have become "altogether artificial, slipshod, effete"; it dramatizes a contemporary crisis of culture-making, played out in contests "between the aristocracy and the mob, – between wealth, refinement, art, learning, all that makes a nation great, and the savage herd . . . below" (Kingsley, xvii, 21). In the guise of historical drama, Kingsley voices deep anxiety about the containment of that populist body, whose energies are all too easily pressed into service of "barbarous" forms of entertainment and political theater (ix).

If these anxieties aptly give voice to Basil Ransom's, they are not easily assignable to James. What is striking about his condensed reference at the climactic moment of *The Bostonians* is the complex positioning it allows James to achieve. Olive Chancellor becomes a newly heroic figure of feminist passion through the agency of Ransom's perspective, itself derived from cultural models that insist on firm distinctions between high and low cultural forms, between authentic expressions of "taste" and the ungoverned appetites of the mob. In turn, the narrator's assignment of this vocabulary to Ransom has the force of calling attention to the undesirability of the latter's cultural commitments: Ransom is here understood to make sense of his world in a static, self consciously literary imagery that remains notably at odds with the inchoate energy of the cultural spectacle at hand. Preoccupied with "strik[ing] Verena dumb" (1098), Ransom simply fails to attend to the possibilities Olive's performance opens up, for some genuinely democratic but regulated kind of cultural exchange. If the dramatic climax of *The Bostonians* strikes us as deeply anticlimactic, this is at least in part because the focus of the narrative on a tear-stained, "muffled" Verena being led away to the destiny of "far from brilliant" union withholds from our view the quality of Olive's address, and of the public's reception of it (1218, 1219). Following Ransom outside the Music Hall, provisionally occupying his vantage point, James's narrative suggests what must be lost, in the way of engagement with emerging forms of modern America, by a politics of agonistic withdrawal into the high style.

It is, of course, James's special (if not perverse) genius to make this very suggestion in distinctly literary, aestheticized gestures: through the manipulation of narrative point of view, imagery, allusion, tone. James, in other words, refuses to concede the literary as a cultural act, striving instead to press the limits of its self-described distinction from other institutions for shaping and representing cultural experience and power. In this specific respect, his text departs from the advertised aims of American realism, as do *The Princess Casamassima, The Reverberator,* and other of James's complexly hybrid texts of the 1880s. But if *The Bostonians* ultimately fails to sustain a commitment to realist literary strategies, it thereby more powerfully probes the boundaries of literature as a participant in "very *American*," "very characteristic" contests over the value of culture and the forging of cultural values.[24] In our own fin de siècle, more than a century after James's forays into realism, we still struggle with such questions about the place of the literary: which canons and texts can fairly be said to represent the range, the complexity, of American social experience? Which narratives encode our shared and competing histories; what kind of national culture do they create or allow us to invest in; what kinds of boundaries – forms of inclusion and exclusion – does the imagination of national traditions draw? Finally, the James we continue to encounter is nothing less than a prescient reader of modernity: anticipating, negotiating, struggling with the possibilities and limits of its new social forms, not least its literary and aesthetic ones. If not strictly a literary realist, James remains an artful combatant in culture wars whose ongoing effects continue to be all too real.

NOTES

1 Henry James, *The Art of the Novel* (New York: Scribner, 1960), 37.
2 Richard Brodhead, *The School of Hawthorne* (New York: Oxford University Press, 1986), xx.

3 James, *The Complete Notebooks of Henry James,* ed. Leon Edel and Lyall H. Powers (New York: Oxford University Press, 1987), 19–20.

4 In an elegant and wide-ranging reading of James's project and *The Bostonians* in particular, "Woman's Voice, Democracy's Body, and *The Bostonians,*" ELH 56:3 (Fall 1989), 639–65, Lynn Wardley similarly focuses on James's "American Girl" as America's "repository of culture," her body the source of both biological and cultural reproduction and thus of innumerable anxieties about engendering culture. Wardley carefully distinguishes the character Ransom from James, who is not, in her reading, arguing for the return of women to a separate and regulated domesticity, but to a new kind of "interior someplace in between" (640) the house and the public sphere. But her suggestive remarks on the novel's social geography (including its uses of New York and Central Park) treat the latter largely as symbolic spaces, linked to biological reproduction and the female body, rather than sites of historically emergent experience. I depart from Wardley, too, in redirecting her ultimate sense of James's anxiety about the "vulnerability" of the social body with respect to cultural production into an examination of James's commitment to literary institutions and strategies as modes of shaping that body's future.

5 James, *The Bostonians,* in *Novels 1881–1886* (New York: Library of America, 1985), 827.

6 James, *Notebooks,* 20.

7 Cultural historians have richly documented the rise of consumerist and theatricalized forms of public identity during this period; in fact, the identification of a shift from a producer-oriented culture organized in and through notions of "character" to a mass-mediated, consumer culture typified by expressions of "personality" has become a truism of American studies accounts of modern social identity. These particular terms are most influentially articulated by Warren Susman in *Culture as History: The Transformation of American Society in the Twentieth Century* (New York: Pantheon Books, 1984), 271–85, which traces the assimilation of theatricality and role-playing as norms not only in middle-class life but throughout modern corporate America. Karen Halttunen, in *Confidence Men and Painted Women: A Study of Middle-Class Culture in America, 1830–1870* (New Haven: Yale University Press, 1982), discusses the emergent conditions of middle-class American life and the complex rituals of display, self-display, and identity-formation they shape; see especially pp. 198–210. More broadly, Philip Fisher's *Hard Facts: Story and Form in the American Novel* (New York: Oxford University Press, 1985), argues that new and consumer-oriented paradigms of identity emerge from the shifting forms of public space. A recent historical study of the techniques that make forms of consumer appeal and desire possible – for example, developments in the uses of plate glass, lighting, and materials that enable the staging and display of consumer goods – is William Leach's exemplary *Land of Desire: Merchants, Power, and the Rise of a New American Culture* (New York: Vintage, 1993).

8 Brodhead, 109; Larzer Ziff, *The American 1890s: The Life and Times of a Lost Generation* (New York: Viking, 1968), 102. James vacationed with Gilder on

Cape Cod shortly before composing the novel, in a town on which "Marmion" is modeled.

9   William Dean Howells, *Criticisms and Fiction* (New York: Harper, 1891), 55, 15.
10 Henry James, *Literary Criticism: Essays on Literature: American Writers: English Writers* (New York: Library of America, 1984), 46.
11 Perhaps most prominent among these readings is Alfred Habegger's "The Return of the Father in *The Bostonians,*" in *Henry James and the "Woman Business"* (Cambridge University Press, 1989), 182–229.
12 Roy Rosenzweig and Elizabeth Blackmar, *The Park and the People: A History of Central Park* (Ithaca: Cornell University Press, 1992), 136.
13 Ibid., 137, 143.
14 Ibid., 307, 239.
15 Frederick Law Olmsted, cited in *Creating Central Park, 1857–1861*, ed. Charles E. Beveridge and David Schuyler (Baltimore: Johns Hopkins University Press, 1983), 9.
16 Rosenzweig and Blackmar, 212, 308.
17 The *New York Times,* cited in Rosenzweig and Blackmar, 226.
18 Rosenzweig and Blackmar, 222, 230.
19 Recent historians of U.S. racial identity and narratives have documented the knotty entanglement of "whiteness," middle-class or genteel codes, bourgeois institutions, and ideologies of gender – particularly femininity. See, for example, Ruth Frankenberg, *White Women, Race Matters: The Social Construction of Whiteness* (Minneapolis: University of Minnesota Press, 1993), and Sara Blair, "'Trying to Be Natural': Authorship and the Power of Type in *The Princess Casamassima,*" in *Henry James and the Writing of Race and Nation* (Cambridge University Press, 1996), 90–122.
20 Rosenzweig and Blackmar, 321.
21 H. E. Scudder, *Atlantic,* June 1886; cited in *Henry James: The Critical Heritage,* ed. Roger Gard (London: Routledge and Kegan Paul, 1968), 168.
22 James to William James, 9 October 1885, in *Henry James Letters,* ed. Leon Edel (Cambridge: The Belknap Press of Harvard University Press, 1980), 3:102; James to William Dean Howells, 2 January 1888, *Letters* 3:209.
23 Kingsley, *Hypatia, or New Foes in Old Clothes* (New York: Harper and Brothers, 1985), 51, 456.
24 James, *Notebooks,* 20.

9

ERIC HARALSON

Lambert Strether's Excellent Adventure

What is there in the idea of *Too late*—of some . . . passion or bond . . . formed too late? . . . It's love, it's friendship, it's mutual comprehension—it's whatever one will.
  —James's Notebook, February 1895[1]

What then did James mean by sensations, passions or pleasure?
  —Maxwell Geismar[2]

"Live all you can; it's a mistake not to": every heart vibrates to that iron string, no doubt, but what on earth does it mean? As James emphasizes in the Preface, the "whole case" of *The Ambassadors* (1903) centers in Strether's tutorial effusion to his young painter-friend, Little Bilham, during Gloriani's garden party, but this is fortune-cookie advice at best: "It doesn't so much matter what you do in particular, so long as you have your life."[3] The key to Strether, apparently, lies in his belatedness – or better, his belated *discovery* of belatedness under the barrage of impressions that play havoc with his "categories" in Europe. It is "simply too late," he feels, too late to repair "the injury done his character" by – well, by just about everything: his proverbial New England conscience, his botched job of parenting, his unbuilt "temple of taste," his cobbled career of all strain and small gain, of much utility for others but meager identity for himself (*A* 131, *AN* 308, *A* 63). There is nothing obscure about *his* hurt – except, after all, in the kind of "Enjoyment" (that's James's capital *E*) that has eluded "poor fine melancholy, missing, striving Strether" (*N* 226, 383).

And yet, as anyone can see from his envy of both the sculptor Gloriani – that "glossy male tiger" stalking his "queer old garden" of Eden – and Chad Newsome – that lucky young man "marked out by women" – Strether's deepest regret is no riddle at all: not enough passion (*A* 133, 118, 98). So what is his problem? Why *can't* he find a nice woman, settle down, warm that old connubial bed? Or, failing that, why not a walk on the wild side –

a romantic fling being just "the typical tale of Paris" (*A* 315)? Has his sex appeal fizzled out? Is he a dissolute cad, an insensitive lout? Or is it lack of opportunity – a bad market, maybe, adverse demographics on the dating scene?

On the contrary. Strether is still "very attractive" at fifty-five, as his friend Waymarsh assures him, with a pleasant demeanor, a feel for "the higher culture" of Europe, yet good American family values, too, whatever his track record as a husband and father (*A* 33, 62). He is sober, frugal, not inclined to those excesses that can spell trouble in a marriage, as he testifies to Maria Gostrey: "I don't get drunk; I don't pursue the ladies; I don't spend money; I don't even write sonnets" (*A* 197). True, this tally of his virtues for domesticity contains an element of self-deprecation, and he taxes himself for being "portentously solemn" and having a quaint "estimate of fun"; but then a quiet reliability can be welcome in a man (*A* 338, 188). So agreeable is Strether to the opposite sex, in fact, that he finds himself constantly in a circle of petticoats – a convenient gentleman in Woollett, Massachusetts, in what is "essentially a society of women," and a popular ambassador abroad, adept at "get[ting] the ladies to work for him," as Bilham teases, though liable to getting worked by them as well (*A* 213, 124).

At least two "ladies" want to marry Strether: the wealthy, handsome Mrs. Newsome, who does the proposing herself, and the discerning Miss Gostrey, who is twenty years younger than he, goes in for décolletage, and polishes pewter with such care that its reflections are (like his, so to speak) "improving to life" (*A* 340). Even the charming countess Madame de Vionnet, with her "almost celebrated" taste in acquisitions, wishes to be "sublime" for him: "You see how . . . I want everything. I've wanted you too" (*A* 123, 324). Indeed, in the scenario of 1899, James worried about "represent[ing] every woman in the book . . . as having . . . 'made up' to my hero" – a man no longer in his prime, when all is said and done, with the modest income and bearing of a provincial magazine editor – but he affirmed his plan to portray each of the main female characters as "favourably affected" (a muted Victorianism for amorous arousal) by Strether (*N* 414).

Yet Strether notoriously bungles his chances. One cannot blame him, perhaps, for backing out on Mrs. Newsome, a stereotype of the post-Puritan dominatrix that James embellishes with élan (and not a little period misogyny). But even here one might ask, prudently if unromantically, whether Strether is not being reckless or overfastidious in letting a "great sponge" wipe out his "opulent future" with her (*A* 293, 297). His rejection of Maria Gostrey seems more puzzling still, since, as James stresses, her offer "might

well have tempted" an aging drifter who ends his European sojourn "as de-
pleted as if he had spent his last sou," with only memory and imagination to
put "a loaf on the shelf." Chock-full of old ivory and brocade, Maria's place
in the Quartier Marbœuf has the makings of a perfect love-nest, with a boun-
ty of "ripe round melon[s]" and a prospect of "exquisite service," including
(her blushes hint) the sexual kind. "It built him softly round, it roofed him
warmly over," Strether feels, sensing how "it was awkward, it was almost
stupid, not to seem to prize such things" (A 317, 339, 341, 344). As for
Marie de Vionnet, we will never know whether her small piece of the Empire held a room and a regular omelette for Strether, who dismisses the possibility of their mutual attraction by fiat: "It . . . has nothing to do, practically, with either of us" (A 291). Yet is *might* have, James strongly implies,
and the oddest thing about the "odd foundation" of their friendship is not
what Strether "rear[s] on it" (as Maria points out) but what he does not (A
331).

So again, what's wrong with Strether?

If I have given the question an invidious spin, it is to highlight the normative bias secreted in its very tenor of familiarity – the way in which assumptions about the nature and proper conduct of gender both influence and flow
from repeated "scenes of engendering" (in Evelyne Ender's phrase) that do
their cultural work even as they "vanish into the quotidian of our existence."[4] Commentary on *The Ambassadors* indicates the efficacy of this
process, for much of the critical tradition builds upon unexamined prejudices
about "normal human biopsychic behavior," underwriting not only a reductive definition of "the recognized, shared experience of the human race"
but a regulatory perspective that can spot deviants like Strether – or James,
with whom he is often confused – from a mile away.[5] From the earliest reviews to the latest scholarship, Strether has been cited for his "typical thinness of feeling wherever passion is concerned"; deemed a virtual castrato,
"incapable . . . of carnality"; faulted for his "lack of masculine reciproca-
tion" to feminine palpitations; admonished for avoiding "more complete
commitments of behavior" like marriage; pronounced "the most maidenly"
of James's protagonists; and, most recently, psychoanalyzed as a man who
moves through the primal scenery of the French countryside – the trysting
ground of Chad Newsome and Madame de Vionnet – as if he were dispossessed of the "accoutrements of masculinity."[6] These accounts vary consid-
erably in subtlety as well as political temper, but as a general rule, the Lambert Strether who emerges seems erotically challenged beyond remedy – a
"perfectly equipped failure" without the equipment, as it were (A 40) – and

The Ambassadors, by the same stroke, gets written off as an "emasculated leisure-class novel."[7]

The cultural warrant for this line of reading is such that attempts to rescue James's hero from aspersions of manly deficiency have historically been thrown on the defensive, scrambling to salvage esteem for his choices under the rubric of "renunciation" – roughly: the pathos of poor old high-minded, nothing-getting Strether – or of "transcendence" – roughly: the evacuation of new improved Strether from the messy intrigue of life – though, of course, these topoi can blend: Strether rises above the sometimes brutal economies of intimacy by thwarting the demands of "the wretched self" (*A* 321). Admittedly, James himself mapped out these avenues of critical recourse, speaking of Strether's final "renouncement" of Maria Gostrey, for instance, as evidence that he has surmounted his "old order" of being and returns to America "really so quite other" (*N* 414–15). But it does not follow, as talk of renunciation suggests, that Strether's eschewal of a "normal" male role in a "normal" male–female relationship concedes the authority of the norm as the sine qua non of experience. Nor does it appear, on the other hand, that his transcendence of an "order" in which such a role in such a relation had once been conceivable – in fact, all but consummated – exempts him from the pressure of the norm or the emotional and practical consequences of resisting that pressure. Significantly, where critics have aimed at shifting the burden of persuasion back upon normative discourse, with its "sophisticated moralisms about Strether's failures," the tendency has been to downplay his personal discomfiture in rubbing the norm the wrong way and to treat his "indifference to sexual liaison" as a natural, even negligible aspect of his winsome "aesthetic dandyism."[8]

But James's mixed signals are crucial here, underscoring both that Strether feels "awkward, . . . almost stupid" for seeming to misprize the sacred institution of heterosexuality and its amenities and that he implicitly devalues "such things" by disengaging himself from Mrs. Newsome, Marie de Vionnet, and Maria Gostrey: "so far as they made his opportunity they made it only for a moment" (*A* 344). In this respect, *The Ambassadors* simultaneously reflects and confronts the power of the modern gender system, especially in its prescriptions and expectations for masculine performance. As Thomas Laqueur has shown, the idea of a "radical dimorphism" of the sexes began as a postulate in the service of Enlightenment patriarchalism but was articulated as scientific fact by James's time – a truism "solidly grounded in nature" rather than a political scheme profoundly shaped by culture. Further, the enforcement methods by which this gender-(d)riven regime molds its subjects and reproduces itself – or what Laqueur calls "the social thuggery that takes a polymorphous perverse infant and bullies it into a heterosexual man or woman" – intensified in the late-Victorian period as the hegemony of that regime came under increasing threats, real and perceived, in both the United States and England (James's adoptive home).[9]

A rising women's movement bent on removing the barriers that hemmed in "woman's sphere" from public life, civil rights, and the socioeconomic prerogatives enjoyed by men; a more visible (because more criminalized and pathologized) homosexual subculture that muddied gender boundaries, finding "no definite place on either side of that incisive line which divides the race into two elemental parts" (thus Henry Blake Fuller, a closeted novelist-friend of James's[10]); a social universe beset by divorce, an alarming trend toward recreational sex, a falling birthrate among middle-class whites, triggering fears of "race suicide": all of these circumstances conspired to give a keen sense of urgency to propping up male privilege, sharpening up masculine self-definition, and firing up men's procreative zeal – making them "anxious to be fathers of families," in the words of Theodore Roosevelt's recruiting call.[11] To adapt the old labor anthem, the question of the day was: which side are you on, boys?

As Strether's habitual inferiority complex makes clear, this challenge to one's gender loyalties took on a distinctive accent on the American scene, where pledging allegiance to manhood demanded not only assuming the roles of husband and paterfamilias but proving oneself as "an immense man of business," like the late Abel Newsome of Woollett, or commanding a "large income" that could "look anyone in the face," like the commercial attorney Waymarsh (*A* 341, 31). Equally clearly, *The Ambassadors* amounts to a brief *against* this package deal as a dubious proposition for masculinity, while "business" itself, as Ross Posnock notes, serves as a sort of Jamesian shorthand for the "congealed status of the American male, whose submission to compulsory heterosexuality results in psychic dessication."[12] Indeed, the central opposition Strether must mediate in his embassy pits Old World charm and variety – figured by Madame de Vionnet – against "the special phase of civilization" represented by "the mercantile mandate" of Woollett and its homogenized drones, "all the Mr. Brookses and Mr. Snookses, gregarious specimens of a single type." Thus, saving Chad, in this novel of conversions, comes to mean saving him not for but from the American way – from being "compressed into the box" of bourgeois marriage and "the advertising-department," or merging into the "monotonous commonness" of "the pushing male crowd" (*N* 408, *A* 249).[13] That way madness lies,

James seems to say, or at the very least a poor choice between the social disfranchisement of a Jim Pocock (the real eunuch in the cast, as Strether eventually recognizes) or the "overwork, . . . prostration," and "strapped down" spirit of that model of manly "success," Waymarsh (A 30, 199).

Yet if *The Ambassadors* bears out John Carlos Rowe's observation that James's works "move relentlessly toward the perversity of family and marital relations,"[14] and if Posnock and others are right that James locates a particularly warped form of these relations at the heart of American capitalist culture, we still fall short of a full explanation of Strether's romantic (non)career. It is one thing, in other words, for Strether to fret about the fate of a "fair young man just growing up" under the cold penal paradigm of Woollettian business-manhood and consequently to take a "vicarious joy" ride in the vehicle of Chad's youthful freedom – a freedom whose highest expression seems to be a "virtuous attachment" to a woman who seems to be the antithesis of Woollett (A 61, 116, N 393). But when Chad himself elects for "advertising scientifically worked" and, in all probability, for life under the "blessed law" of American marital "symmetry," what justification does Strether have for continued noncompliance, especially since wedding Mrs. Newsome will not require him to "touch the business" any more than before (A 339, 391, 50)? Or say that the mere "fact of marriage," Woollett-style, puts a man socially "out of the question" irrespective of his vocation and that Strether refuses to forfeit his share in what James elsewhere calls the "numerous relations with the world . . . that are imputable to civilized being": what is to prevent an expatriate union with Maria Gostrey or a Paris-style compact with Marie de Vionnet (A 213, AS 345)? They are the ones, after all, who help him fashion an alternative status for the American male, their ministrations serving to lubricate his psyche and to teach him new arts of sociality, new fluencies of being.

To put a fine point on it: why was James so adamant that Strether's renovation, unlike Chad's, should have everything to do with women but "nothing to do with any bêtise of the . . . 'tempted' state," an incongruity compounded by the fact that (also by authorial decree) this belated-bildungsroman unfolds in the world capital of temptation: "it must be Paris . . . if he's an American" (AN 316, N 227)? Why did James promise a prospective publisher of the novel that Strether would "not in the least . . . [have] fallen in love" with Marie de Vionnet, whose graces were to "stiffen and harden" only his conviction of her mentorial value to Chad, and that he would not "do anything so vulgar" as "'take up'" with Maria Gostrey (N 395)?[15]

As suggested by references to the objectionable *bêtise* or "vulgarity" of supplying a sexual angle to Strether's evolution, one answer may lie in the longstanding view of his abstinence as an inscription of James's own squeamishness and fear of the female body. This general line of interpreting not only *The Ambassadors* but other writings can be traced from George Moore's early opinion that James "confesses himself on every page . . . a prude" to Geismar's acid comment that in the Jamesian universe "the worst crime, next to being poor, was to be sexual" to Ender's strongly theorized account of the "characteristic prudery" informing James's literary criticism.[16] The most specific statement of the case, however, comes from Carren Kaston, who treats James as virtually indistinguishable from Strether in his "distrust" of seductive women and "condescension" toward sex. On this reading, James's "fixed imagination" is no more prepared than his hero's to accommodate the daunting "vision of sexuality" embodied in Madame de Vionnet, who takes his self-protective moral categories by surprise and must finally be reassimilated to the type of the Bad Woman – "base, venal – out of the streets" – whom Strether first came seeking at the end of Chad's tether (*A* 45).[17]

Leaving aside how well these terms apply to Strether, they need to be enlarged to comprehend James and the gender-political workings of his favorite novel. It seems incontestable that, on one side of his complex being, James agreed with his old friend William Dean Howells – the influential American author and editor as well as, in a sense, the original of Strether – that sex was overrated as the engine of human behavior and that Anglo-American realism should ignore "the cant of the critics who require 'passion' as something in itself admirable" and, worse yet, who had "no conception of any passion but one."[18] James too, that is, was not above warning his fellow writers against imitating the excesses of French naturalism, which found an analogy to human life in "the monkey's cage," or lecturing them for constructing plots with "too great an implication of sexual motives" or characters with a "basely erotic preoccupation."[19] By the same token, he complimented them (and indirectly himself) for being "better psychologists" than the likes of Emile Zola, giving priority to the "subtler inward life, the wonderful adventures of the soul" over the gross life of externality and the superficial adventures of the body (*FW* 870, 483). According to this James, American and English readers were to be congratulated on their "great and . . . just dislike to the egotistic-erotic," for when an author such as Pierre Loti indulged in tales of romantic conquest – pursuing the ladies, as Strether might say, and advertising the results – "the last thing we take him for is a real man of action" (*FW* 494). Then, too, the real man of action in art – being a man as well as a temperate Anglo-American – knew better than to violate the canons of realism, as "the feminine . . . hand" typically did, by exaggerating the role of romance in making the world go round, assigning "the famous 'tender sentiment' . . . a place even greater . . . than that which it holds in life."[20] It is this Henry James whom Kaston rightly hears in *The Ambassadors*.

But as we discover in eavesdropping on Strether's consciousness as it gropes for the truth of Chad's affair, James was also aware of the extreme cultural relativism of attitudes toward sex and capable of (self-)irony in assessing America's "awkward tradition" with its "odious ascetic suspicion of . . . beauty," if less forgiving of its hypocrisies (N 410, A 118). As James said of the writings of Théophile Gautier – whom Strether, ironically, invokes as a *moral* guide during his early fantasy of Chad's degradation (A 67) – the French notion of beauty invariably referred to physical beauty, treating the body with "perfect frankness" and assuming *between* bodies a "full-blown sensuality in conduct" (FW 367). Our pilgrim from Woollett, on the other hand, comes burdened with a heritage that regards bodily passion warily, as a "soilure of the wits," in poet Edwin Arlington Robinson's words.[21] Strether is uncertain, for example, about the term for Maria Gostrey's "cut down" dress, showing the novelty of naked skin at home (A 42); and although he mentally recasts her as Mary Stuart, reputed for using "the [infinite] graces of her body" to undermine Queen Elizabeth (played by the severe Mrs. Newsome), the sexual substratum of his comparison remains unconscious (EL 1276).

Indeed James's sport in *The Ambassadors* is to suggest that if Paris did not exist, Woollett would have invented it – albeit from materials like that *Revue des Deux Mondes* in the Newsome parlor, which did not feature "phallic romances" full of "palpitating divans."[22] Even though Strether has read Maupassant, his puritan nippers have filtered out the substance, which testifies everywhere – in James's telling phrase – to "the empire of the sexual sense" (FW 528).[23] This cross-cultural dissonance inhabits the hero's very name, which derives from Balzac, long censored for his "fantastic explorations of man's carnal nature" (FW 43). In James's deadpan formulation: "Balzac had described many cities, but hadn't described Woollett Massachusetts" (A 24).

This side of James, like Thoreau in discussing Whitman,[24] chided "Anglo-Saxon readers" for pretending to be "scandalised" by functions of their own bodies and becoming "perversely preoccupied" with Zola's erotic preoccupations (FW 528, 880–1). This same James routinely lamented the Anglo-American novel's "immense amount of conventional blinking" in the matter of sex, sometimes blaming it on the mob of scribbling women who geared their work to an audience of "virgins and boys," and sometimes understanding how both such blinking and such blaming were self-serving maneuvers of patriarchal control. Wouldn't it be poetic justice, he wondered aloud, if this "most superstitiously closed" window in the house of fiction were smashed by "the female elbow" in the act of plying the pen (*FW* 540, *EL* 109)?

But to generalize: both Howells in his chagrin at the ascendant "study of exotic shivers and fervors"[25] and James in his more complicated stance on sex in literature were negotiating with an epochal change in the way that Western society explained itself to itself, from the macrolevel of social structure down to the microlevel of the individual life. This was the era, recall, in which the established science of biology, the upstart discipline of psychology (of which William James was the chief exponent in both America and England), and the more dubious offshoot of sexology (popularized by Havelock Ellis) collaborated as well as competed to explicate the "sexual instinct" as the germ of personality and the "sex drive" as the instrumental mechanism of community. This was also the era, not coincidentally, in which medico-juridical discourse (meaning medical authority in concert with statute and case law) sought new taxonomies for discriminating between "proper gentlemen" and dangerous "inverts" and new technologies for policing both – a regulatory environment in which key supporting roles went to journalists, scandalmongers, and literary censors (both official and self-appointed) who decided which fare nourished the growth of "healthy-minded men" but not that of politically ambitious "unsexed women" (a civic morality test failed, in England, by James's own *Italian Hours*).[26]

As Christopher Craft writes, summarizing the totalizing – if not always coherent – impulses of this sexological imperative: "By the late nineteenth century, . . . sex would not just signify, it would signify everywhere and everyhow; no domain of knowledge or feeling, no recess of culture or subjectivity, would be immune to its ramifying effects, its power of insinuation, its general and diffuse causality."[27] It will not do to say that the Victorians *invented* sex, of course; nor that they were the first to appreciate its shaping force or to employ it in drawing gender boundaries and formulating homophobic codes; nor, certainly, that they were the first to pressure men into paternity (go read Shakespeare's sonnets if you are in doubt). But in James's lifetime, both the political stakes and the ideological bearings of sex were systematically ratcheted up to an unprecedented degree, as "heterosexuality" graduated from an ancient practice without a professional nomenclature to a social-disciplinary category par excellence – in Gore Vidal's arch definition, "a weird concept of recent origin but terrible consequences."[28]

In this sense, Strether was present at the creation, and the "only logic" that governs (or perhaps covers) his exit from the text and thus from romantic possibility marks his departure from the script of masculinity just when that script was being suffused with a potent new logic of sexualized being (A 344). In reading *The Ambassadors,* that is, we must follow James's own advice to the would-be historical novelist and try to imagine "the old CONSCIOUSNESS . . . of individuals in whose minds half the things that make ours . . . were non-existent," including this overdetermined discourse of sexuality and its corresponding desiderata, if not dictates, for masculine performance. Not just James's but his entire generation's thinking was "intensely otherwise conditioned" from ours and, more importantly, was undergoing intense reconditioning of a sort that the novel subtly resists.[29] Against the advent of both Sigmund Freud and Teddy Roosevelt, so to speak, James sought to persuade his audience that "the real man of action" could qualify for that title without proving his manhood in a Parisian boudoir or a Woollett bedroom, because "action" could qualify for *that* name in other venues, even in the privacy of one's imagination. In a world where manliness increasingly certified itself by outwardness, Strether's process of becoming "changed and queer" is pointedly one of "quiet inwardness," occurring "deep down" and resulting in what Emily Dickinson called "internal difference, / Where the Meanings, are" – a traditionally feminized space and drama that should not, however, be reserved for women (A 209, 277).[30] By extension, James begged to differ that adventure was not a uniform but an "equivocal quantity" – not the exclusive property of "detectives or pirates or other splendid desperadoes" whose (s)exploits were overt and noisy, but a field that was also open to "the spirit engaged with . . . forces of violence" invisible to the untrained eye, including the operations of gender normativity in both the culture outside and the psyche within (AN 313). In Strether's case, then, Adrienne Rich's now-canonical phrase deserves another turn of the screw, for *The Ambassadors* enters a caveat against compulsory sexuality as such, whether hetero-, homo-, or otherwise.

None of the foregoing is meant to suggest that the novel's gender-political resistance is strictly intentional, or even completely conscious, or that it expresses itself except by dramatic projection. As James playfully responded when Hugh Walpole asked him to expand on the thematic statement of *The Ambassadors,* "How can you say I do anything so foul and abject as to 'state'?"[31] On the contrary, James's disposition to contest the new order of things is profoundly a predisposition already evident in the notebook jottings, inscribed in the germinal idea of the novel: it is a given that Strether will "not in the least" be carnally tempted or fall in love. As with James's "characteristic prudery," this organic structuring of character and plot may be rerouted through biography and seen as the instinctive posture of a celibate "hardened bachelor" whose family and friends spent years coaxing him toward "some conjugal Elizabeth or other" (in Henry Senior's offhand phrase).[32] But consider that the same intonations we now hear as prudish or anxious can also chime as "characteristic" in a larger sense, not only personally but *culturally* expressive of a superseded view of "romantic" options apart from the scene of sexuality. Perhaps it is not so idiosyncratic, in other words, when James defends Strether's famous renunciation of marital opportunities in terms of psychological realism – "the mark of the real never ceases to show in him, and with the real only the real [of representation] consorts" (N 414) – and does so every bit as confidently as later critics who rebuke him for defying gender-role "reality" ("one of the few words which mean nothing without quotes," as Nabokov slyly noted[33]). James's self-assurance should remind us that an earlier age might not have assumed Marie de Vionnet to be the "unarguable romantic relation of [Strether's] life"[34] but might have taken at face value the author's conceit that she "gratifies some more . . . disinterested, aesthetic, intellectual, social . . . sense" in him, stimulating not a sexual shudder but a *frisson historique* (N 392).

But we have contemporary reception of *The Ambassadors* to remind us, too – indeed, to situate Strether as teetering just on the cusp of a new century in which "passion" reduces to "sex" (as Howells had feared) and "'to live' . . . in essence means to live sexually" (as Peter Brooks glosses the novel's big speech).[35] Notably, for every reviewer who cavilled at Strether's "typical thinness of . . . passion," another appreciated his friendship with Maria Gostrey as an exceptional instance of "love at first sight." For every reader who complained that "passion is hardly recognisable through [the] envelopment" of James's style or objected to the interiority of the narrative action, another found Strether's adventures had "a vastly keener poignancy than if they were translated . . . into terms of duels and elopements." And a surprising number of reviewers believed both James and Strether to be operating from "the fulness of experience," and the novel itself to be rendering, if "not precisely life," then "an extremely fascinating . . . analogy." In this respect, critics who subsequently mobilized a humanist vocabulary to disparage the "sensations, passions or pleasure" celebrated in the novel are guilty not only of normative hubris but of a misleading anachronism as well.[36]

How to account, then, for Strether's persistent "envy" of other men? To pose him as the avuncular, only mildly rueful Bartleby of this brave new world of sex ("I'd prefer not to") may seem contradicted by his continual desiring of this man's art and that man's scope. Admittedly, much of this yearning turns on his poor showing on the job market and his dependence on Mrs. Newsome's pursestrings, reemphasizing the composite profile of manly "success"; yet much evidently turns on his shortcomings as a lover, reemphasizing the ascendancy of heterosexual prowess within that profile. But note how modulated Strether's envy is: it is fleeting with respect to that tawny beast in the jungle, Gloriani, a moment's "absurdity" greeted with "depths of critical reserve" by Bilham. It is more animated, to be sure, where the object is "that rare youth" Chad, but only because Strether's "almost envious vision" of his "romantic privilege" has another kind of romance in mind, shrouding the sexual subtext – the "prime producing cause" – of Chad's "famous knowing how to live" (A 133, 65, 102, 312). As for Waymarsh, his "actual adventure[s]" with Miss Barrace and Sarah Pocock – jouncing about in carriages, smothered in flowers – seem merely to reference a chapter neglected in Strether's sentimental education, which missed "the time natural in Boston for taking girls to the Museum" (A 110, 43). Each of these episodes reveals female companionship as something missed in his "general genius for missing [things]," but by the same token, each shows the *texture* of such companionship to be more soft and sociable than anything else: kaffeeklatsching, kibbitzing, sharing Chad's "excellent cigarettes" (A 269, 78). In this regard, Georges-Michel Sarotte was both right and wrong to see Strether's relations with women – including the far-off marriage of his youth – as nominal "tribute[s] to heterosexuality," for while they hover beyond the margins of "actual" romance, they are nonetheless occasions of deep heterosocial pleasure.[37]

Instructively, the gate of Strether's envy swings both ways, as his spectatorship at the "fine free range of bliss and bale" betokened in Madame de Vionnet's "abysmal" passion produces a "vague inward irony" at his own expense (A 323). But the point remains that such an identification, like his response to the spectacle of Chad's "massive young manhood," betrays naive awe – and possibly a homoerotic inflection – more than an active emulative impulse, going no farther than the vague impression of "some sense of power, oddly perverted; something latent and beyond access, ominous and perhaps enviable" (A 99). Perhaps enviable? Almost envious? Only "akin to envy" (A 268)? These questions are not meant to accuse James of (hetero) textual feinting, as Leslie Fiedler does, but to suggest, again, how qualified

Strether's registrations of envy are, and that we must seek elsewhere for a more persuasive manifestation of that emotion.

Partly because Little Bilham serves so unassumingly as *Chad's* ambassador and partly because, to Strether's infatuated eye, he stands in Chad's shadow, it is easy to overlook how the "little artist-man," too, is a focus of envy, forming, in fact, a more plausible youthful alter ego for our hero: "life can hold nothing better" than the term of his life in Paris (*A* 74). The vital difference lies in Bilham's blithe *acceptance* of his own negligibility, his capacity for dodging the standard criteria of manhood and "being contentedly just the obscure and acute little Bilham he [is]," while Strether is "still in search of something that would work" – some identity that is not a "specious shell" for his own deepest needs (*A* 256, 63). Indeed Strether wonders how the young expatriate appears "more American than anybody" when his mode of being "intense" deviates so from the usual intensities. Bilham's occupation is "only an occupation declined" and declined without "alarm, anxiety or remorse," as if he is immune to the inner promptings of the protestant work ethic and the outer pressures of the cult of manly achievement. Like some prodigy of the James family, in which (by Henry's account) "no good word" was ever spoken on behalf of "success – in the sense that was in the general air,"[38] Bilham "isn't a bit ashamed" of his utter indifference to the expectation that he buckle down and "do something" (*A* 83–4).

But most importantly, Bilham's "serenity" extends to his conduct as a suitor, though being "'notoriously' . . . not from Boston," he has reasons for romantic reluctance other than Strether's (*A* 73). Eve Kosofsky Sedgwick sees Little Bilham as "closely related" to another Left Bank artist-figure, Little Billee of George Du Maurier's *Trilby* (1894), who shares not only Bilham's diminutive physique but also his "sexual anesthesia" and his subservience to more virile embodiments like Chad.[39] It would be a stretch to attribute homosexual panic (or any other agitation) to Bilham, and yet his lifestyle of "small sublime . . . independences," in which Strether finds an "odd and engaging dignity," is disjoined from conventional romance (*A* 84). When Strether coaxes him to pursue Jeanne de Vionnet, Bilham replies that only "some great golden sun" could open her "pale pink petals," whereas he is "but a small farthing candle" – a figure that conflates his social and financial inadequacy with his limited sexual enthusiasm. When Strether proposes Mamie Pocock instead, Bilham gazes at the prospect "as a delicate appetite stares at an overheaped plate" (*A* 164, 258). For his own part, Strether may seem to proffer Bilham as a sacrifice to the household gods of Woollett, a proof of his "fidelity" to homestyle heterosexuality, but by the time he packs the young pair off to Switzerland, he is well beyond that "blessed law": "it won't matter a grain" if Mamie and Bilham do not marry (A 291).

Viewed from the unusual angle of vision that James encourages, then, the same attributes that make Strether a failure "as men go" make him the perfect bearer of the novel's argument, its necessarily gentle dissent from uniform masculinity and compulsory sexuality: one doesn't thumb the nose at such a big bully as that, particularly when the project is to get over being a typical man. The rhetorical masterstroke of *The Ambassadors*, that is, lay in hitting upon just this exemplar of male "abnormality" – this endearingly "absurd" Lambert Strether – whose details of personal history and contours of character accomplish such a careful balance. He is too distracted by vocational incoherence to have "battled with his passions" (note the plural), yet possessed of *different* passions that regerminate under the right conditions of cultivation in Europe. He is too old to be invested with replete romantic potencies, yet not too old "to be a source of excitement" to three women who wish to invest in *him*. He is too "awkward" in body matters to know the "fun" of carnality but ultimately less amazed at a world of sexual possibility than at his own "labour" of imagination in "dress[ing] the possibility in vagueness," as a girl muffles her doll's nakedness (N 226, 414; A 313). It is not too much to say that in post-Puritanism itself, James located not only a naturalistic explanation for the Stretherness of Strether, but a readily available ulterior discourse that could serve as a staging ground against the gathered forces of heteronormativity, as well as a probable draw for the reader's cultural nostalgia. Consolidating these narrative coups is James's skill in showing how the very forces against which Strether must eventually define his alterity have made themselves at home within his own (double) consciousness. What Strether himself counts as ridiculous defects – even his penchant for seeing New Englandly – are gradually, seductively inverted to become virtues, the novel making "the manner of Woollett a lovable thing again" in its fund of "true inwardness" (A 251).

Thus the conclusion of *The Ambassadors* finds Strether quite literally in quest of new premises for his masculinity, and its unstated moral would seem to be that the social price of freedom from the new sexual diktat – of an "unaffiliated, uncompromised manhood," in Leland S. Person's terms[40] – is to discover oneself suddenly an unaccommodated man. In retrospect, the fundamental inhospitality of heterosexual culture to a man of Strether's (re)construction, whatever its provisional amenities, has been emblematized throughout the book, from his own Parisian quarters – "all indoor chill" and exuding the "dour presence of Waymarsh" – to Maria Gostrey's cluttered "fireside," where Strether's "fear of . . . misappliance" and lack of "real harmony" with his surroundings have clear symbolic import (A 70, 80, 341). It is no accident, in this context, that the abode which comes nearest to Strether's ideal is Chad's, with its "perched privacy," its vista on cosmopolitan life, its "soft circle" of bachelor domesticity and revery – a space of "super-sensual" delights infused with the taste of femininity ("the place . . . was full of [Marie de Vionnet's] influence") but resolutely discontinuous from romantic liaison or marital attachment (A 70, 281, N 393, 335).

Yet such a habitat is ideal, too good to be true, and that is just the point. It is a testimonial to James's analytical acumen and integrity that his hero must sustain his quest on native ground, in America, where social realities both formative and formidable abide, as if to say that Strether will need to find his new premises not in utopia, "But in the very world which is the world / Of all of us, the place in which, in the end, / We find our happiness, or not at all."[41] In this register, Strether's determination "not, out of the whole affair, to have got anything for myself" figures as a bid to buy out of the heightened heterosexual economy of modernity – to proclaim his disinterestedness (a concept valorized by its recurrence in the novel) and to get precisely himself out of the bargain (A 201, 253). The horror informing Strether's "horrible sharp eye" – of James's, which comes to the same thing – resides just in the tough terms and thorough cultural penetration of this economy, and the "sharpness," in the insight that freedom from the sexual imperative is purchased at a high cost and yet never fully free. "It's you who would make me wrong," Strether tells Maria Gostrey, who represents his last chance at a stake in "normal" passions and pleasures, and on his own, equally rigorous terms, Strether is right. But after such rightness, one might ask, what forgiveness (A 344–5)?

Whether James manages, in the end, to generate "romantic sympathy" on behalf of his unconventional hero and to confer "the grace of intensity" upon Lambert Strether's experience rests not in the keen eye of author or character, but in the eye of the individual beholder, or reader (N 374, AN 318). It may well be that, in the view of the "happily and hatefully young," Strether's repudiation of sexual in favor of "moral glamour" holds small attraction, but bear in mind that his ringing charge to Little Bilham, in its glorious vagueness, leaves room for all sorts of excellent adventures (A 132, 64). In the same spirit, here is a final suggestion, as genially intended as Strether's to his young friend: if *The Ambassadors* does not speak to you just now, return to it later in life and give it another go. You will be pleasantly surprised. In the meantime, live all you can: it's a mistake not to.

NOTES

1 *The Notebooks of Henry James,* ed. F. O. Matthiessen and Kenneth B. Murdock (New York: George Braziller, 1955), pp. 182–3; hereafter cited as N.

2 Maxwell Geismar, *Henry James and the Jacobites* (Boston: Houghton Mifflin, 1963), p. 266.

3 Henry James, *The Ambassadors,* ed. S. P. Rosenbaum (New York: Norton, 1964), p. 132; hereafter cited as A; *The Art of the Novel : Critical Prefaces* (New York: Charles Scribner's Sons, 1934), p. 307; hereafter cited as AN.

4 Evelyne Ender, *Sexing the Mind: Nineteenth-Century Fictions of Hysteria* (Ithaca and London: Cornell University Press, 1995), p. 3.

5 Geismar, *Henry James and the Jacobites,* p. 8.

6 Respectively: Edward Garnett [rev. of *The Ambassadors*], Speaker [England] new series 9 (14 November 1903), 146–7, in *Henry James: The Contemporary Reviews,* ed. Kevin J. Hayes (Cambridge University Press, 1996), p. 400; E. M. Forster, *Aspects of the Novel, and Related Writings* (London: Edward Arnold, 1974), p. 111; Richard Chase, "James' *Ambassadors,*" in *Twelve Original Essays on Great American Novels,* ed. Charles Shapiro (Detroit: Wayne State University Press, 1958), p. 136; Laurence B. Holland, *The Expense of Vision: Essays on the Craft of Henry James* (Baltimore and London: The Johns Hopkins University Press, 1964, 1982), p. 281; Leslie A. Fiedler, *Love and Death in the American Novel* (New York: Stein and Day, 1960, rev. ed., 1966/1975), p. 307 ("we are told [Strether] has been married before, has a son, but we do not believe it"); Kaja Silverman, *Male Subjectivity at the Margins* (New York & London: Routledge, 1992), p. 166.

7 Geismar, *Henry James and the Jacobites,* p. 278.

8 Richard Poirier, *A World Elsewhere: The Place of Style in American Literature* (London: Chatto and Windus, 1967), p. 143.

9 Thomas Laqueur, *Making Sex: Body and Gender from the Greeks to Freud* (Cambridge: Harvard University Press, 1990), pp. 5, 240.

10 See Kenneth Scambray, *A Varied Harvest: The Life and Works of Henry Blake Fuller* (Pittsburgh: University of Pittsburgh Press, 1987), p. 24.

11 Roosevelt quoted in Gail Bederman, *Manliness & Civilization: A Cultural History of Gender and Race in the United States, 1880–1917* (Chicago and London: University of Chicago Press, 1995), p. 202. The rubric in England was "race degeneracy"; see Samuel Hynes, *The Edwardian Turn of Mind* (London: Pimlico, 1968), ch. 8, "The Organization of Morality."

12 Ross Posnock, *The Trial of Curiosity: Henry James, William James, and the Challenge of Modernity* (New York, Oxford: Oxford University Press, 1991), p. 204.

13 Henry James, *The American Scene,* ed. W. H. Auden (New York: Charles Scribner's Sons, 1946), p. 83; hereafter cited as AS.

14 John Carlos Rowe, *The Theoretical Dimensions of Henry James* (Madison: University of Wisconsin Press, 1984), p. 89.

15 Alan W. Bellringer infers from Madame de Vionnet's expressions of gratitude to Strether that "an offer of physical recompense was on the cards"; *The Ambassadors* (London: George Allen & Unwin, 1984), p. 127. Similarly, Poirier hears

tones of sexual availability in Maria Gostrey's confession that Strether makes her "distinctly restless"; *A World Elsewhere*, p. 141.

16 George Moore, *Confessions of a Young Man*, ed. Susan Dick (Montreal and London: McGill-Queen's University Press, 1972), p. 211; Geismar, *Henry James and the Jacobites*, p. 6; Ender, *Sexing the Mind*, p. 87.

17 Carren Kaston, *Imagination and Desire in the Novels of Henry James* (New Brunswick, N.J.: Rutgers University Press, 1984), pp. 102–3, 106–7.

18 William Dean Howells, "Sex in Literature" [1889], in *W. D. Howells as Critic*, ed. Edwin H. Cady (London and Boston: Routledge & Kegan Paul, 1973), p. 153.

19 Henry James, *Literary Criticism: French Writers, Other European Writers, the Prefaces to the New York Edition* (New York: Library of America, 1984), p. 528; hereafter cited as *FW*. Henry James, *Selected Letters*, ed. Leon Edel (Garden City, N.Y.: Anchor/Doubleday, 1960), p. 202.

20 Henry James, *Literary Criticism: Essays on Literature, American Writers, English Writers* (New York: Library of America, 1984), p. 646; hereafter cited as *EL*. Essential to contextualizing Strether's stance toward what even the liberal American clergy termed the "degrading worship" of "aesthetic Paganism" is Jonathan Freedman's *Professions of Taste: Henry James, British Aestheticism, and Commodity Culture* (Stanford, Calif.: Stanford University Press, 1990), ch. 2.

21 Edwin Arlington Robinson, "New England," *Selected Poems of Edwin Arlington Robinson*, ed. Morton Dauwen Zabel (London: Collier-Macmillan, 1966), pp. 221–2.

22 The phrases come, respectively, from James's friends John Hay and Howells. In this 1881 letter to Howells, Hay cites as the main purveyors of this moral "rottenness" and "infection" Balzac and Alphonse Daudet, two of James's favorite authors. See W. D. Howells, *Selected Letters: Volume 3: 1882–1891*, ed. Robert C. Leitz III, Richard H. Ballinger, and Christoph K. Lohmann (Boston: Twayne, 1980), pp. 12–14.

23 Again it is James's fun, at his hero's expense, to make this point as the "deep truth of intimacy" behind Chad's fictionalizing is about to emerge; the "whole episode" of the Lambinet scene reminds Strether of Maupassant in its impressionism (*A* 343), but James knows that the "sexual impulse . . . is the wire that moves almost all M. de Maupassant's puppets" (*FW* 530).

24 Henry David Thoreau, "Letter to H. G. O. Blake," in *The Harper American Literature*, ed. Donald McQuade et al. (New York: HarperCollins, 1994), vol. 1, p. 1361 : "Walt Whitman can communicate to us no experience, and if we are shocked, whose experience is it that we are reminded of?"

25 Howells, "Sex in Literature," p. 151.

26 For background, see Richard Dellamora, *Masculine Desire: The Sexual Politics of Victorian Aestheticism* (Chapel Hill and London: University of North Carolina Press, 1990) and Jeffrey Weeks, *Sexuality and Its Discontents: Meanings, Myths & Modern Sexualities* (London: Routledge & Kegan Paul, 1985). On the apparent instance of suppression of *Italian Hours* in 1909, see Hynes, *The Edwardian Turn of Mind*, pp. 301–2. In England, the newly theorized "sexual instinct" was also known as the "racial instinct," meaning the dominant-group motive of self-preservation, of course.

27 Christopher Craft, *Another Kind of Love: Male Homosexual Desire in English Discourse, 1850–1920* (Berkeley: University of California Press, 1994), pp. 27–8. The view that "sex explains it all" is of course famously addressed in Hemingway's *The Sun Also Rises,* notably in a passage that speculates on James's sexual (in)capacity (New York: Charles Scribner's Sons, *c.* 1926), pp. 115–16.

28 Gore Vidal, "Foreword," Jonathan Katz, *The Invention of Heterosexuality* (New York: Dutton, 1995), p. ii.

29 Henry James, *Letters: Volume IV, 1895–1916,* ed. Leon Edel (Cambridge, Mass.: Harvard University Press, 1984), p. 208.

30 Emily Dickinson, #258, in *The Complete Poems of Emily Dickinson,* ed. Thomas H. Johnson (Boston: Little, Brown, 1960), p. 118.

31 *The Letters of Henry James : Volume II,* ed. Percy Lubbock (New York: Charles Scribner's Sons, 1920), p. 245.

32 Henry James, *Letters: Volume III, 1883–1895,* ed. Leon Edel (Cambridge, Mass.: Harvard University Press, 1980), p. 17: "What strikes me most . . . is the want of application on the part of society of the useful, beneficent, civilizing part played in it by the occasional unmarried man of a certain age. He keeps up the tone of humanity." Henry James, Sr., quoted in Daniel Aaron, *The Unwritten War: American Writers and the Civil War* (Madison: University of Wisconsin Press, 1973/1987), p. 109. As James's admirer Marianne Moore wrote, very much in the spirit of *The Ambassadors,* the cultural prejudice in favor of marriage is such that it "requir[es] all one's criminal ingenuity / to avoid!"; "Marriage," in *The Complete Poems of Marianne Moore* (New York: Macmillan/Viking, 1967), p. 62.

33 Vladimir Nabokov, "On a Book Entitled Lolita," in *The Annotated Lolita,* ed. Alfred Appel, Jr. (New York: Random/Vintage, 1991), p. 312.

34 Kaston, *Imagination and Desire,* p. 106.

35 Peter Brooks, *Body Work: Objects of Desire in Modern Narrative* (Cambridge, Mass.: Harvard University Press, 1993), p. 114.

36 Quotations from *Henry James: The Contemporary Reviews,* pp. 392–4.

37 Georges-Michel Sarotte, *Like a Brother, Like a Lover: Male Homosexuality in the American Novel and Theater from Herman Melville to James Baldwin* (Garden City, N.Y.: Anchor/Doubleday, 1978), p. 203.

38 Henry James, *Autobiography,* ed. Frederick W. Dupee (Princeton, N.J.: Princeton University Press, 1983), p. 123.

39 Eve Kosofsky Sedgwick, *Epistemology of the Closet* (Berkeley: University of California Press, 1990), p. 194.

40 Leland S. Person, Jr., "Henry James, George Sand, and the Suspense of Masculinity," *PMLA* 106, no. 3 (May 1991), p. 525.

41 William Wordsworth, *The Prelude: 1799, 1805, 1850,* ed. Jonathan Wordsworth et al. (New York: Norton, 1979), p. 398.

10

WILLIAM STOWE

James's Elusive *Wings*

I have read *The Wings of the Dove* (for which all thanks!) but what shall I say of a book constructed on a method which so belies everything that *I* acknowledge as law? You've reversed every traditional canon of story-telling (especially the fundamental one of *telling* the story, which you carefully avoid) and have created a new *genre littéraire* which I can't help thinking perverse, but in which you nevertheless *succeed,* for I read with interest to the end (many pages, and innumerable sentences twice over to see what the dickens they could possibly mean) and all with unflagging curiosity to know what the upshot might become. It's very *distingué* in its way, there are touches unique and inimitable, but it's a "rum" way; and the worst of it is that I don't know whether it's fatal and inevitable with you, or deliberate and possible to put off and on.

William James (cited in Matthiessen, 338)

This is, we repeat, an extraordinarily interesting performance, but it is not an easy book to read. It will not do for short railway journeys or for drowsy hammocks, or even to amuse sporting men and the active Young Person. The dense, fine quality of its pages – and there are 576 – will always presuppose a certain effort of attention on the part of the reader; who must, indeed, be prepared to forgo many of his customary titillations and bribes.

Anonymous (*Times Literary Supplement,* 1902)

"He gives you a sense of a tremendous lot going on, for instance, in *The Wings of a Dove* [sic], of things undeniably, though not unmistakably, happening. It is a great book."
   "It is, it is," she sighed again. "It wore me to a thread. . . . My husband and I read the story aloud together, and I wanted to weep. We had such a strange experience with that book. We read it half through together; then we got impatient, and tried to finish it alone. But we could not make anything of it apart; and we had to finish it together. We could not bear to lose a word; every word – and there were a good many! – seemed to tell. If you took one away you seemed to miss something important. It almost destroyed me,

thinking it all out. I went round days, with my hand to my forehead; and I don't believe I understand it perfectly yet. Do you?"

William Dean Howells (487)

"Perverse," but successful; "*distingué*" in a "rum" sort of way; "interesting" but "not easy"; "a great book" but "a strange experience." *The Wings of the Dove* is a contradictory text. It tells the rather sordid, arguably banal, definitely melodramatic story of a well-connected but penniless young Englishwoman, Kate Croy, who encourages her secret fiancé, Merton Densher, to pretend to fall in love with a wealthy, mortally stricken American heiress, Milly Theale, perhaps even to marry her, but in any case to put himself in a position to inherit, on her inevitable demise, some portion of her fabulous riches. Or rather, it tells some of the story. The young man's most important interviews with the two young women take place between chapters; the crucial communication from the dying American is thrown into the fire before anyone finds out what it says; the novel ends before its story is concluded.[1] Despite its melodramatic plot, furthermore, the book's language is notoriously difficult, sometimes even undecidably obscure: sentences wind interminably on,[2] pronouns lack definite antecedents,[3] characters use words like "everything" and "nothing" and phrases like "Well, there you are," which simultaneously suggest and obscure meanings and conclusions that they may or may not have reached.

The Wings of the Dove is a direct descendant of such great works of nineteenth-century melodramatic "realism" as Balzac's *La Cousine Bette* (see Stowe, 130–1; Brooks, 180). It is also, however, a direct progenitor of literary modernism and postmodernism, providing a preview of the worlds of J. Alfred Prufrock and Hugh Selwyn Mauberley and a foretaste of what Allon White (1–2) describes as the willful obscurity of the modernists, and anticipating the playful elusiveness, the joyful *différance* of postmodern theory and fiction (see Bradbury, 82–3, and Rowe, 172) as well as the evasive anti-authoritarianism of *écriture féminine* (see Walton, 120–40). It shares features of what Roland Barthes called the "text of pleasure: the text that contents, fills, grants euphoria; the text that comes from culture and does not break from it, [and] is linked to a *comfortable* practice of reading" and the "text of bliss: the text that imposes a state of loss, the text that discomforts (perhaps to the extent of a certain boredom), unsettles the reader's historical, cultural, psychological assumptions, the consistency of his tastes, values, memories, brings to a crisis his relation to language" (Barthes 1975, 14). It is, in other words, a strange hybrid, a work that can be illuminatingly described in traditional humanistic terms as a moral or spiritual fable and in contemporary theoretical terms as a radically elusive text that entices the reader into an unendable process of supplementation and (over-)reading. In what follows I consider this hybridity as an essential element of the work's moral and textual projects, and as a symptom of its author's paradoxically central and marginal position in literary and cultural history. I begin by showing in some detail how James presents two of the novel's central actions – Milly's fateful interview with her London physician and Merton's final conversation with Kate – in passages that are both overtly melodramatic and textually evasive. I will also be suggesting that this insistent doubleness is both an indication of a turning point in the stylistic history of prose fiction and a symptom of James's uneasy position as an artist and a professional at the turn of the century.

Milly treats her meeting with Sir Luke Strett ("the greatest of medical lights . . . the right, the special man," 140–1) as a highly significant moment in her personal history, an occasion for unaccustomed secrecy and deception, and a moment of melodramatic revelation. She keeps her appointment alone, "putting her friend off with a fraud, giving a pretext of shops, of a whim, of she didn't know what" (147), braving the London streets for the first time "without a companion or a maid" (147). She has come to learn her "doom." Having been "found out about," she is now ready to be "let down." Her very life has been "put into the scales," she thinks, and she is about to hear the fateful reading of the balance (146). By the end of the sequence she acts as if she has heard it, asking the doctor what she can do and inquiring about the prognosis of her illness.

> "Shall I at any rate suffer?"
> "Not a bit."
> "And yet then live?"
> "My dear young lady," said her distinguished friend, "isn't to 'live' exactly what I'm trying to persuade you to take the trouble to do?" (151)

The events that this passage describes constitute a crucial moment in a familiarly melodramatic text of pleasure, the moment in which the heroine acquires that essential knowledge of her condition on which all of her future actions must be based. Any humanistic, moral interpretation of the novel must assume that Milly has this knowledge.[4] Any judgment of her future actions, any interpretation of the dynamics of James's story as a "psychologically" "realistic" depiction of plausible human behavior, depends upon it. In the very next chapter she behaves as if she had it, acting for an hour or two as much like Lear's "unaccommodated man" as any of James's hypercivilized urbanites ever does, wandering through neighborhoods she rather appallingly (see Freedman, 218) "hoped were slums," describing herself as "a poor girl – with her rent to pay for example" (155), and contemplating the fact that "she had been treated – hadn't she? – as if it were in her power to live; and yet one wasn't treated so – was one? – unless it had come up, quite as much, that one might die?" (152).

And yet James nowhere shows Milly learning anything. Every reference to what Sir Luke and Milly actually *know* is terminally vague. Her physical examination is described in terms that are at once outlandish and imprecise: "After much interrogation, auscultation, exploration, much noting of his own sequences and neglecting of hers, had duly kept up the vagueness, they might have struck themselves, or may at least strike us, as coming back from an undeterred but useless voyage to the North Pole" (150). She is convinced that "he had found out simply by his genius . . . literally everything" (145), but we never learn what "everything" *is*. Before *he* tells *her* anything, *she* tells *him* that "nobody can really help" (148), but she never says help *what*. Before he (presumably) discloses his diagnosis (which the reader never hears) she discerns that he is "interested on her behalf in other questions beside the question of what was the matter with her," takes this interest as a sign of pity, and infers from what she takes to be his pity that she is in a pitiable state. Having made this inference, she is ready to hear the worst news he can give her, but she hears, instead, nothing. "He might say what he would now, in fact from this moment she only wanted him to say what he would" (148), but he says nothing. They exchange a glance, "a sign of the eyes only" (148), with no explicit content either for themselves or for the reader, and their communication is taken to be complete. After this, their conversation remains oblique, but there is the sense, just the sense, that their pronouns and their references have common if unstated antecedents. When she agrees at the end of their conversation to "accept any form in which happiness may come" (149), says she has already accepted many, and ends, enigmatically, "Now *this!*" (149), the *this* must refer both to her friendship with Sir Luke ("Now I am accepting *this*") and to her illness ("Now *this* is visited upon me"). When he says a moment later "Don't mind who knows," the implied predicate "how sick you are" remains, even when he goes on to say "Knows, I mean, that you and I are friends" (149).

Milly's solitary visit to Sir Luke is made possible by a lie. Her interview with the great man in conducted, or at least reported, in the most intense and

yet the vaguest of terms, so that any understanding it conveys is both crucially, mortally important and totally inexplicit. In addition to this more or
less overt evasiveness, meaning in this passage is both embodied in and obscured by metaphor. Milly's assessment of her condition is based on what she
takes to be Sir Luke's "pity" for her, but her perception of this pity is as resistant to easy interpretation as Macbeth's much-discussed "pity, like a
naked new-born babe, / Striding the blast" (1.7. 21–22).

> Wanting to know more about a patient than how a patient was constructed or
> deranged couldn't be, even on the part of the greatest of doctors, anything but
> some form or other of the desire to let the patient down easily. When that was
> the case, the reason, in turn, could only be, too manifestly, pity; and when pity
> held up its telltale face like a head on a pike, in a French revolution, bobbing
> before a window, what was the inference but that the patient was bad?
>
> (148)

Milly reads Sir Luke's ostensibly benevolent gaze as a kind of mask, the "telltale face" of some conventional and distant pity, a mask that paradoxically
reveals her concerned physician as both a tattler (a tale-teller) and a mute
clue (a telltale sign) to her condition. Before the sentence is over, furthermore,
Sir Luke's expression of concern has become a grisly taunt and a threat, the
face of pity has been attached to a severed head impaled on a pike as by a
French revolutionary and thrust up to the level of a presumably aristocratic
window as a sign of doom to those within. The motivation for this figure is
difficult to make out. Milly is a besieged princess in a romance, an American heiress with an unnamed life-threatening disease, and a poor girl with
her rent to pay. She is surrounded, as her fate becomes evident, by pitying
"friends," most of whom want to use her in some way for their own benefit, some of whom might well appear grotesque to the poor sufferer, but none
of whom has very much in common with a French revolutionary. Her striking simile can be unpacked up to a certain point, after which interpretation
can only shade off into speculation, revealing more about James's psychological and cultural baggage than about his specific intentions in this passage.[5]

Figurative language expands the suggestiveness of James's text without
making its meaning any more explicit. The "revolutionary" register is highly melodramatic, but the explicit meaning of the revolutionary image is impossible to pin down. The same can be said for the passage's allusions, both
to earlier moments in the novel and to other texts. Milly in Sir Luke's "com-
modious 'handsome'" consulting room (the "handsome" reminds us of her

newest friend and most dangerous enemy, "the handsome girl" [22, 99, et passim]) is like Milly at the Brünig Pass, perched for a view of her prospects, confronted by some version of "abysmal" (79) emptiness – a gulf of air, the "general wreck" in which her whole family has disappeared (149) – which is at the same time a vision of ideal and unlimited freedom (79, 150). She is in both passages a Miltonic figure, like the Christ of *Paradise Regained,* being shown the "kingdoms of the world,"[6] or like Eve at the end of *Paradise Lost,* with the world "all before her" (*Wings,* 87).[7] Like Milly's metaphorical reference to the French Revolution, however, James's Miltonic allusions are direct, literal, but more suggestive than definitive of meaning: Milly is most definitely a mortal woman, like Eve, but she hasn't tempted her partner to break divine law, nor does she seem doomed to live by the sweat of her brow all her days. We are led not only by this passage but by her repeated characterization as a dove and by her long-distance blessing of Densher, timed for Christmas Eve, to associate Milly with both Christ and the Holy Spirit, but we are not sure even at the end of the book how effective her gesture will have been, or whom if anyone she will have redeemed from what.

On one level, James's description of Milly's visit to Sir Luke Strett can be made to fit to fit Barthes's characterizations of the classic novelistic text. Like the "text of pleasure" or the "readerly text," it initiates actions and shows how they turn out, raises questions and either answers them or artfully defers their answers. An anxious patient contrives to visit her doctor alone, receives bad news and a promise of help, and goes out to contemplate her changed prospects on an unaccustomed solitary walk through the city. Previously raised questions are answered, at least by implication: How sick is Milly? Gravely sick. Other questions are raised, presumably to be answered as we read on: Will she live? How will she carry out Sir Luke's injunction, precisely *to* "live"? Like Balzac's *Sarrasine* in Barthes's classic analysis, the passage also alludes to common cultural practice (the doctor's visit), helps characterize a literary voice (Milly as center of consciousness for James's indirect discourse), and suggests wider ramifications through the use of symbols (Barthes 1970, 25–7). Described in this way, James's text seems perfectly conventional and the devices he uses to capture and hold the reader's attention seem identical to those employed by traditional romancers and melodramatists.

On another level, however, James's text blocks the reader's access to these conventional sequences, making "reading for the plot" a terribly frustrating, for some readers a tedious and numbing, experience, tempting them, as Ruth Yeazell puts it, "to approach the late James as if his language were a beautiful and mysterious screen placed between us and the moral facts of the novels" (Yeazell, 13–14). This is a temptation to be resisted. *The Wings of the Dove* may not *be* a "text of bliss," indeed, there may be no such thing as a text of bliss in its purest state, but it certainly invites the kind of reading that "imposes a state of loss," "discomforts (perhaps to the point of a certain boredom), unsettles the reader's historical, cultural, psychological assumptions," and brings to a certain "crisis his relation with language" (Barthes 1975, 14). Instead of seeing it as a literary "product," more or less fit to be consumed, we should perhaps see it as a challenge to read more actively, as Mary Cross suggests (139) or, as Barthes has it, to *write* as we read, to make our own text ("le texte scriptible, c'est nous en train d'écrire"; Barthes 1970, 11).

This challenge is even more pronounced in the novel's final book, which turns even more markedly than the rest of the text on voids, focuses even more intently on blanks. It begins with Merton's unusual and prolonged silence on his return from Venice, and his absence from Lancaster Gate; it centers on Milly's pervasive absence from London, on the process of her dying in Venice, and on the lack of information about her physical and spiritual state; it turns on an unread letter and a rejected legacy. It presents the penultimate scenes of the romance and the melodrama, while leaving the final one unwritten. It insists, as John Carlos Rowe has argued, on Milly's role as a producer, and a "symbol[,] of differences" (Rowe, 172) and underlines the sense that difference, distance, and emptiness are the necessary products of the social and economic situation that all the characters inherit and the moral choices that they make in dealing with them (Rowe, 176; see also Bradbury and Walton).

The action of the last book is sordidly, vulgarly melodramatic. The lovers' plot has been revealed to their intended victim, who has as a consequence given in to her consuming illness and "turned her face to the wall" (331). Densher has returned to London, but delayed seeing Kate or even announcing his presence for a fortnight. When they finally meet, something has changed between them (353). He is as much in love with her as ever, but he is no longer willing to play along with her scheme. "We've played our dreadful game and we've lost," he says to her (372). The only way to make it right, he believes, is to announce their engagement immediately, to avow their love in defiance of their "poverty" and other people's expectations of them *before* any word comes from Venice of Milly's death and the disposition of her estate. She still loves him, too, but continues to calculate. I'll marry you in a minute, she says, if "you really *know* something," if you can give me "your moral certainty," if you have "an idea," but Merton, ever the moral absolutist, denies the idea, demands absolute commitment (373). Kate balks; a letter arrives from Venice, timed for Christmas Eve; they both "know" (393) that it contains a "stupendous" (386) deathbed blessing; Kate throws it into the fire unread, saying that he "will have it all," in any case, "from New York" (394). Two months later he hears from New York. He sends Kate the document, which she opens. The blessing is indeed "stupendous" (402), but he cannot accept it, and gives Kate a clear choice between marrying him and inheriting Milly's money.

> "You'll marry me without the money; but you won't marry me with it. If I don't consent *you* don't."
>
> "You lose me?" He showed, though naming it frankly, a sort of awe of her high grasp. "Well, you lose nothing else. I make over to you every penny."
>
> Prompt was his clearness, but she had no smile this time to spare. "Precisely – so that I must choose."
>
> "You must choose." (403)

Densher has seized the moral high ground in explicitly melodramatic fashion. The stakes are love and money; the decision is to be made in absolute moral terms. Kate, however, turns the tables by setting an impossible condition for her acceptance of Merton's conditions: "'Your word of honour that you're not in love with her memory'" (403). Merton attempts to skirt the issue – "I'll marry you," he replies, "in an hour" – but Kate claims the last word, naming the essential difference in their relationship as his moral unfaithfulness rather than her unbending greed.

> "As we were?" [she asks.]
>
> "As we were."
>
> But she turned to the door, and her headshake was now the end. "We shall never be again as we were!" (403)

Like the classic melodrama, the quintessential text of pleasure, the last book of *The Wings of the Dove* lends itself to summary, invites focus on highly charged, simplified moments with dire moral and emotional consequences. It is easy to imagine these confrontations showing up in an episode of "Dallas" or a couple of weeks' run of a daytime serial, or to visualize them in a pop/Classic Comic version by Roy Lichtenstein, with full-frame close-ups and thought balloons. Such a translation would eliminate many important elements of the text of pleasure, of course – verbal echoes, image patterns, deep psychological realism, refinements of moral judgment, among others – as well as reducing the text's essential contradictions and denying its difficulty. For alongside all the melodramatic explicitness of the last book runs the contradiction of Milly's palpably pervasive absence, her effect and her meaning as a creator of difference, and the text's demand that the active reader become a writer, not so much filling in the text's blanks as elaborating on their patterns and exploring their possibilities. John Carlos Rowe sees the end of the novel as calling into question all preexisting categories of meaning, all such "transcendental signifiers" as "grace" and "love," and substituting for them the consciousness of perpetual difference (172–6; 195–7). Nicola Bradbury similarly reads the whole text under the sign of absence, and declares that Milly's triumph is not simply to have foiled Kate's (and Merton's) "wonderful system" but to have escaped and retrospectively denied the validity of any system whatever (Bradbury, 95–6). Priscilla Walton sees the novel as a struggle among modes of writing, with each of the main characters attempting to write the story in his or her own way, and with Milly finally converting Merton to her brand of radically inconclusive *écriture féminine* from Kate's exploitative "Masculine/Realist" plotting (Walton, 120–40; see also 30–1). If we look again at the book's last few pages, and read them now *literally* as text rather than instrumentally as the record of a preexisting story, we can understand what these critics mean, and see again why William James, and Howells, and the anonymous *Times Literary Supplement* reviewer, found the book such a challenge.

The first thing that a summary reading for the plot would miss would be the continuation and elaboration in the last chapter of the protomodernist thematic of spiritual and emotional hollowness, the depiction of Kate's and Merton's treatment of each other after the burning of Milly's letter as attentive, considerate, correct, but emotionally vacant. The pair meet regularly during this period; their meetings are pleasant, even intimate; he "hold[s] her close to his side" (396); she has "never been more agreeable nor in a way – to put it prosaically – better company" (397), and yet their relationship seems strangely empty. James describes the devices Kate uses to arrange these meetings as ways to "make absences" (396) from home rather than to seek a presence elsewhere. The whole subject of their "working" of Milly Theale hovers over their trysts and yet is "made present to them . . . only by the intensity with which it mutely expressed its absence" (394). Their "contact" is finally "multitudinous as only the superficial can be" (397). They "rumble together to Clapham or to Greenwich" (397) like figures from "The Waste Land," together but alone, sociable but incommunicative.[8] James's treatment of this period in his characters' lives links psychological and social insight with registers of emptiness, nothingness, and absence to provide a rich field for a satisfying if conventional literary reading.

More disturbing, because less decipherable, are two extended figures James uses in the chapter to embody Merton Densher's sense of the crisis he is undergoing. The first of these is actually two related metaphors that appear in the same long paragraph, but whose connection is unclear and whose meaning is obscure. In the first, the current phase of Densher's relationship with Aunt Maud, a phase marked by his comparative absence from Lancaster Gate, is characterized in such a contradictory fashion as to constitute on the literal level a moment of indecipherable nonmeaning.

> Another phase had taken its place, which he would have been painfully at a loss to name or otherwise set on its feet, but of which the steady rising tide left Mrs. Lowder, for his desire, quite high and dry. (395)

There are two problems here. First, what would it mean to "set" a phase "on its feet," and what would this have to do with naming it? What are the feet of a phase, and why does James attribute such appendages, properly belonging to animals, to such an abstraction? Second, how does a phase, once on its feet, become a "tide," and how can a *rising* tide leave someone "high and dry"? Both characterizations of the phase suggest that it has an independent existence, that it can move on its own. I can take the first no further, but the second seems to suggest the existence of some kind of reciprocal dynamic between Densher and Maud. The only way a rising tide can leave anyone high and dry is if that person is in another part of the world altogether, so far away that the increment of whatever fluid was rising in one place (water, emotion, interest, honesty) would decrease the level of the same fluid elsewhere: whatever it is that threatens to engulf Densher, in other words, would leave Aunt Maud "high and dry." As with Milly's association with Eve, it would probably be possible to concoct a minute explanation of this figure, but I doubt if the result would tell the reader anything more useful than the unexplicated figure suggested.

The appearance of a closely related figure later in the paragraph complicates the reader's problem rather than solving it. Here Densher thinks of his correspondence with Susan Stringham, a "transatlantic commerce" whose very existence he has kept a secret from Kate, as his one act of duplicity, "the one connexion in which he wasn't straight," and sees it as "a small emergent rock in the waste of waters, the bottomless grey expanse of straightness" (395). Several questions immediately arise. Whatever can Densher mean by thinking of his trivial correspondence with Susan Stringham as his one deviation from straightness? Is straightness the same as dullness? Is it bottomless and grey? Does it threaten one with drowning? Does one need a refuge from it, a life-saving island of deviance or dishonesty in a sea of stultifying conformity? And then, how does this figure relate to the earlier one? Does Densher risk drowning in a sea of straightness while Aunt Maud is left high and dry on an island, or perhaps a whole continent, of crookedness?

In suggesting possible readings for these figures I have been attempting, like a classical textual interpreter, to convert what appears to be an opaque passage, a failure of meaning, a moment of textual aporia, to a moment of plural but graspable meaning. In the spirit of the text of pleasure I have substituted a limited number of potential signifieds for a troublingly obscure signifier, reducing radically plural signification, in Barthes's terms, to manageable connotation (Barthes 1970, 11–14). Such a reading is probably necessary but not, I think, sufficient. James's figures do both more and less than connote: the very ingeniousness they demand from an interpreter suggests that in most readings they stand as nodes of unreduced plurality – islands, perhaps, of deviant bliss in a rising tide of pleasure.

The second figure affirms this reading by resisting reduction even more strongly. It begins with an outlandish image of Kate moving with the stiff but graceful posture of a woman with a basket on her head and of Densher "in his own person . . . swaying a little aloft as one of the objects in her poised basket" (398). This is followed by a description of the strange period of suspension between Milly's death and the arrival of her lawyer's letter, that period of arid but apparently friendly contact between the (former?) lovers. Such periods, Merton thinks, "are in general supposed to keep the time slow," but this one had gone all too quickly for him because

> he was aware of how, while the days melted, *something* rare went with them.
> This *something* was only a *thought,* but a *thought* precisely of such freshness
> and such delicacy as made the precious, of whatever sort, most subject to the
> hunger of time. The *thought* was all his own, and his intimate companion was
> the last person he might have shared it with. He kept it back like a favourite
> *pang;* left *it* behind him, so to say, when he went out, but came home again the
> sooner for the certainty of finding *it* there. Then he took *it* out of its sacred cor-
> ner and its soft wrappings; he undid them one by one, handling them, handling
> *it,* as a father, baffled and tender, might handle a maimed *child.* But so it was
> before him – in his dread of who else might see it.   (398, emphasis added)

"Something," "a thought," "a pang," a holy fetish, a household god hidden away in its "sacred corner," swaddled in its "soft wrappings," a "maimed child." It would certainly be possible to suggest some referents for this list of signifiers. It would be possible, too, but I think ultimately unsatisfying, to try to pin down once and for all the connections among the registers from which they are taken, the abstract, the intellectual, the emotional, the domestic, the "primitive," the magical, the paternal, the violent, and to relate them to Densher's earlier vision of Kate walking straightly away, as if with a basket on her head, and of himself, as if in the basket. But whether an actual reader stops to make such connections, pauses a page or two before the end of the book to think about them, notes them in passing as "typical" Jamesian circumlocutions, or skips them in his or her hasty desire to find out what happens, the figure itself remains, like many other such figures, images, words, and sentences, an obstacle to comfortable reading, a discomforting challenge to "the [conventional] reader's historical, cultural, psychological assumptions, the consistency of his taste, values, memories" (Barthes 1975, 14).

This unsettling effect is what *The Wings of the Dove* is about, both thematically, as a text of pleasure, and more radically, as a text of bliss. It is about a new world, a new market, a new system of exchange in which money has become the universal signifier, and other traditional tokens of signification – words, figures, works of art, religious symbols and practices, conventions of courtesy, "standards of decency" – have been set adrift, their meanings no longer set and clearly motivated but shifting and arbitrary, up for grabs, for sale to the highest bidder. And it is about signification itself, and the possibility of writing in what is to become the modern and then the postmodern age. As Nicola Bradbury has suggested, Kate's famous last line is eminently appropriate to this evasive, self-contradictory text (Bradbury 83). "We shall never be again as we were," she says, predicting an indeterminate future (about which nothing is sure except that it will not much resemble the already retreating past) and skipping the present altogether, as an infinitesimal abyss between two times – the abyss where we, and James's characters, live.

The Wings of the Dove was written just after the turn of the century, at the high tide of "an age in which," as James put it, "everywhere, more people than ever before buy and sell, and read and write, and run about" (James 1898, 651). It was the age, he went on to say, of "literature for the billion" (James 1898, 653), of potentially enormous profits for popular writers, but also of the threatened disappearance, or at best the practical invisibility, of more refined writers. Their only hope, James wrote, was the possibility of defining small, select "individual publics positively more shifted and evolved than anywhere else, shoals of fish rising to more delicate bait" (James 1898, 654).

The central contradictions that inhabit and energize *The Wings of the*

Dove can be understood as traces of two incompatible impulses, James's perennial desire for a thumping triumph in the literary marketplace,[9] and his permanent need to do something fine, to distinguish himself as a literary artist, to please the happy few. James's frank comments to two of his fellow novelists, William Dean Howells and Mrs. Humphry Ward, underline his commercial ambitions. The book, he tells Howells, "has a prettyish title" and is "a prettyish inspiration – a 'love-story' of a romantic tinge, and touching and conciliatory tone. I pray night and day for its comparative prosperity" (*Letters*, 224). "The subject is a poor one," he writes self-deprecatingly to Mrs. Ward, "the result of a base wish to do an amiable, a generally-pleasing love-story" (*Letters*, 242). His preface testifies to his more serious ambitions for the book, however, and it does so in language that suggests an appeal to a refined public by stressing the resistance of the text to mere hurried perusal, and associating more appropriate reading with the social distinction implied by "luxury" and leisure:

> The enjoyment of a work of art, the acceptance of an irresistible illusion, constituting, to my sense, our highest experience of "luxury," the luxury is not greatest, by my consequent measure, when the work asks for as little attention as possible. (15)

James was never unaware of the lucrative literary marketplace, never unenvious of "the fortune apparently open now, any year, to the lucky book – usually the lucky novel – that happens to please" (James, *Letters*, 1898, 651), never theoretically unwilling to descend into the fray in hopes of garnering the impressive financial success of a *Trilby* or a *Quo Vadis?* When it came to the writing, however, and especially the writing of novels as opposed to the occasional pot-boiling short story, he went in for distinction, for a difficult, resistant writing that frustrated some of his friendliest readers and opened him to claims of literary ancestorship by the abstrusest of modernist and postmodernist writers.

It would be a mistake, however, to divide the elements of James's novel into the vulgar and the refined, the melodramatic and the aesthetic, and to attribute the former to his desire for commercial success and the latter to his sense of himself as an artist. *The Wings of the Dove* may be a hybrid, contradictory text, but this does not mean that it would be "better" if it were simply, resolutely one thing or the other. Much of the strength of James's work derives from its hybridity. *The Wings of the Dove* is, in one sense, the culmination of a long tradition of literary realism, a Balzacian "text of pleasure" with roots deeply set in nineteenth-century popular fiction. Cut off from these roots, it would wither; its life depends in part on the vitality of this tradition. The distinction of late Jamesian prose, of obscure metaphors, undecidable references, and uncertain morals, of James's approach, in other words, to the text of bliss, would be of little interest, would probably, in 1902, be inconceivable, without the counterbalancing "vulgar" interest provided by the exquisitely dying heiress and her gentle, loving, cold-blooded assassins.

Literary history, furthermore, is never very far removed from social history, and James's understanding of the necessary hybridity of literary distinction – of the necessity, even the positive value of the vulgar – may be read back into his sensitive and, I think, affectionate understanding of the ways in which his characters strive to distinguish themselves from the "billions" around them. Each of them seems to me both admirable and flawed; each has virtues – energy, idealism, naiveté – but all are implicated in the network of exploitation, of the "workers" and the "worked," that is their social and economic milieu. Energetic Aunt Maud is distinguished from her surroundings by epitomizing them so intensely: "Mrs. Lowder *was* London, *was* life – the roar of the siege and the thick of the fray" (38). Her idea is to work the prodigious market from within: she is ruthless and without a charm, but memorable for her monumental strength. Mrs. Stringham, poor soul, is distinguished by her superior "culture." James satirizes her Bostonian confidence in the power of this brand of distinction (78), and takes note of her willingness to attach herself to Milly's train, without reducing her to caricature. Kate and Merton are distinguished, perhaps, by love, but James's first description of their affair suggests the brief power even of their strong love to hold them above the fray. Their first meeting is described as the encounter of two sensitive souls fleeing the vulgar *furore* of a London party by climbing two matching metaphorical ladders, hoping for a view of the adjoining garden, and getting a view of each other. They remain "perched" for quite some time, but when they come down they part, not to meet again until six months later; by chance, they enter the same crowded carriage on the Underground Railway, as vulgar a spot, as little like a garden ladder as it is possible to imagine. Similarly, of course, their love cannot keep them from their sordid exploitation of their American friend. It encourages them, in fact, in their "working" of the dying girl, draws them back into the same world – the world of the Lionel Croys, the Maud Lowders, the Lord Marks – that it had temporarily enabled them to transcend. Not even Milly finally succeeds in distinguishing her influence entirely from the forces of the social and economic marketplace. Her final blessing is not divine grace, as some have argued,[10] but a "stupendous" check drawn on her "thumping bank account," a check that ends by dividing its intended recipients rather than facilitating their union.

One of James's subjects in *The Wings of the Dove* is the complicated combination of nobility, pathos, beauty, and futility that necessarily attends every attempt to transcend social and economic "reality." Jonathan Freedman has argued that the failure of Milly's deathbed gesture, the ultimately disempowering effect of her generous gift represents James's critique not only of the decadent role that Milly seems to be self-consciously adopting, but of his own attempt, or better, perhaps, his temptation, to write

> a narrative of cultural decline and redemption which suggested that an aesthetically supple, culturally advanced, and intellectually sophisticated consciousness could escape through the very perfection of its being from the larger processes of social decomposition. (226)

The illusion that one can escape from the fray, from the world of the workers and the worked, through love or culture or art or illness or fanciful role-playing cannot last. No one is totally pure, totally unsullied, totally abstract. Similarly, there is, in James's literary world at least, no text of bliss that is not rooted in a text of pleasure, no celebration of "everything," "nothing," and "the abyss" without a dying heiress with a thumping bank account looming on the horizon to be exploited by an author and his characters. *The Wings of the Dove* is elusive by design.

NOTES

1   "Do you think Kate took the money from Densher at last and married Lord Mark?" Howells has his troubled reader inquire. "Why should you care?" comes the reply, and the lady admits that "one oughtn't to care, of course, in reading Mr. James," but adds that "with any one else, you would like to know who married who. It is all too wretched." (Howells, 486)

2   For example: "She had come on from Boston for that purpose; had seen little of the girl – or rather had seen her but briefly, for Mrs. Stringham, when she saw anything at all, saw much, saw everything – before accepting her proposal; and had accordingly placed herself, by her act, in a boat that she more and more estimated as, humanly speaking, of the biggest, though likewise, no doubt, in many ways, by reason of its size, of the safest." (76)

3   Most famously in the scene at Matcham, where the crucial final word of Milly's "I shall never be better than this" (137) is undecidably vague. See Bradbury, 94.

4   See, for example, Krook, 212–13.

5   James's obsession with the French Revolution shows up again in Book 10, where

he pictures Milly hanging on to her "dream of a future" "not shrieking indeed, but grimly, awfully silent, as one might imagine some noble young victim of the French Revolution, separated at the prison door from some object clutched for resistance" (369).

6 *Paradise Regained*, IV, 89. Cf. *Wings*: "She was looking down upon the kingdoms of the earth" (87).

7 Cf. *Paradise Lost*: "The World was all before them" (XII, 646).

8 Cf. T. S. Eliot, "The Waste Land": "Speak to me. Why do you never speak? Speak / What are you thinking of? What thinking? What? / I never know what you are thinking. Think." (ll. 112–114)

9 Fred Kaplan emphasizes this in *Henry James: The Imagination of Genius*.

10 See, for example, Krook, 229.

WORKS CITED

Anonymous. "Mr. Henry James's New Book." *Times* (London) *Literary Supplement* (September 1902), 263. Rpt. in Henry James, *The Wings of the Dove*. A Norton Critical Edition, ed. J. Donald Crowley and Richard A. Hocks, pp. 481–3. New York: W. W. Norton, 1978.

Barthes, Roland. *S/Z*. Paris. Seuil, 1970.

Barthes, Roland. *The Pleasure of the Text,* trans. Richard Miller. New York: Hill & Wang, 1975.

Bradbury, Nicola. "'Nothing That Is Not There and the Nothing That Is': The Celebration of Absence in *The Wings of the Dove*." In *Henry James: Fiction as History*, ed. Ian F. A. Bell. New York: Barnes and Noble, 1985.

Brooks, Peter. *The Melodramatic Imagination: Balzac, Henry James, Melodrama, and the Mode of Excess*. New Haven: Yale University Press, 1976.

Cross, Mary. *Henry James: The Contingencies of Style*. New York: St. Martin's Press, 1993.

Freedman, Jonathan. *Professions of Taste: Henry James, British Aestheticism, and Commodity Culture*. Stanford: Calif.: Stanford University Press, 1990.

Howells, William Dean. "Mr. Henry James's Later Work." *North American Review* 176 (January 1903), 126–31. Rpt. in Henry James, *The Wings of the Dove*. A Norton Critical Edition, ed. J. Donald Crowley and Richard A. Hocks, pp. 483–7. New York: W. W. Norton, 1978.

James, Henry. *Letters,* Vol. 4, 1895–1916. Ed. Leon Edel. Cambridge: Harvard University Press, 1984.

James, Henry. "The Question of the Opportunities," *Literature* (March 16, 1898). Rpt. in *Literary Criticism: Essays on Literature; American Writers; English Writers*. New York: Library of America, 1984.

James, Henry. *The Wings of the Dove*. A Norton Critical Edition, ed. J. Donald Crowley and Richard A. Hocks. New York: W. W. Norton, 1978.

Kaplan, Fred. *Henry James: The Imagination of Genius*. New York: William Morrow, 1992.

Krook, Dorothea. *The Ordeal of Consciousness in Henry James.* Cambridge University Press, 1962.

Matthiessen, F. O. *The James Family.* New York: Alfred A. Knopf, 1947.

Rowe, John Carlos. *Henry Adams and Henry James.* Ithaca, NY: Cornell University Press, 1976.

Stowe, William W. *Balzac, James, and the Realistic Novel.* Princeton: Princeton University Press, 1983.

Walton, Priscilla L. *The Disruption of the Feminine in Henry James.* Toronto: University of Toronto Press, 1992.

White, Allon. *The Uses of Obscurity: The Fiction of Early Modernism.* London: Routledge and Kegan Paul, 1981.

Yeazell, Ruth Bernard. *Language and Knowledge in the Late Novels of Henry James.* Chicago: University of Chicago Press, 1976.

11

MARGERY SABIN

Henry James's American Dream in *The Golden Bowl*

Well, we're tremendously moral for ourselves – that is for each other; and I won't pretend that I know exactly at whose particular personal expense you and I for instance are happy. What it comes to, I dare say, is that there's something haunting – as if it were a bit uncanny – in such a consciousness of our general comfort and privilege . . . as if we were sitting about on divans, with pigtails, smoking opium and seeing visions. "Let us then be up and doing" – what is it Longfellow says? That seems sometimes to ring out; like the police breaking in – into our opium den – to give us a shake.

(24:92)[1]

James composed *The Golden Bowl* during 1903, the year when he was planning his extended return trip to America, and writing to American friends of his great curiosity, his eagerness to *see* the country after two decades of living abroad: "The idea of *seeing* American life again and tasting the American air, that is a vision, a possibility, an impossibility, positively romantic."[2] Although the direct impressions from the trip would later go into *The American Scene*,[3] the indistinct anticipatory vision corresponds to the vagueness of the place called America in *The Golden Bowl*. The two married couples – first, the rich American girl, Maggie, and her husband, Prince Amerigo; then Maggie's father, Adam Verver, and his wife, Charlotte – go off for long, vague wedding journeys to remote American City, its generic name obviating any realistic description of a particular American place. Nobody in the book specifically describes America. At the very beginning, penniless Charlotte Stant sardonically remarks her rediscovery of her native land as a "country for interests" of the sort that she doesn't have (23:56). As for her later wedding journey as the wife of the millionaire, Adam, we learn only that Charlotte "by all accounts . . . had wondrously borne the brunt; facing brightly, at her husband's side, everything that came up – and what had come, often, was beyond words" (23:317). At the end, what is likely to come up for Charlotte in her permanent return to America as Mrs. Verver seems equally unspeakable, except in the vague terms of doom set out by long-expatriated Fanny Assingham: "I see the long miles of ocean and the dreadful great country, State after State – which have never seemed to me so big or so terrible" (24:303–4).

Because "the dreadful great country" of America at the turn of the century was still more visionary then real to James in 1903, he conjures the taste of the American air in *The Golden Bowl* through the elaborate inward faculties that were, in any case, the essential instruments of his artistic imagination. Many of his actual later impressions curiously conform to the verbal shapes already conferred on the American scene in advance of the trip. One letter from America echoes Fanny's image of American emptiness in characterizing the thousand miles seen by train from Boston to St. Louis as "a single boundless empty platitude." Phrases for Charlotte's doom in *The Golden Bowl* also come to mind in a letter where James describes Milwaukee as "a place of desolation and dreariness," while Adam Verver's dream of liberating his compatriots from "the bondage of ugliness" sounds through another letter where James laments the Middle West: "the ugliness, the absence of any charm, is like a permanent plague – chronic and miserable."[4]

James's compatriots responded variously both to James's visit and to his American vision in *The Golden Bowl*, published in New York during his trip.[5] A sympathetic commentary by H. G. Dwight of the New York Authors' Club explains the mainly hostile public notice of James at this time by remarking that he is simply too difficult, too involved with "the dark drama of the inner life" for popular American taste.[6] In "Henry James – 'In His Own Country,'" Dwight speculates that Americans prefer Kipling because "the more elemental qualities of man and the less tamed aspects of nature" in Kipling's art more recognizably correspond to the conditions of American life: James "speaks for all . . . that is the fruit of time, of consciousness, of civilization"; Kipling, "with that in his veins which civilization never yet has quenched, is more at home in the hinterlands of civilization, where adventure wears a more open face than in boulevards and ballrooms." According to Dwight, Americans prefer "the literature of colonization" to "the literature of civilization."[7]

Yet Dwight goes on to predict some greater future appreciation of James's American identity on the very grounds of his subtle, secret, and dramatic probing of America's troubled relation to civilization. Breaking down the categorical distinction between the literature of colonization and of civilization, Dwight sees Henry James as the consummate artist of what we would now call the postcolonial predicament of America.

We are not, as some of us would like to think, a legendary race in its infancy face to face with the primal problems of man. Neither are we, as others of us would like to think, a historical race rich with the accumulations of ages. We are, rather, the younger sons of the ages, with a tradition and a country that do not match. Our feverish activity, our prodigious progress, are the haste of pioneers with civilization in their blood to create anew – and more perfectly! – the world from which they came. And Henry James, instead of blinking it or failing to perceive it, has discovered the dramatic possibilities of the case.[8]

To identify James's postcolonial character goes against not only early but also recent complaints about his preoccupation with private, inner dramas. Marxist critics, such as Raymond Williams and Terry Eagleton in England and Fredric Jameson in the United States, disparage James's psychologizing themes and techniques as epitomizing the cult of the personal in bourgeois capitalist ideology.[9] In his provocative essay, "Third-World Literature in the Era of Multinational Capitalism" Jameson scorns the "host of fragmented subjectivities" that populate the advanced psychological novel in the West with an impatience reminiscent of James's hostile critics at the start of the century. Jameson's alternative to decadent subjectivity, however, is not the colonialist adventure-writer, Kipling, preferred by James's contemporaries, but the postcolonial challengers to imperialist oppression from embattled national cultures outside the West. Even superficially private stories from postcolonial cultures represent collective struggles, Jameson argues, because in what he labels "third-world fiction," "*the story of the private individual destiny is always an allegory of the embattled situation of the public third-world culture and society.*"[10]

In this essay, I join more recent cultural critics who have begun to break down Jameson's kind of polarization by recognizing the social and historical self-consciousness of James's own fiction.[11] In 1907 H. G. Dwight already perceived the public implications of James's dark dramas of the inner life. My reading of *The Golden Bowl* here follows the lead of his early recognition that James's psychological narratives allegorically dramatize America's embattled postcolonial position at the end of the nineteenth century.

In contrast to contemporary third-world writers, however, an American at the turn of the century could see (with the aid of popular journalism and political commentary on both sides of the Atlantic)[12] that the westward movement of empire had already made the former colonies in America a fabulous economic if not cultural force. The question that haunts the psychological, moral, and cultural situation depicted in *The Golden Bowl* is whether America's new wealth would sponsor a new and superior civilization or whether America was doomed merely to replicate the worst patterns of its earlier masters and rivals. Was the American dream of novelty in the arts of wealth and power an inspired vision or merely a self-deceiving hallucination? A higher and holier Idea, or only a new version of earlier imperial depredation and decadence, as Adam Verver momentarily contemplates in his image of a Chinese opium den?

In addition to restoring historical self-consciousness to James, emphasis on the haunting anxiety about the dynamics of American power in *The Golden Bowl* goes against recent critical tendencies to hurry past troubles on the surface of texts in order to ferret out a more insidious and hidden "complicity" with power that authors and earlier critics allegedly conspire to disguise.[13] *The Golden Bowl* stays way out ahead of the interrogational reader in its own manifest obsession with evidence of complicity and strategies of covert manipulation. The aggressive coercions just below social decorum are precisely what create the dramatic intensity of this novel, as well as the fierce division in responses to it. On almost every page, frightening images of violence, crime, and punishment darken Maggie's dreams of love and salvation: wild beasts locked in or escaping from cages, expensive materials fashioned into halters, collars, and other instruments of torture and control; silent voices screaming in agony or disguising misery (and satisfaction) in grotesque postures of humility. The mounting impression of covert violence in Volume Two of the novel has famously shattered the equanimity of most readers, even while holding them with the suspense of a horror story. The ostensibly happy ending of new marital union might be compared to an opium dream that confirms that drug's reputation for inducing wonder and terror in equal measure.

James's aspiration to write national allegory contributes to the tensions that all but break down the novel as it proceeds. The psychology strains against the allegory, or at least obscures its public meanings. When the two marriages are finally reconstituted, they have lost the earlier public significance that depended on the peculiar combination of the innocent American girl and her millionaire father. In Volume Two, Adam Verver disappears into inscrutability, except as the supporting base, as it were, of the marriages. When he ambiguously chooses to go, or complies with Maggie's will that he go, back to American City with Charlotte, their removal to America mainly confirms Maggie's victory over her rival, Charlotte, and her new, total possession of her husband. The cultural significance of Adam Verver with his brilliant wife in America becomes almost as hard to locate as American City itself. Likewise, Adam's project of a museum for American City, never quite thoroughly palpable as an idea even in Volume One, recedes from the book's consciousness at the end, leaving only Maggie's expatriate marriage supported by Verver money to represent American success.

At the start of *The Golden Bowl,* the terms of the psychology and the national allegory work together more openly. The book begins with Prince Amerigo on the verge of his marriage to Maggie, in language that both evokes and moves beyond Conrad's *Heart of Darkness* (published two years before):[14]

> The Prince had always liked his London, when it had come to him; he was one of the Modern Romans who find by the Thames a more convincing image of the truth of the ancient state than any they have left by the Tiber. Brought up on the legend of the City to which the world paid tribute, he recognized in the present London much more than in contemporary Rome the real dimensions of such a case. If it was a question of an *Imperium,* he said to himself, and if one wished, as a Roman, to recover a little the sense of that, the place to do so was on London Bridge, or even, on a fine afternoon in May, at Hyde Park Corner. (23:3)

The perception of London as the successor to the Roman *Imperium* connects Prince Amerigo to Conrad's Marlow, telling his story on a cruising yawl in the Thames, but James quickly moves forward to the historical recognition that America was displacing Britain as the new *Imperium.* For despite his "Anglomania" (23:99), the impoverished Italian Prince has sold himself as a treasure of European civilization to the rich American Patron of Art and his enthusiastic little daughter.

At the start, the novel separates rising American power from British imperial decline through the marginal figure of the retired Colonel, Bob Assingham. *Heart of Darkness* hovers right behind James's account of Bob Assingham's cynicism:

> The infirmities, the predicaments of men neither surprised nor shocked him, . . . he took them for granted without horror, classifying them after their kind and calculating results and chances. He might in old bewildering climates, in old campaigns of cruelty and licence, have had such revelations and known such amazements that he had nothing more to learn. But he was wholly content, . . . and his kindness, in the oddest way, seemed to have nothing to do with his experience. He could deal with things perfectly, for all his needs, without getting near them. (23:67)

In Bob Assingham, Conradian "horror" has declined into grim contentment and placidity. Although James's portrait of a sensibility dissociated from its experience might refer to British imperialism at any moment of its history, the Dickensian detail for Bob Assingham portrays diminished rather than disguised power: his "bad words" like a "box of toy soldiers" (23:64); his leanness, with "abdominal cavities quite grim in their effect," and the reduction of military discipline in him to a habit of admiring his elegantly slender foot, "jerking in its neat integument of fine-spun black silk and patent leather" (23:66).[15] In the Assingham marriage, authority belongs to the American wife, Fanny, who disdains her husband's "complete incapacity" for moral and intellectual reaction. He is capable of appreciating money, however, and his cynical conviction that "pecuniary arrangement" (23:67) is the greater part of life offers its own tribute to new American power.

It is left to more imaginative Fanny to see allegorical romance in the arrangement of the Prince's marriage to Maggie. She explains to her husband how Prince Amerigo succeeds even better than his historical namesake by attaching himself to Americans (rather than to the land itself) as an infinitely rich source of gold. Fanny even helps the slightly bewildered Amerigo to understand the mythic dimensions of his successful adventure: "'Your tossings are over – you're practically *in* port. The port,' she concluded, 'of the Golden Isles'" (23:27). Fanny also understands how the charm of this imperialist romance arises from the perfect reciprocity of exploitation. For if the Prince is bound for "the golden Isles" of the Verver wealth, Maggie and her father are also launched on an adventurous voyage, with Europe and the loot of all previous empires of the world as their ambition.

James devises a variety of tones in Volume One for America's doubleness as both the object of European exploitation and a new acquisitive power itself. The amusing and childlike fun of the American adventure comes through Maggie's lighthearted banter to the Prince, as when she gaily compares her father and herself, stowing away art treasures, to "stage pirates, the sort who wink at each other and say 'Ha-ha!' when they come to where their treasure is buried" (23:13). Maggie even jokes to the Prince about his status as a "*morceau de musée*" for their collection. Her gaiety rests not only on naive trust in the Prince, but on the jolly fact of her father's power to purchase an authentic Italian treasure (backed by documents in the British Museum, like others of their acquisitions).[16]

The historical situation represented by Maggie's marriage fundamentally revises the design of *Heart of Darkness*. Both Kurz's "Intended" and the African "natives" in Conrad's story are in a sense pure victims of Europe's "idea" of civilization, the European fiancée because she is kept in the dark by lies, the natives because they are being invaded and plundered. The American "natives," Maggie and Adam Verver, have ventured away from their natural habitat on a plundering expedition of their own. They have not only adopted the European idea of civilization, but have aggressively reversed its geographic and mythic coordinates. Once Adam Verver had gotten the inspiration for his museum that would be filled with European treasure, "to rifle the golden Isles had become on the spot the business of his future" (23:141).

James's attitude toward his romantic American millionaire remains the most elusive riddle of the novel. Descriptive detail in Volume One – his diminutive stature, "concave little stomach," and unchanging "little black 'cutaway' coat" (23:171) – identifies a fatherly mildness at odds with great creative ambitions, whether civic or sexual. But James shifts to a higher key for Adam's vision of himself as American Patron of Art. For this "supreme idea," James relinquishes even the mediation of Fanny, as if the ardor of Adam's American dream transcended her vulgar romanticism and needed to be confided directly on his own narrative authority.

Yet the tone of this narration seems insecure. Somewhat implausibly endowing Adam with a sublime moment of "wild surmise" while reading Keats, James describes him as reconceptualizing Keats's analogy between cultural translation and imperial conquest in the sonnet "On First Reading Chapman's Homer." Like "stout Cortez," or even more like the translator, Chapman, or the poet, Keats himself, Adam Verver has envisioned how he might attain his own "peak in Darien" (23:141), not in the presence of the Pacific, but by turning back to Europe and transporting its artistic treasures for the blessing of the New World. The alchemical Genius of the connoisseur, the collector, the Patron of Art, might transform American realms of gold into cultural rather than merely literal wealth. Adam Verver has the passion of a cultural missionary to his own land, which he pictures in need of blessing and of liberation from savagery and bondage:

It hadn't merely, his plan, all the sanctions of civilisation; it was positively civilisation condensed, concrete, consummate, set down by his hands as a house on a rock – a house from whose open doors and windows, open to grateful, to thirsty millions, the higher, the highest knowledge would shine out to bless the land. In this house, designed as a gift primarily to the people of his adoptive city and native State, the urgency of whose release from the bondage of ugliness he was in a position to measure – in this museum of museums, a palace of art which was to show for compact as a Greek temple was compact, a receptacle of treasures sifted to positive sanctity, his spirit to-day almost altogether lived, making up, as he would have said, for lost time and haunting the portico in anticipation of the final rites. (23:145)

It is hard to be certain how much irony James intends in this portrait of Adam's fantasy of himself as a combination of Moses leading his people out of bondage and Peter building a new city on a rock. The whole account of Adam's visionary moment of vocation recalls the birth of Lydgate's intellectual passion in *Middlemarch,* but George Eliot's mixture of respect and ironic reservation is clearer, especially since her emphatic point is that Lydgate is a young man, with faults and virtues still in the making. James is less clearly diagnostic. The impression of something immature in this middle-aged Adam, at once grandiose and pathetic, feels less like irony than like a specter haunting the site that Adam's own spirit is haunting in a dream of sanctification. Some ghostly specter of Jamesian irony surely lurks in the incongruity of "sifted" to describe the transmutation of material treasure into spiritual blessing: "a receptacle of treasures sifted to positive sanctity." As Adeline Tintner has demonstrated in detail, James's own devotion to art museums did not prevent his criticism of crude confusions between the figurative and the literal in American (as well as British) plundering of real temples to furnish temples of art.[17] This irony becomes more substantial later in the chapter in Adam's wish to pack up the whole village church at Fawns in a glass case and transport it "to one of his exhibitory halls" (23:305–6).

The much less subtle and indeed glaring irony in Adam's vision of sanctity comes from the simple fact that in Volume One two human beings are the principal treasures currently being "sifted" by the Ververs. After her marriage, Charlotte brilliantly expostulates to the Prince on the Ververs' errors and failures of imagination about their (and especially *her*) humanity:

> "What do they really suppose," she asked, "becomes of one? – not so much sentimentally or morally, so to call it, and since that doesn't matter; but even just physically, materially, as a mere wandering woman: as a decent harmless wife, after all; as the best stepmother, after all, that really ever was; or at the least simply as a *maitresse de maison* not quite without a conscience. They must even in their odd way," she declared, "have *some* idea."   (23:305–6)

In Volume One, the American father and daughter have very few ideas about other people as human beings, or even as artistic treasures. They are content merely to enjoy the privileged intimacy with each other that they have purchased through the double marriages. Charlotte not only names their fault, but also demonstrates in her own wit and charm an alternative and entirely different American possibility. From the very beginning of the novel, when she shows up to haunt the bridegroom with memories of their former love affair, she is Maggie's rival and (except for her poverty) the superior example of how to integrate Europe into an American identity. Charlotte's independence, curiosity, and readiness for larks have an American freshness, while her wit (in more than one language), her taste, and her sexiness differentiate her cosmopolitanism from Fanny's overcolorful incoherence. Charlotte dazzles not only Amerigo but everyone, from ambassadors to Maggie herself. That is why Maggie gets the idea of acquiring her to compensate her father for her own marriage, and why it becomes so easy instead for father and daughter to end up leaving the whole social "work" of their position to Charlotte in joint service with the Prince.

For many readers, the most persuasive part of the novel is James's unfolding of the social, psychological, and sexual logic of the ensuing adultery, with all its nuances of self-justification and betrayal, success and ultimate failure. From the point of view of national allegory, the fundamental question is what cultural logic James represents by dooming to ultimate failure the mature and cosmopolitan American figure of Charlotte and her passionate union with the handsome Italian Prince – what F. R. Leavis calls the only natural passion in the book?[18]

Charlotte descends from a distinguished line of cosmopolitan failures through whom James simultaneously admires and punishes Americans who have thoroughly given themselves to European worldliness. Charlotte seems even more extravagantly punished than such predecessors as Eugenia in *The Europeans* or Madame Merle in *The Portrait of a Lady,* for her social immorality goes beyond charm and opportunism to serve the interests of a genuine passion. Maggie, moreover, seems a less worthy champion of American idealism than Isabel Archer in the conflicts between the sacred and the profane, the innocent and the worldly, the pure American and the cosmopolitan that James likes to stage in his rivalries between women. Isabel has more manifest charm and vitality than Maggie, and, in any case, ends up suffering her own punishment. *The Golden Bowl* bestows full victory on a meager and even repellent American figure, and leaves the meaning of her unique success buried in the silence of the book's confusing final marital embrace.

The structure of the novel prepares for Maggie's success by first demonstrating the logic of Charlotte's failure. Although Amerigo's telegram to Charlotte at the time of Adam's proposal to her praises a "courage" in her that the narrative has directly dramatized, James in Volume One also builds the point that Charlotte's cosmopolitanism is insufficiently courageous, not ambitious enough. Marriage to a rich man as a solution to the problem of existence is itself unoriginal for an impoverished, unattached female, as Charlotte acknowledges to Adam in her candor about the "dreadful" state of spinsterhood, "except for a shopgirl" (23:219). To be sure, the situation of becoming the stepmother-in-law of her former lover and her schoolfriend presents novel risks, but Charlotte herself emphasizes not the originality but the passivity of her responses. The freedom given to her and Amerigo, she makes a great point of explaining, derives from how they have been "placed" by the preference of Maggie and Adam to play house with each other and the baby Principino: "Haven't we therefore to take things as we find them?" (23:303) she asks, and again later, "The thing is for us to learn to take them as they are" (23:307). By the end of Volume One, James has fully exposed the weakness as well as the charm of a talent for mere adaptability, even when it takes ingenuity almost to the point of genius.

The climax of Charlotte's apparent success occurs during the country-house weekend at Matcham when, in the absence of Adam and Maggie, the lovers consummate their illicit passion. The very name of Matcham undercuts the romance of plans that are constrained to match already existing structures. At Matcham, Charlotte and the Prince can snatch minutes of privacy only by dressing more quickly than others for dinner, and the fine details of *Bradshaw's Railway Guide* organize their passion according to the minute timing of the trains; their adulterous expedition must fit in between the local leaving for Gloucester at 11.22 and the 6.50 "in" to Paddington. James ironically accompanies his display of Charlotte's romantic glamour with these inglorious signs of civilization's constraints. Although Charlotte can seduce Amerigo into a renewal of their earlier romance, their passion can create no stronger structure than what had already failed them previously in Rome.

The general decadence of English high society further vulgarizes their specialness as lovers "meant for each other," and underlines the unoriginality of adultery itself. At Matcham, their need for an alibi all too neatly matches the convenience of their hostess, Lady Castledean, who needs to cover her little affair with somebody named Mr. Blint. This vulgar correspondence degrades even Charlotte's genius for arrangements. Amerigo marvels at her effectiveness as if it were the rare essence of the cosmopolitan: "Blood? . . . You've that of every race!" (23:362). Fanny, however, can already foresee at the end of Volume One how this cosmopolitan affair will follow the commonplace pattern of "nine cases out of ten" (23:399). The penniless cosmopolitan woman will be discarded by the fashionable but impoverished cosmopolitan man, according to the conventions of civilization. It will be for Maggie, Fanny sublimely predicts, to come up with an "original" (23:386) method of saving them all.

For a wife to retrieve her husband from adultery is no more original than adultery itself, as Edith Wharton shows in *The Age of Innocence* by rewriting the plot of *The Golden Bowl* as the victory of social convention over passion. If the wife's father is supporting the whole enterprise of two marriages, a cynical reading might identify in Maggie's success merely the force of "pecuniary arrangement," in accord with Bob Assingham's grim philosophy. Amerigo's anxiety in Volume Two about what Adam might "know," and Maggie's sense of Charlotte's concern for her "security," both fit this materialist interpretation. Maggie's "saving" of Amerigo and Charlotte by manipulating the breakup of their liason might signify only that she arranges for them both to retain the Verver support that they initially married in order to enjoy.

The Verver power to "save" might equally signify nothing more original than the power of great wealth to keep what it has bought. James sustains this cynical interpretation of American power to the very end, as the "lingering view, a view more penetrating than the occasion really demanded" (24:360). At their stiff moment of final separation in the last chapter, Charlotte and the Prince figure as "human furniture," along with the sofas, chairs, and cabinets in Maggie's Portland Place house. All of it "might have figured as concrete attestations of a rare power of purchase" (24:360). The crude destructiveness of this power appears further in the comparison of the two noble figures being admired by Maggie and her father to wax effigies on "one of the platforms of Madame Tussaud": "Ah don't they look well?" Maggie exclaims to her father. Of all the Verver purchases, none so clearly exposes the failure of money to transmute body to spirit than this admiration by Maggie of the wax figures she has managed to make out of the former lovers. The historical fact that Mme. Tussaud began her successful career producing noble heads of the doomed during the French Revolution adds a further ironic point to Maggie's earlier comparison of both Charlotte and Amerigo in their suffering to "noble captives in the French Revolution, in the darkness of the Terror" (24:341).

The almost intolerable ambiguity of Volume Two, however, is that while James keeps insinuating a "penetrating" cynicism, he also strenuously follows Maggie's own drive to displace cynicism with a higher, if not deeper, vision. Images of Amerigo and Charlotte "saved" by Maggie's radical love and pity compete with equally vivid yet somehow discounted images of them tortured and doomed by ruthless American Terror. The same situations serve both visions, as when the Portland Place House where Amerigo retreats to solitary confinement figures simultaneously as the "locked cage" of a prison and a "monastic cell" (24:338) for his penitence and conversion to Maggie's new order of love. This ambiguity of judgment about Maggie's power would upset James's readers less if James himself did not seem to endorse Maggie's refusal of ambiguity. In Volume Two, James shows Maggie at her most original when her consciousness refuses the penetrating view of her own experience and when she chooses between alternative interpretations that his own more variegated narrative art cannot help but continue to blend inextricably together.

The correspondence between conversion and a restrictive fixity of meaning is supported by Maggie's religious identity as Catholic, and even more by her psychological and aesthetic preference for allegory as a creative method. This bias becomes most explicit in the crucial cardgame scene, where Maggie assumes responsibility as "author" of the play her family seems to her to be rehearsing in their quiet game of bridge. Maggie here rejects the morality of accommodation to impure social realities that Charlotte and Amerigo have devised to reconcile adultery with the decent performance of their marital duties. To Maggie, such shuffling simply signifies the sophistry of evil: "The horror of finding evil seated all at its ease where she had only dreamed of good; the horror of the thing hideously *behind,* behind so much pretended nobleness, cleverness, tenderness" (24:337).

Maggie's formulation of "evil" stabilizes and simplifies the "thing" behind the surface of experience, while her "horror" follows upon her awakening from a "dream" of absolute moral identity between social grace and the Good. Her alternatives of response are equally absolute and simplistic: either violent destruction or thorough reconstruction of the scene: "It was a scene she might people, by the press of her spring, either with serenities and dignities and decencies, or with terrors and shames and ruins" (24:236).

Maggie's creative opportunity has the freedom but also the excessive clarity of moral allegory. In her "play," something of the fixed and arbitrary assignment of values in cardplay limits the impression of freedom suggested by a stage, "spacious and splendid." The actual people in Maggie's "play" are already on the scene, like the set figures in a deck of cards, and she doesn't want to give up any one of them. But instead of fitting into the game as structured by others (the best Charlotte can do), Maggie envisions creatively revising the relationships within the scene by "peopling" it with different meanings. The same people must be made to enact a new set of moral personifications in a new allegory.

Maggie's discovery of betrayal has made her see the apparent serenity of the scene before her as an allegory of falsity. Although she initially feels this

falsity as "horror," she quickly redefines the moral meaning of falsity itself
in the method she will adopt. The natural alternatives, such as open rage or
protest, appear to her barbaric, like "a wild eastern caravan, looming into
view with crude colours in the sun, fierce pipes in the air, high spears against
the sky, all a thrill, a natural joy to mingle with, but turning off short before
it reached her" (24:237). In the metaphors of Maggie's imagination in Volume Two, "natural" responses become associated with an exotic and savage
Orientalism whose destructiveness she shuns. Her creativity instead moral-
izes falsity into a strategy for restoring the inward decency and dignity of civilization that the others have secretly betrayed. Maggie's redemptive idea
strangely resembles her father's vision of sanctifying the plundered fragments
of earlier imperial conquest through the construction of a new American
temple. In Maggie's case, the corrupt social and sexual falsity of civilization
will be sifted to sanctity through her creative power of love.

For the reader, another kind of horror enters to haunt Maggie's dream of
sanctification by the way the psychological narrative exposes savage passion
as "the thing *behind*" Maggie's own high manner. Rage, jealousy, and resentment are passions she has chosen to reject, yet James keeps peopling his
own narrative with images of these passions in her, even as components of
her love. In the competitive economy of Maggie's psychology, her freedom
of movement requires the imprisonment of those who have caged her. She
refuses to allow them to confront her power directly. Yet they must be im-
mobilized by feeling her seizure of control. Only once she has attained this
silent assent to her power, is she liberated to pity, admire, embrace, and even
passionately love them.

The brutality of Maggie's love in *The Golden Bowl* comes from the universal unconditional surrender it demands. "They're paralyzed, they're paralyzed!" Maggie comments to herself with satisfaction, when the success of
her method begins to show Charlotte and Amerigo "cornered," so that she
"might still live to drive [them] about like a flock of sheep" (24:51-2). The
aggressive drive behind Maggie's redemptive love makes her a horribly fierce
shepherd, even if Biblical precedent sanctions such violence for a holy end.[19]

Maggie shuns direct expression of her unholy natural passions, but James
marvelously renders her barely suppressed savagery through her inner
speech. Resentment and shame sharpen Maggie's unspoken wit, and poison
the "bare blade" that passes across her vision "ten times a day" (24:9). At
the post-Matcham dinner for the Castledeans, Maggie sees them all passing
her about "like a dressed doll" who could talk if pressed on her stomach,
"Oh yes, I'm *here* all the while; I'm also in my way a solid little fact and I

cost originally a great deal of money: cost, that is, my father, for my outfit, and let in my husband for an amount of pains – for my training – that money would scarce represent" (24:51). Maggie's inner speech in Volume Two vibrates with tightly controlled aggression, as she sarcastically parodies the pathetic figure the others have constructed her to be: meager, sick, infantile, nothing more than "the dearest little creature in the world" (23:316), in Fanny's ambiguous reference to her cost as well as her goodness.

James's challenge in Volume Two is a version of Maggie's own. What kind of original new human being could result from the awakening to life of a dear little doll? Shall he people the scene of this American consciousness with rage and shame or with dignity and decency? I believe that James intends to endorse Maggie's own rejection of destructive passions, but that his penetrating narrative imagination compels him to author a less benign drama of American awakening to passion and to power.

For the combination of pathos and aggression in this drama, James introduces metaphors from the whole scale of art and life, regardless of how they cohere in a stable allegorical design. The recurrent circus imagery seems especially important for breaking down aesthetic and moral hierarchies, and giving popular American color to Maggie's newly impassioned inward activity. Even the term "humbuggery," for Maggie's manipulative duplicity, draws on the slang associated with P. T. Barnum of circus fame.[20] To be sure, the book's analogue (and corrective) to Barnum is Adam Verver rather than Maggie, since P. T. Barnum was even more famous in the nineteenth century for his American Museum of human and animal "curiosities" than for his later establishment of the three-ring circus.[21] Verver's project of a fine art museum is at the opposite cultural pole from the tasteless commercial hodge-podge of Barnum's American Museum, so that James's irony undercuts Adam's dream. Near the end, the great countryhouse, Fawns, becomes like a circus tent of forced labor, with the door into the central chamber resembling "the aperture through which the bedizened performers of the circus are poured into the ring" (24:289).

The circus imagery in *The Golden Bowl* separates Maggie's labor from Adam's high idea of himself and his museum, allying her effortful daring with a popular art of skill and risk that is yet without high style. Maggie is never pictured as the owner of the circus, but only one of the performers, the "overworked little trapezist girl – the acrobatic support presumably of embarrassed and exacting parents" (24:302). Little-girl circus performers work hard and are sometimes thrilling to watch, but not with reverence. They suggest the pathos of exploited child labor rather than pretentious power or ease.[22]

James's proliferating metaphors at the end of *The Golden Bowl* keep the inner meaning of Maggie's adventure from settling into any stable allegory, whether sacred or profane. Some of the images show James straining to identify her with a specifically American drive to domesticate savagery, in her case the savagery of her own nature. Thus, in relation to Amerigo, she becomes like a "settler, or a trader in a new country," even more strangely, like "some Indian squaw with a papoose on her back and barbarous beadwork to sell" (24:323–4). The American West offers a wildness off the social and aesthetic map of Europe that is less foreign and less purely destructive than the eastern caravan of high spears and fierce shouts Maggie earlier rejected. While out beyond the frontier of civilization, the trader, the settler, and in James's image, even the Indian squaw are there to survive in a new life rather than to destroy. As figures for the decency and dignity of Maggie's creative love, however, these images may seem dubious, too far-fetched and artificial in relation to the dramatic particulars of this marriage. The problematic distinction between marauder and victim in America's own Western history further destabilizes any consolidation of Maggie's identity into a positive figure of American creativity.

The fullest and most interesting dramatic ambiguities in Maggie's role as Wild Western heroine appear in relation to Charlotte. At the end of Book 5, Maggie "tracks" her defeated rival out of public view into the depths of the garden at Fawns, where Charlotte has sought private refuge. Maggie goes after her, armed only with the civilized pretext that Charlotte has borrowed the "wrong volume" of a novel and needs to be given the "right" new beginning. Maggie holds to a sense of her harmless and even "abjectly mild" intention, as if her role in this pursuit were purely to surrender, like "people she had read about in stories of the wild west, people who threw up their hands on certain occasions for a sign they weren't carrying revolvers" (24:310). But the exact nature of this occasion is obscure; since Maggie has already won her husband back and resolved to relinquish her father, any show of surrender to Charlotte has a strong air of humbug.

Heart of Darkness again helps James, this time to infuse his curious version of an American Western with the uncanny horror of imperialist adventure. Maggie begins from the civilized outpost of her room, as from "some castle-tower mounted on a rock" (24:306). In the "immensity of light," the hot garden of Fawns looks almost tropically sinister: "the peacocks on the balustrades let their tails hang limp and the smaller birds lurked among the leaves" (24:306). Maggie recognizes a moving spot of green and white to be Charlotte fleeing into the "unvisited" dark of the gardens. Earlier in the day, Maggie had already imagined Charlotte's desperation so intensely that the thwarted and confused passions of her defeated rival had become entirely merged with her own anxieties "in a darkness of prowling dangers that was like the predicament of the night-watcher in a beast-haunted land who has no more means for fire" (24:299). Now Maggie's earlier vague anxiety becomes a still-confused compulsion to pursue Charlotte into the dark. As she confusedly hears echoes of ancient myths: "Io goaded by the gadfly or . . . Ariadne roaming the lone sea-strand" (24:307), the ambiguity of who is the attacker and who is the prey intensifies. The mythic images of female suffering seem to apply mysteriously to both women. I don't think James means us to understand exactly what drives Maggie here any more than Conrad specifies exactly what demons drive Marlow or Kurz, or how these figures are related to each other. In the James scene, the tension comes from the discrepancy between Maggie's insistence on her "harmlessness" and the narrative's evocation of more confused and primitive impulses that she consciously denies. In this instance, the "horror of the thing hideously *behind*" Maggie's own high intentions usurps the surface with nameless intensity.

Maggie obscurely knows that she is "turning the tables" (24:308) on the Charlotte whom she earlier experienced as stalking her on the terrace like a wild beast, but she also rejects the analogy from consciousness, "allowing, oh allowing, for the difference of the intention! Maggie was full of the sense of *that*" (24:309). This kind of overemphatic disclaimer belongs to what James calls "the upper air" of Maggie's artificial speech on the balcony with her father near the end, when she feels how reality "would have torn them to pieces, if they had so much as suffered its suppressed relations to peep out of their eyes" (24:362). The blind obscurity in the garden exceeds the darkness of both the terrace at Fawns earlier and the balcony of Portland Place later. Maggie is in the grip of a confused need to see Charlotte and to receive as well as inflict pain. She knows that she has already defeated Charlotte: she has seen the "silken halter" of her father's power, and the "knife in her heart" (24:311) from Amerigo's rejection. This security seems to release in Maggie a compulsion to experience (and positively provoke) the punishment by Charlotte that she so intensely feared earlier. Charlotte's fierce and lying accusation that Maggie has "worked against" her free possession of Adam Verver seems to be what Maggie even more than Charlotte wants, and it sends Maggie into a paroxysm of "supreme abjection": "'Oh, Oh, Oh!' the Princess exclaimed" (544), and then, "Maggie took it and for a moment kept it; held it, with closed eyes, as if it had been some captured fluttering bird pressed by both hands to her breast" (24:317).

Maggie's sadomasochistic rapture with Charlotte in the garden surpasses any moment of passion with Amerigo. Charlotte's play-acting of power allows Maggie to reexperience her earlier humiliations in the form now of "a secret responsive ecstasy" (24:313). Charlotte is the one who brutally breaks decorum; Maggie in her ecstasy of pain can believe that she is herself in control. She has "pressed the spring" (24:317) of Charlotte's words, as earlier she had controlled the "spring" of meaning in the cardgame scene. "Yes, she had done all" (24:318) ends the chapter, in one of James's maddening flights from specificity. For the reader, "all" here inevitably includes the perverse psychological dynamic that makes Maggie's ecstasy a horror fully evoked but beyond exact articulation.

Maggie's consciousness does even more trapeze acts than usual to convert the irrationality of her last encounter with Charlotte into a sublime "saving" of Charlotte's pride. Yet the figurative geography of the scene as well as its emotional coloration take Maggie off the social map into uncharted territories of passion. The passion in question seems rooted in what James calls "abjection," a condition of dependence and humiliation that Amerigo at the start specifically associated with Charlotte and with the hidden condition of women, generally, no matter how they "muffled and disguised and arranged" to dissimulate it (23:50). At the end, Maggie has successfully retaliated against her own cultural and sexual abjection by forcing Charlotte into the dark. Yet at the same time as she wants to see and taste this victory, Maggie in her new safety is also driven to an intimate identification with the pain she has herself provoked Charlotte to express. By comparison with this compulsive mixture of desire, fear, vengeance, and sadomasochistic ecstasy, the normalization of passion with Amerigo at the end may seem hardly more than a version of the "Lie" that protects civilization at the end of Conrad's story.

Leon Edel offers this Conradian perspective when he argues that the "lies" involved in the renewed marriages at the end of The Golden Bowl are "'constructive lies' – the lies by which civilization can be held together."[23] Such a proposition seems as feeble an affirmation for the ending of The Golden Bowl as it is in Heart of Darkness, for neither book has represented any values of civilization worth preserving through these terrible lies. I prefer Philip Weinstein's differentiation between the "ostensible assent and implicit rejection," in what he calls James's "perversely brilliant" art.[24] Although Laurence Holland accepts the embrace as a "promise" of "commitment to the communion it affords and to the larger community of purpose it can make possible,"[25] these terms recall Maggie's own earlier willful effort to change the allegory of her situation through the "press of a spring." James's allegorizing itself suffers from the mechanical quality implicit in his characterization of Maggie. At the very end, James seems to back Maggie's way of pressing the spring of an Amerigo now converted into a perfect doll of a husband, who says no more than what is prompted by his wife's cue: "'See'? I see nothing but *you*" (24:369).

James's more haunted total vision, however, shows how Maggie's triumph over abjection not only requires brutal domination of others, but also remains dominated by specters of what she has sought to banish and control. Far from perfecting the civilization whose immorality has made her suffer, the American heroine's willful spirit (backed by her father's wealth) succeeds only in taking possession of a civilization that she at once envies, desires, and fears. Her ritual reenactments of abjection disguise both her power and also the perversity of her ecstasies. For she uses her power to stage repetitions of the abjection she has ostensibly overcome. Charlotte's more straightforward suffering, as she is condemned to an American exile among what even Maggie calls "the awful people" (24:266), further confirms the book's insuperable anxiety that America could not naturally come into a marriage with civilization. The very idea of civilization would have to be "sifted to sanctity" in America by more mysterious and horrifying translations, suppressions, and conversions before America could safely possess or even handle it.

NOTES

1. Quotations from *The Golden Bowl* are from *The Novels and Tales of Henry James,* New York Edition, Vols. 23 and 24 (New York: Scribner's, 1909), and are referred to by volume and page in the text.
2. Letters to Grace Norton, 22 Jan. 1902, 27 July 1903, and to Louise Loring, 22 September 1903, cited by Leon Edel in *Henry James: The Master, 1901–1916,* Vol. 5 of *The Life of Henry James* (Philadelphia: J. B. Lippincott, 1972), pp. 227–8.
3. *The American Scene* (London: Chapman and Hall, 1907).
4. Letters to Elizabeth Jordan, cited by Edel in *Henry James: The Master,* p. 277.
5. *The Golden Bowl* was published in two volumes by Scribner's in 1904, without prior serialization.
6. H. G. Dwight, from "Henry James – 'In His Own Country,'" *Putnam's Monthly* (May and July 1907): 164–70 and 433–42; cited in *Henry James: The Critical Heritage,* ed. Roger Gard (London: Routledge and Kegan Paul, 1968), p. 432.
7. Ibid., p. 445.
8. Ibid., p. 448.

9 Raymond Williams, *The English Novel from Dickens to Lawrence* (New York: Oxford University Press, 1970), p. 133; Terry Eagleton, *Criticism and Ideology* (London: Verso, 1978), pp. 141–5; Fredric Jameson, *The Political Unconscious: Narrative as a Socially Symbolic Act* (Ithaca, NY: Cornell University Press), pp. 221–2.

10 Jameson, "Third-World Literature in the Era of Multinational Capital," *Social Text* (Fall 1986): 69. A brilliant Marxist critique of Jameson's analytic categories appears in Aijaz Ahmad's *In Theory: Classes, Nations, Literatures* (London: Verso, 1992), pp. 95–122.

11 Among recent commentators newly attentive to James's historical consciousness, see Ross Posnock, *The Trial of Curiosity: Henry James, William James, and the Trial of Modernity* (New York: Oxford University Press, 1991), Jonathan Freedman, *Professions of Taste: Henry James, British Aestheticism and Commodity Culture* (Stanford, CA: Stanford University Press, 1990), and "The Poetics of Cultural Decline: Degeneracy, Assimilation, and the Jew in James's *The Golden Bowl*," *ALH* 7 (1995): 477–99.

12 See, for example: J. P. Seeley, *The Expansion of England* (London, 1883), Brooks Adams, *The New Empire* (New York, 1902), B. H. Thwaite, *The American Invasion* (London, 1902), W. T. Stead, *The Americanization of the World* (London, 1902), Fred A. McKenzie, *The American Invaders* (New York, 1901). In "The Poetics of Cultural Decline" (p. 480), Freedman discusses the "profusion of books and articles," contemporaneous with *The Golden Bowl*, in which the decline of England is measured against the rise of America.

13 Mark Seltzer examines *The Golden Bowl* and other fiction by James to expose "the criminal continuity between art and power and the ways in which the novelist and critic – through an aesthetic and theoretical rewriting of power – have worked to disown it." *Henry James and the Art of Power* (Ithaca, NY: Cornell University Press), p. 24 and passim.

14 Echoes and allusions to *Heart of Darkness* in *The Golden Bowl* are noted by Edel in *Henry James, The Master*, p. 215. See also, Thomas Galt Peyser, "James, Race, and the Imperial Museum," *American Literary History* 6 (Spring 1994): 53.

15 Colonel Assingham as a figure of British imperial decline is suggestively discussed by Stephen D. Arata, "Object Lessons: Reading the Museum in *The Golden Bowl*," in *Famous Last Words: Changes in Gender and Narrative Closure*, ed. Alison Booth (Charlottesville, VA: University of Virginia Press, 1993), pp. 205–6.

16 Arata, pp. 203–4, remarks on the new importance of "authenticity" in the aesthetic of the American art museum in the 1880s and 1890s.

17 Adeline R. Tintner, *The Museum World of Henry James* (Ann Arbor and London: U.M.I. Research Press, 1986), pp. 199–235. Peyser's identification of the Verver museum with American political and cultural aggression against Native American (Indian) culture and in the Philippines (pp. 48–9, 56, 64) ignores the emphatically European idea of "treasure" in *The Golden Bowl* (including, to be sure, the artifacts of Persian, Indian, and Chinese civilization already appropriated by earlier European purchase and conquest). The American fine arts museum evolved in the late nineteenth century in competition with the models

Peyser cites of scientific and ethnographic museums where conquered races are turned into objects of ethnographic curiosity. See Arata, pp. 201–3.

18 F. R. Leavis, *The Great Tradition* (London: Chatto and Windus, 1950), p. 160. Champions of Charlotte's claims were especially numerous among critics of the 1950s and 60s who upheld the standard of social and psychological realism in fiction. See, for example, R. P. Blackmur, "The Loose and Baggy Monsters of Henry James" (1951), rpt. in *The Lion and the Honeycomb: Essays in Solicitude and Critique* (New York: Harcourt Brace, 1955), pp. 276–9; Sallie Sears, *The Negative Imagination* (Ithaca, NY: Cornell University Press, 1968); Jean Kimball, "Henry James's Last Portrait of a Lady: Charlotte Stant in *The Golden Bowl*," *American Literature* 28 (January 1957), 450–68. See also Ruth Yeazell, *Language and Knowledge in the Late Novels of Henry James* (Chicago: University of Chicago Press, 1976), pp. 103–27, and my own discussion of critical division in response to Charlotte in "Competition of Intelligence in *The Golden Bowl*" in *The Dialect of the Tribe: Speech and Community in Modern Fiction* (New York: Oxford University Press, 1987), pp. 65–81.

19 R. W. B. Lewis, in *The American Adam: Innocence, Tragedy, and Tradition in the Nineteenth Century* (Chicago: University of Chicago Press, 1955), pp. 154–5, astutely identifies the paradoxes of "aggressive innocence" in *The Golden Bowl*.

20 See Neil Harris, *Humbug: The Art of P. T. Barnum* (Boston: Little Brown, 1973).

21 "Humbuggery" was especially associated with Barnum's advertising techniques for his American Museum. See Harris, pp. 57–78.

22 Charges of child exploitation in the Barnum and Bailey circus are discussed by Harris, p. 277.

23 Edel, p. 215.

24 Philip Weinstein, *Henry James and the Requirements of the Imagination* (Cambridge: Harvard University Press), p. 194.

25 Laurence Holland, *The Expense of Vision: Essays on the Craft of Henry James* (Princeton, NJ: Princeton University Press), p. 350.

12

ROSS POSNOCK

Affirming the Alien: The Pragmatist Pluralism of *The American Scene*

Given his reputation as the impeccably patrician high priest of Art, Henry James would have seemed a prime target for demolition in the regime of multiculturalism that began in the 1980s. It sought to redefine literary criticism as cultural studies and to create an intellectual climate generally skeptical of both aesthetic value and canonical white male elitists. As a novelist said to regard Art as a saving consolation amid the vulgarity of modernity, Henry James would seem doubly damned. Yet his critical fortunes have held steady in the 1990s. Moreover, by and large, he has avoided serving as a nostalgic refuge for those in flight from the multicultural dispensation of race, class, and gender. Instead, cultural studies has in many ways been a tonic, stimulating revisionary readings that set aside his image as genteel aesthete to reveal the depth and originality of James's response to the social and cultural upheavals that marked his fin de siècle transatlantic world. Various aspects of the Jamesian sensibility and a number of works in his oeuvre can be, and have been, enlisted to argue for his continued currency. Here I examine only one of these aspects and works – James the cultural analyst, author of *The American Scene* – and argue that it has something especially important to contribute to ongoing contemporary debates about ethnicity, pluralism, and what it means to be an American in our era of identity politics.

The American Scene has emerged as a central Jamesian text in the nineties, a renewal of interest inspired partly by the historicist temper of contemporary literary study. The book's currency is ironic given the fact that for most of the century it has been regarded as, at best, an intriguing oddity in the James canon, and, at worst, the eccentric travelogue of a reactionary aesthete. James was drifting "dangerously close to a doctrine of racism," in the words of F. O. Matthiessen's influential judgment of 1947. The received wisdom (encapsulated in Matthiessen's remark) believes that upon returning to New York, his city of birth, James reacts with horror after finding it invaded by recently arrived ethnics. Appalled at the threat to a uniform Anglo-Saxon Christian culture, James confesses to seeking an "artful evasion of the actual" (87).

The immediate value of James's contribution to contemporary debates about American identity is to put in question the very terms of the debate. For James finds that a "fatal futility" shadows the effort to assume or define an authentic, preordained American identity. He articulates that futility in the form of a question precipitated by his 1904 visit to Ellis Island, the site of immigrant entry to New York: "Which is the American . . . which is not the alien," he asks himself, in a "country peopled from the first . . . by migrations at once extremely recent, perfectly traceable and urgently required?"[1] The question poses an unsettling challenge – "where does one put a finger on the dividing line" between alien and native? And by blurring the boundaries of coherence, this challenge haunts him as the "reminder not to be dodged," the reminder of how precarious is his own – or anyone's – claim to a genuine American identity (Scene, 85, 124). We will see that James's question, pondered at a pivotal moment in The American Scene, exemplifies a distinct, if underrated, interracial tradition that interrogates the cultural pluralism with which it is often misleadingly aligned. I call this tradition pragmatist pluralism because all its participants were influenced by William James's critique of the "logic of Identity," whose twin beliefs are that "what a thing is, is told us by its definition" and that reality "consists of essences, not appearances." William James conceives experience as nothing but "overlap" – "all shades and no boundaries."[2]

Henry James's preference for open questions is part of his larger commitment to breeding in readers a skepticism of nothing less than our inordinately human compulsion to achieve identity. To think is to identify, and we habitually use concepts as the instrument of thinking and identifying. Yet James hopes to disrupt our propensity to arrest meaning in identity, an arrest made possible by ignoring or dismissing the remainder or residue that escapes the concept's grasp. James champions "the obstinate, the unconverted residuum" for it is an ally in his campaign against "American simplicity." With characteristic bravado he declares: "I hate American simplicity. I glory in the piling up of complications of every sort. If I could pronounce the name of James in any different or more elaborate way I should be in favor of doing so."[3] James's passion for difficulty – "the only thing at bottom . . . that interests me" – is obvious to any reader. And ambiguity is the hallmark of his art. Indeed, since his death in 1916 critics have fetishized ambiguity as the very essence of the aesthetic spell he casts on character and reader alike, a spell that makes of Art a hymn of imaginative salvation, a redemption of modernity's philistine vulgarity.

But contemporary readers, encouraged by cultural studies, are suspicious of aesthetic idealism and tend to pillory it as inherently and inevitably the loyal servant – or the dupe – of power, of class privilege and hierarchy. This reaction against the aesthetic has devalued James in the eyes of some critics, particularly those taken in by his status as sacred icon. But for critics who do not confuse Henry James with the cramped aura of sanctity that comprises his cultural myth, the contemporary turn against aesthetic idealism finds an echo in James's own. The prime difference between James's and current skepticism is that his is rigorous; hence he avoids the tendency of cultural studies to essentialize the aesthetic as intrinsically regressive socially. Instead, James constructs the aesthetic not as entity but as action, stripping it of any inherent identity or posture, for instance, solipsistic withdrawal or Olympian disdain. That is, he conceives it not as substance but as activity: "It is art that makes life, makes interest, makes importance" he said in a famous reply to H. G. Wells, rejecting Wells's distinction between literature as an end and literature as a means, as having use.[4] Above all, the aesthetic functions as a form of conduct that feeds on what identity represses – the chaos and contingency of experience.

A worshipper of what he called "the religion of doing," James topples the aesthetic from contemplation to make it practice, a move completely unaccounted for in the image that his cultish admirers (commencing with Percy Lubbock) propagated – James the genteel aesthete. This image was a caricature, and profoundly unJamesian; it ignored not only his skepticism of static identity, but also how he embeds that skepticism in his understanding of literary genius. The interest of a genius is greatest, notes James, "when he commits himself in both directions; not quite at the same time or to the same effect . . . but by some need of performing his whole possible revolution, by the law of some rich passion in him for extremes."[5] James's immediate concerns here are realism and romance, but the words reverberate beyond this context to suggest his equation of genius with passion, contradiction, and mobility, with mutually conflicting impulses that at once incite and doom efforts at resolution.

James represents the agonism of genius nowhere more viscerally than in *The American Scene,* his account of his 1904 repatriation to the country of his birth after a twenty-year absence. In this book he puts his own genius on display, dubbing himself a "restless analyst." This epithet, which he uses

throughout the book, challenges the conventional and hierarchical opposi-
tions of activity and passivity, the hazardous and assured. Rather than being
distanced in static contemplation, James actively solicits and corporeally experiences shock as the imprint of the material pressure of historical change.
Indeed, on the first page of *The American Scene* James is assaulted by "instant vibrations" of curiosity prompted "at every turn, in sights, sounds,
smells, even in the chaos of confusion and change" (1). This noncognitive,
nonconceptual stratum of experience, charged with the primal, childlike
avidity of insatiable curiosity ("I want to see everything," he wrote in anticipation of his trip), is the level at which James will most intensely live
throughout his journey.

The American Scene constitutes a calculated act of affiliation with the new
century and its endless possibilities. Addressing the United States near the
end of his book, James distinguishes his perspective from that of the "painted savages you have dispossessed." While they rightfully begrudge "every
disfigurement and every violence" that America has inflicted upon the land,
James declares: "I accept your ravage" (436). Because he situates his response to modernity as necessarily belated rather than aboriginal, he is not
drawn to a prelapsarian Eden of solitude and wholeness. Instead, James is
skeptical and ironic toward all that purports to be natural, and believes in
the primacy of imitation and theatricality. James, at sixty-one, bears direct
witness to the transition from a Victorian culture of hierarchy and homogeneity to a more unsettling urban modernity. Yet his engagement with urban modernism is not without profound, freely confessed ambivalence and
even acute unease.

Until recently, critics have seen only the unease and disgust, while ignoring that it occurs within a frame of acceptance founded on an uneasy but un-
flinching sense of affinity with the alien. Henry James may be mired in the
nativist prejudices of his class, yet he is unique in submitting them to the
"tonic shock" of total immersion. When he literally confronts and interacts
with the object of his disgust in 1904, he complicates his snobbery with sympathy. In exploring New York City his powers of discrimination are put to
their severest test, yet they grow more inclusive than exclusive. His wayward,
avid curiosity, which brings him to "the very heart of the New York
whirlpool," embodies a dynamic of mobile involvements that puts him in
contact with a variety of people, classes, institutions, and locales in his year
of traveling from New Hampshire to California, Richmond and Charleston
to Seattle, and from Florida to Chicago (134). To this array of experiences
James reacts variously, alternately expressing contempt, condescension, ex-

hilaration, fear, respect, pleasure, and nostalgia. But rather than surrendering to nostalgia, that prime antimodernist emotion, James savors it as a subject. He muses "on the oddity of our nature" which makes us tender toward "ghostly presences" such as those that haunt his walk down Charles Street in Boston (243–4).

The American Scene has been a beneficiary of contemporary historicism in at least two ways: critics have contextualized James's alleged racism as well as perceiving what formalism was blind to – namely that James's aesthetic practice is simultaneously political practice. This equation is implicit in the fiction but explicit in *The American Scene* where he adroitly deploys ambiguity to disrupt the ideological containments of "American simplicity." Such containments are the business of bureaucracy, which Max Weber regards as the engine of modernity. In Weber's famous definition, modernity disenchants the world by imposing the reign of bureaucracy – its enemy is ambiguity and its watchword is "without regard for persons." Bureaucracy prizes "precision, speed, unambiguity . . . unity, strict subordination, reduction of friction."[6] Turn-of-the-century America is modernity incarnate, the era of Taylorism (Scientific Management), social control, and of the imperialism and nativism that marked the presidency of Theodore Roosevelt. Preaching "the gospel of efficiency" as a campaign theme, Roosevelt had a zeal for the predatory expansion of the American empire and for assimilating the immigrant into the melting pot of the "'American' character." In 1898, prior to Roosevelt's ascendancy to the White House, James had scorned his demand for one hundred percent Americanism as threatening to "tighten the screws of the nationalist consciousness as they had never been tightened before." He regarded Roosevelt's disciplinary imperative of identity as expressing the "puerility of his simplifications."[7]

Roosevelt instances what James calls the country's "genius for organization" that keeps the nation "in positively stable equilibrium." To this "ubiquitous American force" of management James gives the name "hotel-spirit." And he stands in awe of its power to convert any potential disruptions into new energy for the circulation of commodities and the production of social ebullience, such as the "gregarious state" of "immense promiscuity" that he encounters in a New York hotel. In dissolving difference into a "gorgeous golden blur," the spirit melts together the general and the particular, "the organized and the extemporized," naive joy and "consummate management" (105). "Imposing the standard, not submitting to it," the hotel-spirit is "omniscient," capable "not only of *meeting* all American ideals but of *creating* . . . new and superior ones" (440). One of its creations is a new subjectivity that at one point – when watching the gregarious scene in the hotel lobby – James images as a human "army of puppets" who "think of themselves as delightfully free and easy," so adroitly manipulated are they by what he calls the "master-spirits of management" (106–7).

"Absolutely a fit to its conditions," the hotel-spirit is a closed system, a seamless totality. However, this spirit only appears serene and in control. Its incessant need to devour heterogeneity is precisely what makes it vulnerable. Late in *The American Scene* James realizes this when he describes all he sees around him as "perpetually provisional": "You are not final. . . . Distinct as you are, you are not even definite" (408). James recognizes that American society is a system simultaneously closed and open; its essence is definable only as lacking essence, which he calls the "margin." The margin of the future dwarfs "the total of American life, huge as it already appears. America seems but a scant central flotilla . . . on the so much vaster lake of the materially possible" (401). The margin is the volatile space of potential and possibility that James believes survives in America despite the best efforts of "hotel-spirit" to depoliticize the social order and to tranquilize subjectivity.[8] But in a society preoccupied with business, with getting and spending, the margin remains untapped, smothered by a "neutrality of respectability" that renders nearly impotent any "experimental deviation from the bourgeois" (455). Against this "great gray wash" of serenely imperturbable "bourgeois propriety," Henry James seeks to preserve "the obstinate residuum" of incalculability.

The project of *The American Scene* might be summed up as the effort to foster active democratic citizenship and the messy heterogeneity of what I call a pragmatist pluralism. A "margin" of plasticity remains in American life, potentially able to fashion looser, more flexible social and psychic structures. But this potential remains blocked by America's fixation on the "will to grow" at any price. Far from retreating from modernity, James pleads for a more varied modernity – less disciplined and disciplinary. A marginal social order of "hotch-potch" would modify the repressive controls of a totalizing system by generating the "friction" that occurs as a result of "having to reckon with a complexity of forces" rather than the reigning "sterility of aspect . . . where a single type has had the game . . . all in its hands" (427).

What makes *American Scene* a pivotal late work is that the "restless analyst" enacts with compelling actuality many of the central preoccupations of the ghostlier but no less haunting personages of these years: the fictional Lambert Strether of *The Ambassadors;* the small boy, son, and brother of the autobiographies; and the revisionary narrator of the Prefaces. Like Strether's adventure a year earlier, James's 1904 experience begins with a primal ritual of disembarking at a dreary harbor after a long sea journey. Docking at Hoboken, New Jersey, James describes himself "emerging from the comparatively assured order of the great berth of the ship" (1). With the pun on "great berth," he initiates a long process of growth, as if he had just been "struck from the float ever held in solution," ejected from the snug security of prenatal oneness. These words by Walt Whitman, who speaks of the "float" in "Crossing Brooklyn Ferry," anticipate James's own sense of being floated by sensations. He feels imbued with the vulnerability of a child innocent of language and the cognitive grids and categories that fix experience even as they render it intelligible.

Legibility is precisely what James often seeks nearly to defeat. "Forgive the fierce legibility," he once apologized to a recipient of his typed letter. Taking pleasure in the "chaos of confusion and change" that attends his arrival in New Jersey, James notes that "recognition became more interesting and more amusing in proportion as it became more difficult, like the spelling out of foreign sentences of which one knows but half the words" (1). This simile connects James's pleasure in difficulty with experiencing language in its materiality, freed (at least partially) from the bondage of meaning. Later James will describe the indeterminacy of the nation's future as "belonging to no known language" and thus expressible only onomatopoetically, as "something . . . abracadabrant" (121–2).

His return to America might be described as a project of exposure, an oxymoronic phrase, since it mingles intentionality and spontaneity. But it was precisely this mixture that proved crucial in his decision to travel home. His brother William had warned him that he would be likely to find America too loud and vulgar, and that it "might yield . . . little besides painful shocks." Yet Henry insisted that it was "absolutely for . . . the Shocks in general . . . that I nurse my infatuation."[9] Henry's "craving for millions of just such shocks," as a corrected William phrased it, represented a conscious attempt to cast off the burden of deliberation and to be "led on and on," subject at all times to the "hazard of flanerie" (Scene 189). His project simultaneously manages to accept the obligation of order and selection (what he calls the "treating," not the "feeling," of impressions) and to devise a way to resist the potentially coercive rationality of the ordering impulse.

He honors this double obligation by improvising a literary form that embodies the waywardness of his experience. James conceives "treating" and "feeling," not in opposition to one another, but as complementary, as phases (rather than competitors) in an encounter that from the start overwhelms the ordering impulse and forces him to redefine the meaning of "decent form." Measured and harmonious – decent – form is imperiled as early as the third page when James admits that impressions "were not for the present . . . to be kept at bay." There will be "more of them heaped up than would prove usable, a greater quantity of vision, possibly, than might fit into decent form." Faced with this contingency, James's response is the opposite of fastidious and economical. Here "wisdom," he says, means putting in "as much as possible of one's recklessness while it was fresh." This decision to represent excess by making "the largest surrender to impressions" results in a radically digressive, improvised form (3–4).

James permits these qualities to shape his form of cultural analysis because they mime the dissonant rhythms of his radical curiosity, which feeds on shocks, contingencies, and the attractions of transitory urban moments of fugitive communion. His preference, he avers, is not for perspectives "that may be followed, more or less, at a distance" but for those that grant "revelations . . . only on the spot." And in New York the revelations never cease, given the fact that there "almost any odd stroll, or waste half-hour, or other promiscuous passage" leaves one "tangled" in an excess of impressions (108). The access to entanglement is afforded only those who are "open to corruption by almost any large view of an intensity of life," but this receptivity comes at a price: "his vibrations tend to become a matter difficult even for *him* to explain" (74).

James narrates a remarkable New York moment when his openness to corruption finds him nearly overwhelmed by the sight of a "dense" New York crowd. Here he seems to surrender to a kind of homoerotic moment of fusion: "The assault of the turbid air seemed all one with the look, the tramp, the whole quality and *allure* . . . of the pushing male crowd, moving in its dense mass – with the confusion carried to chaos for any intelligence, any perception; a welter of objects and sounds in which relief, detachment, dignity, meaning, perished utterly and lost all rights" (83). Finding his cognitive capacities routed, James leaves uncertain just where he is in relation to the alluring crowd, whether in its midst or at the fringe. But this very obscurity amply conveys his exhilarated sense of disorientation and absorption. Swept up in the chaos, James seems carried along by the sheer energy of the moving, "dense mass" whose "grim, pushing trudging silences" are the sound "of the universal will to move – to move, move, move, as an end in itself, an appetite at any price" (84). This nearly self-shattering experience ignited by the "male crowd" is a heightened instance of what has assaulted him from the start: a bombardment of stimuli that leaves "no touch of experience irrelevant" (3). James desires the "touch of experience" as he feels a "perpetual sense of precipitation" that banishes any notion of the irrelevant (3).

James's tentative, open stance suggests one of his central merits as a cultural critic: a willingness to recognize and submit to a new scale of values and new "importances" rather than to continue measuring by older standards. "Truly the Yiddish world was a vast world, with its own deeps and complexities," notes James. His respect for its integrity is part of his recognition that the scale of "importances" seems "strikingly shifted and reconstituted, in the United States, for the visitor attuned, from far back, to 'European' importances" (138). This rearrangement is perhaps most drastic in the New Jerusalem of the Lower East Side, where a "new style of poverty" is "everywhere insistent" (135–6). James's inordinate receptivity replaces theory with practice, the a priori with contingency, clarity with shock, information with immersion, and places the fact of urban modernity at its center.

The American Scene extends the deepest concerns of James's fiction by making his skepticism of identity logic into a tool of cultural critique. That critique articulates a pragmatist pluralism that conceives American identity as radically miscegenated, hybrid against which notions of "American simplicity" or of authentic Americanism, become quixotic at best, antidemocratic and intolerant at worst. Pragmatist pluralism is a countercurrent still underappreciated in American cultural thought. It began, we shall see, with Crèvecoeur's answer to his question posed in 1782, "What then is the American?" and, at the turn into the twentieth century, forms a nexus of Henry James, his brother William James, William's student W. E. B. Du Bois, and his pragmatist colleague John Dewey. In the twenties the current moves to Alain Locke and in our own time to Ralph Ellison. This countertradition shares cultural pluralism's distaste for the melting pot of coercive homogeneity enforced by Roosevelt's progressivist demand for "one hundred per Americanism," but dissents from pluralism's equation of the American with immutable ethnicity. Rejecting both nativism and its presumed antidote, cultural pluralism, the pragmatist pluralist unsettles what conventionally counts as coherence and identity. And this unsettlement generates a vision of an alternative melting pot, one irreducibly heterogeneous, a "vortex of discordant ways of living and tastes," in Ralph Ellison's words. For the pragmatist pluralist, America is a "radically unfinished society" that "doesn't aim at a finished or fully coherent Americanism."[10]

Rather than a theory he imposes, Henry James's pluralism is improvised face to face with the "swarming" immigrant presence in New York. As he reflects on his visit to the teeming streets of the Lower East Side, James becomes the first to use the word "ethnic" in English.[11] As he sees the "great 'ethnic' question" rise before him, he ponders the "elements in the cauldron – the cauldron of the 'American' character," and asks himself: "What meaning, in the presence of such impressions, can continue to attach to such a term as the 'American' character? – what type, as the result of such a prodigious amalgam, such a hotch-potch of racial ingredients, is to be conceived as shaping itself?" (121). He finds the "challenge to speculation" aroused by the "'ethnic' question" "so intense" as to be irritating, but eventually takes comfort in the very "impossibility" of reaching conclusions. "'American' character remains the "*il*legible word" hanging "in the vast American sky" (121).

Instead of ratifying a unitary "American character," that fabled ideological instrument of discipline so dear to the social control designs of progressivism, James dwells in the "hotch-potch," the interrogative and the illegible. This is apparent from the very beginning of *The American Scene,* where he seems to prefer hovering between identities: "If I had had time to become almost as 'fresh' as an inquiring stranger, I had not . . . had enough to cease to be, or at least to feel, as acute as an initiated native" (1). Instead of feeling distressed or weakened by his liminal status, he finds it a "great advantage," for fluidity maximizes his receptivity.

Although James values the illegible, the partisans of assimilation do not. Indeed, illegibility is the opposite of what assimilation aims to produce. "Working with scientific force," the "process of shedding" expunges foreign traits and turns out a standard-issue product – a "tolerably neutral and colourless" American (128–9). "'American' identity" (James invariably puts quotes around "American" when he uses the phrase) is a product of "sacrifice": though it appears to possess "confidence and consistency," it is a fragile contrivance, permanently shadowed by "doubt" that the "extinction of qualities . . . is to be taken for quite complete" (129). What was repressed may return; the properties shed "may rise again to the surface, affirming their vitality and value." James savors the indeterminacy that frustrates the bid for closure embodied in "'American' identity."

The mandate of social control must grapple with an America that, in James's phrase, is "perpetually provisional," resisting all finality (408). This struggle is a source both of fascination and of a dynamism that imparts the vertiginous tempo of modernity where "all that is solid melts into air," as a famous phrase from the Communist Manifesto runs. James implies a similar turbulence in "the very *donnée*" he grants twentieth-century America. He will witness the "great adventure of a society" where "fluctuations and variations, the shifting quantity of success and failure" render experience bewilderingly inconclusive. The country affords him at once a "peculiar interest" and "peculiar irritation" because "with so many things present, so few of them are not on the way to become quite other, and possibly altogether different things" (402).

In a moment of irritation James seeks an "artful evasion of the actual." This phrase is worth pausing over. Some critics pounce on it as an alleged smoking gun to prove that James was in flight from modernity. Yet to examine the passage in which it is embedded suggests something more complicated. In the New York streets James pauses after having just been "shaken" by the sight of a procession of immigrants being processed at Ellis Island (a scene to which we return below). He reflects on the "occasional excursions of memory . . . which ministered, at happy moments, to an artful evasion of the actual. There was no escape from the ubiquitous alien into the future, or even into the present; there was an escape but into the past" (87). But the escape is no sooner made than it is undermined. First, the past is but "absolutely comparative," for "it is all recent history enough, by the measure of the whole." What is more, it is full of "flaws and defacements" that ominously loom even as James wanders around his boyhood neighborhood near Washington Square. There he enjoys "felicities of the backward reach, which, however, had also its melancholy checks and snubs" (91). The sharpest snub occurs when James finds his place of birth "ruthlessly suppressed." The "effect on me," says a startled James, "was of having been amputated of half my history." The abrupt alienation not only ruptures James's "artful evasion of the actual" but also implicitly joins him with the very figure from whom he sought relief – "the ubiquitous alien."

The point of James's effort to escape is to demonstrate the impossibility of evasion – not only from the abstract present, but from the present's most astonishing concrete fact: the teeming presence of recently arrived immigrants. To James's disconcerted sense, they seem as quite "at home" in New York as he is, and this "equality of condition" is impossible to ignore (125). In revisiting Washington Square, evasion becomes its opposite as James realizes that "the affirmed claim of the alien" is "not to be dodged." Indeed he is at pains to specify that "we, not they, must make the surrender and accept the orientation" of the alien's right to share the "American consciousness" (85–6). Grandson of an immigrant, James is a self-described "resorted absentee," and, like all Americans, is a product of the dispossessions of "extremely recent migrations."

For James, the "great fact about the alien" in America is that the members of this group "were *at home,* really more at home . . . than they had ever in their lives been before; and that he [James] was at home too, quite with the same intensity" (125). What it means to be "at home" is what James questions and redefines here. For an alien to be at home is as oxymoronic as calling oneself – as James does – a "restored absentee." James and the alien embody this paradox, which defies conventional understanding. "Being at home" for James and "his companions" is not to rest securely in the stable continuity of tradition but to embrace a strange contradiction – that being at home and being an alien are identical. The "immensity of the alien presence" as the defining fact of American life dissolves the "dividing line" between alien and native and empties the word "home" of positive content. The sense of unity, continuity, and closure the term usually evokes is negated, with home becoming the locus of the alienating, the absent. The deconstruction of home as a stable point of origin is dramatized when James confronts not only his Washington Square "birth-house." He acknowledges an even more shocking loss in Boston when he finds a "gaping void" where once had stood his "whole precious past" (229). "It was as if the bottom had fallen out of one's own biography, and one plunged backward into space without meeting anything." This plunge is emblematic, for it gives James "the whole figure" of his "connection with everything else about [him]." It is a "sense of the rupture, more than of anything else," that he will carry with him (230). "Connection" in disconnection, continuity in "rupture" – as with the sense of being at home, only paradox can express James's decentered relationship to America.

James discovers that to leave the comforts of "American simplicity" and "one hundred percent Americanism" and to enter the shifting, disorienting terrain of the American scene is to surrender to the zone of uncertainty he dubs "margin," a veritable quicksand engulfing all pretensions to mastery, control, stable identity. In other words, in his marginality he comes to embody a version of de Crèvecoeur's answer to the famous question "What then is the American, this new man?" De Crèvecoeur's answer to the question he poses in *Letters from an American Farmer* (1782) is indifferent to origins or roots; for him, the American is one who already possesses a "strange mixture of blood . . . here individuals of all nations are melted into a new race of men" (39). De Crèvecoeur's miscegenated or hybrid American is echoed in James's analogous discovery that alien and native are not opposed but entwined. Although James reaches this epiphany by way of his bruising experiences upon returning to homes of his youth, only at Ellis Island does this discovery make him tremble.

His reaction occasions one of the most remarkable passages in *The American Scene:*

> The simplest account of the action of Ellis Island on the spirit of any sensitive citizen who may have happened to "look in" is that he comes back from his visit not at all the same person that he went. He has eaten of the tree of knowledge, and the taste will be forever in his mouth. He had thought he knew before, thought he had the sense of the degree in which it is his American fate to share the sanctity of his American consciousness, the intimacy of his American patriotism, with the inconceivable alien; but the truth had never come home to him with any such force. In the lurid light projected upon it . . . it shakes him . . . to the depths of his being . . . I positively *have* to think of him about ever afterwards with a new look . . . in his face, the outward sign of the new chill in his heart. So is stamped, for detection, the questionably privileged person who has had an apparition, seen a ghost in the supposedly safe old house. Let not the unwary, therefore, visit Ellis Island. (85)[12]

What James's melodramatic excess restages here is his fall into knowledge of the miscegenated American social order, that is, a society whose identity is not a given but rather born of shared intimacy with the alien. This intimacy exposes one's cherished belief in the sanctity of a unitary, settled consciousness (national and individual) as a narcissistic fiction of transparent self-identity. Rather than a virgin birth bathed in Edenic innocence, "American consciousness," that "supposedly safe old house," is already haunted by the ghost of the alien. This is the knowledge that James eats from the tree. Yet the taste is strangely familiar, for it recalls the "force" of an old truth now acutely sharpened, a truth that James late in life described as his "instinct" for "fusions and interrelations, for framing and encircling . . . every part of my stuff in every other" (*Letters* 4: 803). What generates some of the shock of Ellis Island is that his instinctive antagonism toward the impoverishment of mere identity, the sterility of "American simplicity," collides with another – "our instinct," nurtured by nationalism, that a country should be "simple and strong and continuous." This nationalist sentiment must be revised under pressure of seeing "that loud primary stage of alienism which New York most offers to sight" (86). Watching this "visible act of ingurgitation" by and of the other revives his instinct for fusions and interrelations and enables James to "make the surrender and accept the orientation" – "the affirmed claim of the alien . . . to share in one's supreme relation . . . one's relation to one's country" (85).[13]

Having seen the "ghost in his supposedly safe old house," James will abide with his postlapsarian "after-sense" of "dispossession." Hence he concludes his reflections on Ellis Island by renouncing "the luxury of some such close and sweet and whole national consciousness as that of the Switzer and the Scot," even though, in his "exasperated" imagination, he finds it an enviable ideal (86). His envy fades when he visits a place where a hermetic ideal of community has actually been achieved – with monstrous results.

On his visit to the South James witnesses the pathetic spectacle of a people unwilling to renounce the "luxury" of purity and wholeness. They still cling to the deluded ideal of living in a "safe old house" – the "Confederate dream" of white supremacy for "which hundreds of thousands of men had ever laid down their lives" (371). In Richmond, Virginia, James tastes of "the very bitterness" of the "old Southern idea" – "The project, extravagant, fantastic, and today pathetic in its folly, of a vast Slave State (as the old term ran) artfully, savingly isolated in the world that was to contain it and trade with it" (371). "That that absurdity had once flourished there" is the lesson of Richmond's sad, poor blankness. And forty years after the collapse of the Confederacy James still detects "the incurable after-taste of the original vanity and fatuity" of the "conception that, almost comic in itself, was yet so tragically to fail to work, that of a world rearranged" for the "complete intellectual, moral and economic reconsecration of slavery" (373). The "Slave-scheme" of the "Confederate Dream" maintained itself by "active and ardent propaganda," a "general and a permanent quarantine" that kept "the light of experience" and the "reality of things" at bay. Thus the South shut itself into an "eternal 'false position,'" a perverse provincialism comprised of a "hundred mistakes and make-believes, suppressions and prevarications" (376).

The suppression enabling the "Confederate Dream" was, of course, the inhumanity of slavery. And James notes that, despite the passage of forty years, the Jim Crow South remains as "imprisoned" as ever in denial of the "thumping legacy of the intimate presence of the Negro" (375). And James doesn't flinch from confessing his own denial of black Americans. Recalling his sight, a few days before, in the Washington train station, of "an African type or two" – a "group of tatterdemalion darkies lounged and sunned themselves" – James admits having had his own "ease of contemplation" threatened. For in Washington James is forcefully reminded that, though plantation days are long gone, to see free blacks in public is to see "the Southern black as we knew him not . . . and to see him there, ragged and rudimentary, yet all portentous and 'in possession of his rights as a man' was to be not a little discomposed, was to be in fact very much admonished" (375).

In admonishing himself for having failed until now to recognize "the Southern black" as fellow citizen (though at best a minimal citizen in 1904

Jim Crow America), James restages in a minor key the histrionics of Ellis Island, when he came to grips with the fact that he shares the "sanctity of his American consciousness . . . with the inconceivable alien" (85). The affirmed claim of the black man is another "reminder not to be dodged," and James is tempted to urge the South to "make the surrender and accept the orientation," as he had done on Ellis Island and now is doing in the South. But James resists preaching a "sweet reasonableness" about blacks; such counsel, though needed, would be wasted on the "afflicted South." It would be wasted because the South is condemned to its "eternal 'false position,'" enslaved, that is, to the ironclad separatism of Jim Crow, which draws a curtain over the fact of intimacy between black and white, the fact that "the negro had always been, and could absolutely not fail to be, intensely 'on the nerves' of the South" (376). Figuratively, "on the nerves" tells us that blacks are an irritant; but read literally the phrase imparts James's sharper point by injecting the Negro inside, making him disconcertingly present within the body, life, and mind of the white Southerner.[14] James will "tread" on "tiptoe" around this scandalous truth, but does not shy from uttering the "immitigable fact" of how much the Negro "must loom, how he must count, in a community [the South] in which . . . there were comparatively so few other things" (375).

Certainly, within the context of our own time, James's decision to remain silent rather than to condemn American racism is disappointing. It is hard not to concur with Kenneth Warren's judgment that "James's contribution to the discourse of race in America is at best ambivalent."[15] In comparison, William James twice publicly denounced lynchings. Yet we should not ignore that in this scene Henry James is doing more than tip-toeing; his acid portrait of the white ruling class South stretches his ambivalence to the breaking point, and his silence expresses a stinging rebuke. In Richmond, James makes a double move: he affirms the claim of blacks to their "rights," and recognizes the Negro as looming and counting, as being "really at home" (378). And he consigns the South to its "prison" of vanity and fatuity, its "horrid heritage" of white supremacy. James's final image of the South renders it as more dead than alive – a "blighted," stricken invalid "fixing one with strange eyes that were half a defiance and half a deprecation of one's noticing, and much more of referring to, any abnormal sign." Demanding obedience to its twin fictions – of its own "'high' tone" and of black invisibility – the South remains obsessed with "the keeping up of appearances" (377). Maintaining such an "excruciating posture" of hypocrisy has left the South a "painful" wreck of humanity, beyond the reach of "sweet reasonableness" or indeed of reason itself. Ultimately, James's silence is his way of confirming how irreversible is the South's senility; it is useless pretending otherwise. He departs, leaving the South, that "very heaven of futility," in the "very convulsions of its perversity" (394). He also leaves having complicated his initial intention to perform "a sort of ingenuity of tenderness" on the South's behalf (375). James's actual ingenuity is in managing to mix solicitude with indictment; even while humiliating the South he honors its genteel code of "discretion."

James's accumulated metaphors reveal how devotion to creating an economic and social order founded on white supremacy has left the master class morally, spiritually, and intellectually devastated. The "immense, grotesque, defeated project" of establishing a "vast Slave State" within the United States would have required, James points out, that "history, the history of everything, be rewritten" since "nothing in the Slave-scheme could be said to conform . . . to the reality of things" (374). This meant "the reorganization of the school, the college, the university." The South's fanatical allegiance to the "provinciality of the Confederate dream" has left it stranded in a void. In their mass exodus from reality, white Southerners, to James's sense, are left with only their "solitude and their isolation," like "lone and primitive islanders" (374). This unrivaled effort to achieve "American simplicity" has proved lethal.

As a "social order founded on delusions and exclusions," the South is a grievous example of the cultural disaster of homogeneity (391). Ominously, the South's barrenness is threatening to become the national norm: James describes "the country at large . . . as the hugest thinkable organism for successful 'assimilation'" (124). He images this "assimilative force" as an "immense machine" that is "identical with the total of American life" (124). In its relentless production of the "single type," American life risks becoming as enslaved as the South to an "eternal 'false position'" – a "provincialism" vigilantly enforced. For the plague upon the American scene is a static "sterility of aspect" due to the absence of a "due proportion of other presences, other figures and characters . . . representatives of other interests, exemplars of other possibilities" (427). Only by "contact with other kinds, by a sense of the existence of other kinds" and by reckoning with a "complexity of forces" does an individual or a social order attain a richness of "proportion." To be "unrelated" is to be "unformed, undeveloped" and to risk becoming as blank and helpless as the South (428).

If America is flirting with becoming a "social order founded on delusions and exclusions," its prime delusion is to believe that one has the choice of excluding or affirming the claim of the alien. James's pivotal questions expose this delusion: To ask "which is the American . . . which is not the alien . . . where does one put a finger on the dividing line . . . and identify any particular phase of the conversion?" is to suggest that affirming the alien is, ultimately, not a freely considered option or a concession to an Other: "We, not they, must make the surrender and accept the orientation" (86). To affirm the alien is to affirm one's own Americanness, to embrace the immigrant in oneself (124).[16] And the creation of dividing lines blocks this crucial embrace. The dividing line the South erects between black and white, James realizes in Richmond, is built on a willed blindness to the fact that "the negro had always been, and could absolutely not fail to be, intensely" present in the Southern psyche.

James's pointed skepticism about dividing lines, his understanding of them as instruments of repression masquerading as natural boundaries designating an alleged "'American' identity," aligns *The American Scene* with a book William James had sent to Henry in 1903, a "decidedly moving book by a mulatto ex-student of mine."[17] Addressing white America near the end of *The Souls of Black Folk*, W. E. B. Du Bois asks, "Your country? How came it yours? Before the Pilgrims landed we were here. Here we have brought our three gifts and mingled them with yours. . . . Actively we have woven ourselves with the very warp and woof of this nation – we fought their battles, shared their sorrow, mingled our blood with theirs."[18] Du Bois's pinpoint pressure on the possessive pronoun "your" begins to loosen white America's stranglehold on an American history they would prefer to keep buried. He puts white America on notice that they do not have the choice to reject black America; their bloods are already mingled. Henry James and Du Bois both portray American identity as never anything but miscegenated.

The affinity between Henry James and Du Bois has seldom been remarked on and it is easy to understand why, given James's condescending and misinformed mention in *The American Scene* of *The Souls of Black Folk* as "the only 'Southern' book of any distinction published for many a year" (418). Du Bois was teaching in Atlanta when his book appeared, but he was a native of Massachusetts with a Harvard doctorate. Kenneth Warren regrets the missed opportunity embodied in James's perfunctory mention, for the novelist's reading of Du Bois's book "could have been one of the signal moments" in American literary history. As Warren notes, *The Souls of Black Folk* might have suggested "an alternate trajectory" for *The American Scene* such that its cultural critique would have also become "a powerful brief against American racism."[19] The present essay's emphasis on James's multifaceted interrogation of the notion of a natural, a priori American identity has intended to suggest that James's book does indeed trace an "alternate trajectory," although one not precisely of the sort Warren asks for. Although James's trajectory is hardly a frontal assault on racism, he does show that the obsession with forging a homogeneous "'American' identity" is a suffocating project "founded on delusions and exclusions," and bound radically to impoverish democracy in America. Always groping, ambivalent, at times acutely uneasy in his effort to affirm the claim of the alien, James nevertheless holds steady to this commitment to reinstate the margin, the residuum, that progressive America would prefer to repress.

What Du Bois and James have in common is William James. All his life Du Bois revered his Harvard philosophy professor, and Henry James, after reading *Pragmatism*, realized that he had always "unconsciously pragmatised." Du Bois and Henry James's shared skepticism of authentic American identity strikingly accords with William James's critique of "the logic of identity." This logic holds that a concept "means just what it singly means, and nothing else" and it also "means a particular kind of thing"; thus "once classed, a thing can be treated by the law of its class."[20] James's lifelong project is to disrupt this logic, to end the parsimonious rule of the concept. In "A World of Pure Experience," an essay published in 1904, the year of his brother's repatriation, William James describes experience when "the divine right of concepts to rule our mind absolutely" is revoked. He compares his philosophy to a "mosaic" where pieces cling together not by "their bedding" of cement but by their "edges." Experience unconstrained by identity grows by its edges, with one moment "proliferating into the next by transitions." Or, as James would later say, "each part hangs together with its very next neighbors in inextricable interfusion." His mosaic philosophy depicts experience as nothing but overlap, overflow, flux and fringe, "all shades and no boundaries."[21]

In William James's world of pure experience, dividing lines and exclusions are banished, yielding to a utopic vision of freedom. James's revolt against the bondage of classification parallels Du Bois's own revolt against identity logic's ugly incarnation in Jim Crow – a regime whose implacable identitarian compulsion is embodied in the one-drop rule. Du Bois and Henry James could be described as working by the light William James's philosophy generates, extending his mosaic of edges and interfusions to inform each of their attacks on America's mania for invidious classification and its refusal to face up to its own hybridity.

Certainly, Du Bois and Henry James were not alone in being inspired by William James. A student of his, Horace Kallen, coined the term "cultural pluralism" in 1915, but actually began to formulate it as early as 1905 in response to nativist demands for pure Americanism. Kallen, a German-born Jew at Harvard, refused to submit to the melting pot and turned his anti-assimilationist views into a pluralism whose watchword is "the right to be different." Kallen was directly inspired by James's pluralism (and was at Oxford to hear James deliver his lectures on *A Pluralistic Universe*). Yet what Kallen retained from James's lectures was a comparatively minor point – that the pluralistic world is more like a "federal republic than an empire or kingdom." Kallen interpreted this to mean separate ethnic nationalities coexisting harmoniously in an "orchestration of mankind." It has often been observed that Kallen's pluralism is rigid, a quality deriving from his well-known belief that men "cannot change their grandfathers," for "what is inalienable in the life of mankind is its . . . psycho-social inheritance."[22] Like the racists and nativists he opposed, Kallen believes in immutable ethnicity; because his pluralism remains within identity logic it ends up being a purism. In sum, Kallen's cultural pluralism (which was reborn as multiculturalism in the 1970s) perpetuated precisely what James had repudiated, and Kallen did so while proudly proclaiming his pragmatist lineage.[23]

In 1916 John Dewey offered a pragmatist pluralism as, in effect, a corrective to Kallen's pseudo-Jamesian pluralism. Writing during mounting war hysteria about patriotism and loyalty oaths for ethnic Americans, Dewey reminded his fellow citizens that far from being an ideal to uphold, "authentic Americanism" is a "dangerous thing." Although many many still discounted the fact, the American nation, said Dewey, "is interracial and international in its make-up," which makes the "genuine American, the typical American, himself a hyphenated character." The mistake made by proponents of a "supreme and unified Americanism" is to "assume something which is already in existence called America" to which some "foreign ingredient" may be "externally hitched on." Yet the pluralist vision of an array of discrete, genuine ethnicities harmonizing in America is, ultimately, as purist a goal as the nativist one of total assimilation. Dewey's rejection of static pluralism is unmistakable: "the dangerous thing" is for each ethnicity "to isolate itself, to try to live off its past, and then to attempt to impose itself upon other elements, or at least to keep itself intact and thus to refuse to accept what other cultures have to offer, so as thereby to be transmuted into authentic Americanism."[24] Dewey's statement, which reads like a gloss on Henry James's assessment of the South, crystallizes the importance of pragmatist pluralism as an enemy of the ideology of American simplicity. That the nation is "itself complex and compound" becomes the starting point of all inquiry. Dewey's stance also permits us to see that a decade before his own intervention, Henry James enacted a version of pragmatist pluralism in *The American Scene*.

Although pragmatist pluralism never achieved anything like the popularity of Kallen's cultural pluralism, it did endure as a creative countercurrent, especially among black intellectuals. Also on hand at Oxford in 1907 to hear James was Alain Locke, then the first black Rhodes scholar, who was to become a philosophy professor at Howard, editor of the landmark anthology *The New Negro* (1925), and an impresario of the Harlem Renaissance. Locke came away from James's lectures with an understanding very different from Kallen's. Unlike Kallen, Locke entered into what is radical in James's pluralism – his effort to think beyond identity logic. James's critique influenced Locke's affirmation of racial hybridism and rejection of "cultural purism." Locke's hybridism, shared by his elder rival Du Bois, flourished in the Harlem Renaissance.[25]

Locke's admirers in a later generation, Ralph Ellison and Albert Murray, carried forward this pragmatist lineage that, in Murray's words, thrives on "complexity and confusion" and is allergic to whatever "has any presumptions of purity."

In this context Ellison's 1978 essay "The Little Man at Chehaw Station" is particularly noteworthy. Its skepticism of American identity informs a critique of cultural pluralism that is conducted in a spirit that recalls both Henry and William James. Critics of *Invisible Man* tend to overlook Ellison's skepticism, either absorbing it into a thematics of existentialist despair (the anguish of invisibility) or assuming that identity is the prize for which the narrator quests. Ellison's skepticism of identity conceives democracy as experience that requires a form of conduct which spurns the comforts of the already given for immersion in what he calls the "turbulence of the present." In "Chehaw" Ellison redescribes the melting pot as an image not of coercion but of liberating release from hierarchy. In contrast, he depicts pluralism as grounded in "blood magic and blood thinking," which encourages people to "cling desperately" to their "own familiar fragment of the democratic rock" as the only way to achieve "psychic security." Such security represses "an underlying anxiety aroused by the awareness that we are representative not only of one but of several overlapping and constantly shifting social categories." This reality of "motley mixtures" is embodied in "our cultural wholeness," which Ellison images as a maelstrom which "offers no easily recognizable points of rest, no facile certainties as to who, what, or where (culturally or historically) we are." In electing ethnic identity, we retreat from this experience of evanescence and lubricity, this "psychic uncertainty" that is the condition of participating in the "mysteries and pathologies of the democratic process."[26]

Not simply the cry of its occasion (a dissent from black nationalism), Ellison's essay is an exemplary act of retrieval, recovering what Kallen's cultural pluralism erased – the motley mixtures alive in James's and Locke's pragmatist pluralism. William James's anarchic mosaic of edges and transitions that ruptures identity and purity becomes in Ellison "our complex and pluralistic wholeness." In Ellison's rendering, democratic experience is replete with risk, with anxieties and insecurities that require near acrobatic negotiation of a "whole" that "is always in cacaphonic motion . . . a vortex."[27] This recalls the vertiginous texture of the New York chapters of *The American Scene,* particularly that moment of aftershock on Ellis Island when James realizes that a stable "whole national consciousness" is a "luxury" of "the Switzer and the Scot" but one that the American cannot afford (86). Daring to topple that pillar of American simplicity – the "dividing line" separating American and alien – Ellison's essay revives and advances James's inquiry. Nearly twenty years after "The Little Man at Chehaw Station," we are at a cultural moment when the tide of multiculturalist pluralism – identity politics – shows signs of having finally crested. Replacing it is a mobile, postethnic cosmopolitanism that bears compelling affinities (implicit and explicit) with the pragmatist pluralist tradition. In other words, at last we find ourselves in a position to appreciate and to apply the lessons of *The American Scene.*[28]

NOTES

1 *The American Scene,* p. 124. Subsequent references noted parenthetically in the text.
2 William James, *A Pluralistic Universe,* in *Writings 1902–1910,* pp. 728, 761. Henry James read his brother's *Pragmatism* (1907) and *A Pluralistic Universe* (1909). Of the latter he tells William: "I am with you, all along the line. . . . As an artist and a 'creator' I can catch on, hold on, to pragmatism and can work in the light of it and apply it." This eminently pragmatic response echoes his earlier enthusiasm for *Pragmatism,* which revealed to him how great the "extent" to which all his life he had "unconsciously pragmatised." *The American Scene* embodies Henry's creative application of William's pragmatist pluralism. Henry James" responses to his brother are quoted in Perry 1:428.
3 *Letters* 4: xxxi.

4　*Letters* 4: 768, 770. James's emphasis on the aesthetic as action is evident in his early memory, at age eleven, of first hearing the phrase "making a scene." "Epoch-making" was this idiom, James recalls, for "it told me so much about life," principally that "we could make" scenes "as we chose" (*Autobiography*, p. 107).

5　James, *The Art of the Novel*, p. 31.

6　Max Weber, p. 214.

7　Henry James, *Literary Criticism*, pp. 663, 665.

8　James invents the name "hotel-spirit" after marveling at the efficiency of management displayed in the lobby of the Waldorf-Astoria. There the "supremely gregarious state" is consummately produced as an image of "perfect human felicity," a simulacrum of freedom. See Posnock for analysis of "hotel-spirit" in it cultural context.

9　Quoted in Matthiessen, *Family*, pp. 310–11.

10　Walzer, p. 614. Although Walzer's essay does not discuss the countercurrent I am calling pragmatist, his conclusions, from which I've quoted, coincide with it.

11　See Thomas Bender, p. 249.

12　This passage on Ellis Island, like others on the alien, is usually cited as proof of "what an unbearable and odious social snob James clearly revealed himself as being," in the words of his severest critic, Maxwell Geismar, whose verdict many readers assent to, albeit in more temperate terms (cited in Posnock, p. 280).

13　For a reading of the Ellis Island episode that emphasizes how James entangles himself in a web of primal connections, particularly his childhood memories of sharing his consciousness with his brother William, memories that suffuse *A Small Boy and Others*, see Posnock, pp. 279–81.

14　W. J. Cash's is the classic formulation of how blacks and whites in the South are reciprocally entwined: "Negro entered into white man as white man entered into Negro – subtly influencing every gesture, every word, every emotion and idea, every attitude" (*The Mind of the South*, p. 51).

15　Kenneth Warren, *Black and White Strangers*, p. 22.

16　Stanley Cavell describes Emersonian abandonment as an embracing of one's own immigrancy (*The Senses of Walden*, p. 156).

17　William James, quoted in Warren, p. 112.

18　W. E./ B. Du Bois, *The Souls of Black Folk*, p. 214.

19　Warren, *Black and White Strangers*, p. 112.

20　William James, *Writings*, pp. 728, 1180–1.

21　William James, Writings, pp. 756, 778, 761, 728.

22　Horrace Kallen, *Culture and Democracy*, p. 94.

23　For an influential discussion of Kallen's contradictions, see Werner Sollors.

24　John Dewey, *The Middle Works*, pp. 204–5.

25　See Ann Douglas, *Terrible Honesty*, for a rich history of the Harlem Renaissance written, in effect, from a pragmatist pluralist perspective.

26　Ralph Ellison, *Going to the Territory*, pp. 25, 21, 16, 20.

27　Ellison, p. 20.

28　David Hollinger makes the case for a postethnic perspective.

WORKS CITED

Bender, Thomas. *New York Intellect.* New York: Knopf, 1987.
Cash, W. J. *The Mind of the South.* New York: Vintage, 1941.
Cavell, Stanley. *The Senses of Walden.* San Francisco: North Point, 1981.
Crèvecoeur, Hector St. John de. *Letters From an American Farmer.* New York: Dutton, 1957.
Dewey, John. *Middle Works, 1899–1924.* Carbondale: Southern Illinois University Press, 1980. 15 vols., 1976–83.
Douglas Ann. *Terrible Honesty: Mongrel Manhattan in the 1920s.* New York: Farrar, Straus and Giroux, 1995.
Du Bois, W. E. B. *The Souls of Black Folk.* New York: Penguin, 1990.
Ellison, Ralph. *Going To the Territory.* New York: Random House, 1986.
Hollinger, David. *Postethnic America.* New York: Basic Books, 1995.
James, Henry. *The American Scene.* Bloomington: Indiana University Press, 1969.
James, Henry. *The Art of the Novel.* New York: Scribner's, 1962.
James, Henry. *Autobiography.* New York: Criterion, 1956.
James, Henry. *Letters:* Vol. 4. Cambridge: Harvard University Press, 1984.
James, Henry. *Literary Criticism: American and English Writers.* New York: The Library of America. 1984.
James, William. *Writings 1902–1910.* New York: The Library of America, 1987.
Kallen, Horace. *Culture and Democracy.* New York: Boni and Liveright, 1924.
Matthiessen. F. O. *The James Family.* New York: Knopf, 1961.
Perry, Ralph Barton. *The Thought and Character of William James.* 2 vols. Boston: Little, Brown, 1935.
Posnock, Ross. *The Trial of Curiosity: Henry James, William James, and the Challenge of Modernity.* New York: Oxford University Press, 1991.
Sollors, Werner. "A Critique of Pure Pluralism." In *Reconstructing American Literature,* ed. Sacvan Bercovitch. Cambridge: Harvard University Press, 1986.
Walzer, Michael. "What Does It Mean to Be an 'American'?" *Social Research 57* (1990):614.
Warren, Kenneth. *Black and White Strangers: Race and American Literary Realism.* Chicago: University of Chicago Press, 1993.
Weber, Max. *From Max Weber.* New York: Oxford University Press, 1946.

Suggestions for Further Reading

COLLECTED NOVELS, STORIES, PLAYS

The textual chaos of James's work (so elegantly charted by Philip Horne) is such that no one standard edition exists. Some readers, for example, prefer the New York Edition, in which can be found revised versions of many but not all of James's major novels and tales, done late in his career and in his most baroque manner; others opt to sample the development of James's prose as it shaped and reshaped itself over time. I list below the best editions (mainly hardcover) of the work currently available at bookstores or easily obtainable at libraries. Fine paperback editions of many of the works also abound (from Oxford, Penguin, and a host of others), including Norton Critical Readers of *The Ambassadors*, *The Wings of the Dove*, and major tales, with excellent textual and critical commentary.

Henry James: The New York Edition. 24 vols. New York: Charles Scribner's Sons, 1907–1909. Reprinted New York: Augustus Kelley, 1971.

Novels, 1874–1880. *Watch and Ward, Roderick Hudson, The American, The Europeans, Confidence*. New York: Library of America, 1983.

Novels, 1881–1886. *Washington Square, The Portrait of a Lady, The Bostonians*. New York: Library of America, 1985.

Novels, 1886–1890. *The Princess Casamassima, The Reverberator, The Tragic Muse*. New York: Library of America, 1989.

Complete Plays of Henry James. Philadelphia: Lippincott, 1949.

Complete Tales of Henry James, 12 vols, ed. Leon Edel. Philadelphia: Lippincott: 1962–1964.

Tales. 2 vols. New York: Library of America, 1995.

NON-FICTION

The American Scene. New York: Penguin, 1994.

The Art of the Novel: Critical Prefaces, ed. R. P. Blackmur. New York: Charles Scribner's Sons, 1962. Contains all the Prefaces to the New York Edition and a helpful introduction by Blackmur.

Autobiography, ed. F. W. Dupee. New York: Criterion, 1956. Contains *A Small Boy and Others* (1913), *Notes of a Son and Brother* (1914) and *The Middle Years* (1917), left unfinished at James's death.
The Future of the Novel, ed. Leon Edel. New York: Vintage, 1956.
Literary Criticism, 2 vols. New York: Library of America, 1985.
The Notebooks of Henry James, ed. F. O. Matthiessen and Kenneth Murdock. New York: Oxford University Press, 1947.
Theory of Fiction: Henry James, ed. James Miller, Jr. Lincoln: University of Nebraska Press, 1972.

BIOGRAPHICAL

Edel, Leon. *Henry James*. 5 vols. Philadelphia: Lippincott, 1953–1972. A strong, Freud-inflected reading of James's life: magisterial, painstaking, and sometimes misleading.
James, Henry. *Letters*. 4 vols., ed. Leon Edel. Cambridge: Harvard University Press, 1974–1984. Despite some omissions, the best edition of James's amazingly eloquent and often quite moving correspondence.
Kaplan, Fred. *Henry James: The Imagination of Genius*. New York: Morrow, 1992. A more recent biography than Edel's, reflecting newer understandings of James's sexuality.
Lewis, R. W. B. *The Jameses: A Family Narrative*. New York: LSG, 1991.
Matthiessen, F. O. *The James Family*. New York: Knopf, 1947. A marvelous collection of works from the entire family.

CRITICISM OF JAMES

James is perhaps the most thoroughly commented-on novelist of the nineteenth or twentieth centuries, and one of the most volubly written-about authors of any time. And more than just about any writer I know, his reputation has suffered regular periods of neglect and revival. I include below an assortment of the most compelling responses to his work, organized roughly by what I take to be the four distinct (if occasionally overlapping) moments of critical endeavor. Needless to say, not every significant work of James criticism can be listed here, and not every work listed below fits into these paradigms – but this list can give a good sense of both the dominant issues that inflect James criticism and its twists and turns over the past century.

The 1920s and 1930s

Immediately after James's death, some of the most elegant responses to his work emerged from the classic high modernists – Eliot, Pound, etc. Yet the critical tide quickly turned against him, as Van Wyck Brooks and Vernon Parrington's disparaging views became dominant.

Beach, Joseph Ward. *The Method of Henry James.* New Haven: Yale University Press, 1918.
Brooks, van Wyck. *The Pilgrimage of Henry James.* New York: 1914. Still remains best denunciation of James.
Eliot, T. S. "Henry James." In *The Little Review* (see below); also Kermode, Ed. *Selected Prose of T. S. Eliot* (New York: Harcourt Brace Jovanovich/Farrar Strauss, 1975), pp. 151–2.
Kelley, *The Early Development of Henry James.* Urbana: University of Illinois Press, 1930, 1965.
The Little Review. January 1918. Memorial issue for James, containing a number of important essays by Pound, Eliot, Ford Maddox Ford, and others.
Parrington, Vernon. *The Main Currents in American Thought: An Interpretation of American Literature from the Beginnings to 1920.* New York: Harcourt Brace, 1930.

James Revived: 1940–1975

In the 1930s and early 1940s, James was out of critical fashion; the efforts of F. O. Matthiessen, Leon Edel, and a number of other critics reversed this course and returned him to the center of critical esteem. And James remained at the center of critical practice undertaken via the "New Criticism" – the close reading of literary texts without explicit reference to extrinsic factors, which dominated in the American academy for the next twenty years. Here, curious readers will find some of the best treatments of the themes and imagery, the methods and the manner, of James's work, as well as powerful critiques of the formalist method and a foreshadowing of a new, more historically vigilant James criticism.

Bayley, John. "Love and Knowledge: *The Golden Bowl.*" In *The Characters of Love: A Study in the Literature of Personality,* pp. 203–62.
Banta, Martha. *Henry James and the Occult: The Great Extension.* Bloomington: Indiana University Press, 1972.
Bewley, Marius. *The Complex Fate: Hawthorne, Henry James, and Some Other American Writers.* London: Chatto and Windus, 1952.
Blackmur, R. P. *Studies in Henry James.* Veronica Makowsky, ed. New York: New Directions, 1983.
Booth, Wayne. *The Rhetoric of Fiction,* Chicago: University of Chicago Press, 1961.
Crews, Frederick. *The Tragedy of Manners: Moral Drama in the Later Novels of Henry James.* New Haven: Yale University Press, 1957.
Dupee, F. W. *Henry James.* New York: Sloan, 1951.
Geismar, Maxwell. *Henry James and the Jacobites.* New York: Harcourt Brace, 1963.

Holland, Laurence. *The Expense of Vision: Essays on the Craft of Henry James.* Princeton: Princeton University Press, 1964.
Howe, Irving. "Henry James: The Political Vocation." In *Politics and the Novel.* New York: Horizon, 1957, pp. 139–56.
Krook, Dorothy. *The Ordeal of Consciousness in Henry James.* Cambridge University Press, 1962.
Leavis, F. R. *The Great Tradition: George Eliot, Henry James, Joseph Conrad.* London: Chatto and Windus, 1948.
Matthiessen, F. O. *Henry James: The Major Phase.* New York: Oxford University Press, 1944.
Poirier, Richard. *The Comic Sense of Henry James: A Study of the Early Novels.* New York: Oxford University Press, 1960.
Trilling, Lionel. *The Princess Casamassima.* In *The Liberal Imagination.* New York: Viking, 1950, pp. 55–88.
Van Ghent, Dorothy. "On 'The Portrait of a Lady'." In *The English Novel: Form and Function.* New York: Holt and Company, 1953.
Watt, Ian. "The First Paragraph of *The Ambassadors.*" *Essays in Criticism* 10 (1960): 250–74.
Winner, Viola Hopkins. *Henry James and the Visual Arts.* Charlottesville: University Press of Virginia, 1970.

James Theorized

Under the impact of the turn to theory in the mid- to late 1970s, James criticism was given a different spin: still highly formalist in orientation, it undertook to reread James under the dispensation of narrative theory, psychoanalysis, deconstruction. And readings of James took a more contextual turn, bringing in other arenas of knowledge than the merely verbal. Yet the center of inquiry remained the James's texts themselves in all their challenging knottiness.

Bersani, Leo. "The Jamesian Lie." In *A Future for Astyanax: Character and Desire in Literature,* pp. 128–55. Boston: Little, Brown, 1976.
Brooks, Peter. *The Melodramatic Imagination: Balzac, Henry James, Melodrama, and the Mode of Excess.* New Haven: Yale University Press, 1976.
Donadio, Stephen. *Nietzsche, James and the Aesthetic Will.* New York: Oxford University Press, 1978.
Felman, Shoshona. "Turning the Screw of Interpretation." *Yale French Studies* 55–56 (1977): 94–207.
Miller, J. Hillis. "The Figure in the Carpet." *Poetics Today* 1 (1980): 107–18.
Goode, John, ed. *The Art of Reality: New Essays on Henry James.* London: Methuen, 1972.
Veeder, William. *Henry James – The Lessons of the Master: Popular Fiction and Personal Style in the Nineteenth Century.* Chicago: University of Chicago Press, 1975.

Rowe, John Carlos. *The Theoretical Dimensions of Henry James*. Madison: University of Wisconsin Press, 1984.

Yeazell, Ruth. *Language and Knowledge in the Late Novels of Henry James*. Chicago: University of Chicago Press, 1976.

Our Henry James(es)

In the 1980s and 1990s, James's work has been systematically reread by critics who stress the power of the social in the making of literary form and value; the construction, deconstruction, and reconstruction of sexed and gendered identities; the role of the author in the literary marketplace. To be sure, elegant close readings of James's work continue to emerge, and writers resistant to these tendencies frequently stage that resistance through the figure of James. Reading this work in the light of the previous eighty years of James criticism, however, makes two things clear: that the very possibilities and problems of the critical act continue to get assessed through the figure of James; and that this habit of thought shows no sign of abating.

Agnew, Jean-Christophe. "The Consuming Vision of Henry James." In *The Culture of Consumption: Critical Essays in American History, 1880–1980*. Richard Fox and T. J. Jackson Lears, eds. New York: Pantheon, 1983.

Bell, Millicent. *Meaning in Henry James*. Cambridge: Harvard University Press, 1991.

Blair, Sara. *Henry James and the Writing of Race and Nation*. Cambridge University Press, 1994.

Brodhead, Richard. *The School of Hawthorne*. New York: Oxford University Press, 1986.

Cameron, Sharon. *Thinking in Henry James*. Chicago: University of Chicago Press, 1989.

Freedman, Jonathan. *Professions of Taste: Henry James, British Aestheticism, and Commodity Culture*. Stanford: Stanford University Press, 1990.

Griffin, Susan. *The Historical Eye: The Texture of the Visual in Late James*. Boston: Northeastern University Press, 1991.

Habegger, Alfred. *Henry James and the "Woman Business."* Cambridge University Press, 1989.

Horne, Philip. *Henry James and Revision*. Oxford: The Clarendon Press, 1990.

Ozick, Cynthia. *What Henry James Knew and Other Essays on Writers*. London: Jonathan Cape, 1993.

Porter, Caroline. *Seeing and Being: The Plight of the Participant Observer in Emerson, James, Adams and Faulkner*. Middletown: Wesleyan University Press, 1988.

Posnock, Ross. *The Trial of Curiosity: Henry James, William James, and the Challenge of Modernity*. New York: Oxford University Press, 1991.

Rivkin, Julie. *False Positions: The Representational Logics of James's Fiction*. Stanford: Stanford University Press, 1996.

Sedgwick, Eve. *Epistemology of the Closet.* Berkeley: University of California Press, 1990.

Seltzer, Mark. *Henry James and the Art of Power.* Ithaca, N.Y.: Cornell University Press, 1985.

Stowe, William. *James, Balzac, and the Realistic Novel.* Princeton: Princeton University Press, 1983.

Wardley, Lynn. "Woman's Voice, Democracy's Body, and *The Bostonians.*" *ELH* 26 (1989): 639–65.

Warren, Kenneth. *Black and White Strangers: Race and American Literary Realism.* Chicago: University of Chicago Press, 1993.

Wicke, Jennifer. *Advertising Fictions: Literature, Advertising, and Social Reading.* New York: Columbia University Press, 1988.

INDEX

Cambridge Companions to Literature